THE
EXPLORER
GENE

TOM CHESHIRE
WITH A FOREWORD BY
JAMES CAMERON

THE
EXPLORER
GENE

First published in 2013 by Short Books
Short Books, 3A Exmouth House, Pine Street, EC1R 0JH

10 9 8 7 6 5 4 3 2 1

A CIP catalogue record for this book
is available from the British Library.

ISBN 978-1-78072-089-0

Printed in Great Britain by CPI Group (UK) Ltd, Croydon, CR0 4YY
Cover design: Two Associates

———

Image and photo credits:

p. 1 © Piccard family
p. 5 © Piccard family
p. 35 © Corbis
p. 39 © AP/Press Association Images
p. 44 © Piccard family
p. 108 © Piccard family
p. 111 © Piccard family
p. 134 © Getty
p. 154 © Getty
p. 213 © Solar Impulse
p. 282 © Solar Impulse
p. 288 © Piccard family

To my parents

Author's Note

The Piccards have explored the entire planet. As a result, they calculated and published using a variety of imperial and metric measurements, as did the people who reported on and corresponded with them. This book aims to present a consistent hodgepodge that will be familiar to UK readers. Altitudes, of people, balloons and planes, are recorded in feet, with the metric equivalent somewhere nearby. Depths follow the same rule. Longer distances are in miles, with metric equivalents supplied; shorter distances are metric with no imperial equivalent. Volumes and weights are all metric.

Contents

Foreword	ix
Introduction	xv
Prisoners of the Stratosphere	3
The Extra Decimal Point	8
Lighter Than Air	24
Up	40
Back Down to Earth	52
The Piccards in America	69
Down	90
Jacques	107
A Race to the Bottom	124
The *Trieste*	133
Project Nekton	146
The Deepest Dive	164
Middle Waters	179
Bertrand	196
Around	216
The Third Watch	231
The Last Great Adventure	248
A Greater Adventure	270
Epilogue	283
Appendix	285
Acknowledgements	287
Bibliography	289
Index	291

Foreword

This book is the story of three extraordinary men, representing three generations of a family whose name will resound through history as synonymous with exploration. The first, the scientist Auguste Piccard, followed his questing intellect into the stratosphere to touch the edge of space, while the second, his son Jacques Piccard, went the other direction, ever deeper into the ocean until his quest took him, ultimately, as deep as any human can go on this planet. Both paved the way for decades of oceanographic and atmospheric researchers that followed, and inspired subsequent generations of explorers, myself included.

The third man, Jacques's son Bertrand Piccard, chose a middle path, exploring the atmosphere horizontally with a series of envelope-pushing balloon and experimental-aircraft flights, while simultaneously questing inward – examining the soul and spirituality of exploration.

All three men have quintessentially expressed the Explorer Gene, travelling first a journey of the mind in which their imaginations conceived something barely possible and then, with exceptional will, made it happen in the real world – pitting their strength, their resolve, and indeed their very mortal existence, against the great unknown, and prevailing.

I have known only one of these men personally, and am grateful to be counted among Bertrand's friends and fellow explorers. He asked me to write this foreword, and I was honored to do so, having personally followed quite consciously in the footsteps of his father and grandfather. When I dove in my own submersive to the bottom of the Challenger Deep, the deepest point on earth at the bottom of the Mariana Trench in the Pacific Ocean, in March 2012, one of my goals was to celebrate the pioneers who had made that historic dive 52 years earlier, and to draw attention to the fact that no one had done such a thing since then, despite all the subsequent advances in ocean technology. In a time when the world seems fully explored, and we can call up a satellite image of any spot on the Earth's surface using Google Maps, it is vital for people to realize that a vast unknown territory – the size of North America – remains totally unexplored in the extreme depths of the world's ocean trenches.

The dive made by Jacques Piccard and Don Walsh in the bathyscaphe Trieste on January 23, 1960 was very much on my mind as I made my own attempt to revisit the deepest realm on Earth. I had become friends with Don Walsh over the years while pursuing my own dreams of exploration and through him, I got to know what Jacques was like. I could picture Jacques: serious, thoughtful, focused and driven, in his own quiet and methodical way, to challenge the impossible. As I was being bolted into my own vehicle just prior to launch, knowing that once the hatch was sealed my fate was in a sense already determined by our engineering, I pictured Jacques closing and sealing a similar massive steel hatch half a century earlier. He would have been quietly confident that the calculations and construction methods were correct, but perhaps still wondering in the back of his mind if some tiny but crucial factor had been overlooked.

Jacques was the pilot but his scientist father, Auguste, was the designer of the Trieste, and it was the veracity of his calculations that would keep his son alive. The challenge of this sort of exploration is quite different than that of, say, an Arctic explorer of previous generations driving a team of sled dogs across the icy wastes. It is less a physical challenge of pitting one's body against the elements, but instead a mental challenge of pitting one's intellect against the physics of the natural world – in this case the ocean's extreme pressure at depth, and the limitations of materials such as steel and acrylic that must withstand those pressures to keep the explorer safe within his craft.

Auguste Piccard was inspired by Jules Verne to imagine the extraordinary machines that might one day explore the deepest reaches of the oceans, at a time when what lay down there in that vast blackness was an absolute terra incognita, literally unseen by human eyes. He visualized a revolutionary machine that would function like a balloon, a balloon of steel filled with lighter-than-water gasoline, whose buoyancy would bring it back from the depths. Before he could build such a machine, he tested his principles with aerial balloons, going higher and farther than any human had ever gone.

Not content to simply design these balloons, his questing intellect compelled him to get inside them and go into the stratosphere, to see for himself what was there. An important aspect of the 'expression' of the Explorer Gene is this requirement to see for oneself – to bear witness, personally, to the unknown, to see that which has never been seen before by human eyes. And to project not only one's consciousness on a journey of imagination, but to project one's physical body, with full knowledge of the attendant risks, to some extreme vantage point from which no human being has ever looked out upon unknown vistas.

Auguste was interested in cosmic rays, not in altitude records or publicity. His humility was such that he would have been appalled if his work was seen as driven by a need for notoriety. The quest of the explorer is simply To Go, as a thing in itself, to challenge oneself and satisfy one's own curiosity, not as a means to such a paltry end as fame or fortune. Yes, the explorer is aware that to succeed is to set an example for others who may follow and further expand the sphere of human knowledge. That is an important part of the goal. So one must succeed, not die trying, and that is a huge part of the challenge: to do that which is inherently risky with the greatest level of safety possible. This is where the intellect and will are pitted against the unknown. Those with the Explorer Gene must be wise in their preparation, or their gravestones will only be signposts to other explorers of the path not to be taken.

But any explorer also knows, quite keenly, that in going far beyond where others have already dared, they are entering a realm in which it is impossible to mitigate against all risk. The risk of death walks with every true explorer, and they stare that risk in the eye, knowing that the goal of expanding our reach and knowledge is worth it.

While exploring the stratosphere in balloons filled with helium, Auguste still dreamed of his steel balloon exploring the depths. He would build it, years later, but it would be his son Jacques who would pilot it into the abyss, going far deeper than any human had gone before and ultimately, to the very deepest place on Earth. The son trusted the father's design and calculations, and the father trusted the son to fulfill his dream by diving the machine to the ultimate unknown. This was certainly the most extraordinary father-son relationship in the history of exploration.

Auguste's design was visionary. In fact half a century later, when we were designing the Deepsea Challenger, we could not find better solutions to certain problems like the acrylic viewport or the steel-shot ballast system than those pioneered by Auguste. Despite all the advances in technology and materials-science since then, parts of our vehicle almost exactly followed his designs. It is not an exaggeration to say that many of his engineering principles paved the way for all of the research submersibles to follow, opening up the Golden Age of deep ocean exploration of the '60s, '70s and '80s.

When I gazed out on the lunar plain of that seafloor, almost seven miles down, I was connected in spirit with Jacques, who had looked out on a similar landscape half a century earlier.

The Explorer Gene

My dive was made 34 miles to the east of where Jacques and Don touched down. Their dive was in the west basin of the Challenger Deep, while mine was in the east basin, and it turned out that both depressions were equally deep, at least within the margin for error of their instruments and mine. As we gazed out on the two deepest spots on Earth, we each saw something out our thick acrylic viewports that no human has seen before or since. I believe I experienced what he must have felt, a sense of awe at the mystery of the world, at the vast darkness that lies beyond the limits of our feeble lights, and the sheer scale of all that remains to be explored and understood. It was exhilarating and deeply humbling.

Bertrand, as the Piccard next in line, had big shoes to fill. Despite being gifted with his own full sequence of explorer genes, he initially sought a different path – inward, into the human mind and spirit – studying both psychiatry and eastern mysticism. Where his father and grandfather were logical and analytical, bringing Swiss precision and empirical science to bear on the world they saw, Bertrand followed instinct and spirituality on his quest. His eastern approach notwithstanding, he eventually found himself following the family tradition: setting balloon records (using Cameron-built balloons, ironically further entwining our family names) in daring crossings of the Atlantic and a circumnavigation of the globe.

I met Bertrand at a cocktail party at the Jules Verne film festival years ago, which is fitting given that the works of the Father of Science Fiction had inspired Bertrand's grandfather and set the whole Piccard saga in motion. He told me then of his dream to build a solar-powered airplane, and to fly it solo around the world, as a symbol of the vital role of renewable energy in the future of human civilization. We promptly ignored all those around us who were clamoring to talk to us, and began geeking out discussing engineering principles of photovoltaics and high energy-density battery systems. We bonded not only over our common spirit of adventure and exploration, but our love of the technical challenges that go with that, in our present age.

Only last week, as this is written, Bertrand finished his cross-country flight of the Solar Impulse airplane here in America, an important leg of his round-the-world journey. He is fulfilling the dream he expressed to me years ago, and fulfilling the promise of not only his family's legacy, but the Explorer Gene he carries in his DNA.

Bertrand is also following his father's principle that it is not enough to explore and bring back the scientific data, one must also communicate and inspire, so that exploration continues to expand through public support. Just as Jacques spent his later years designing subs like the August Piccard which could take large numbers of the public into the depths, Bertrand used social networking and digital connectivity to bring the public along with him on his historic flights, to help inspire the next generation of explorers and engineers.

Most importantly, Bertrand is not only carrying forward the family tradition of innovation and exploration, but he has incorporated the equally important message of sustainability and the stewardship of our planet. His ongoing adventure will highlight the importance of solar technology in the destiny of the human race, as the fossil fuel age enters its twilight, and a perilous future lies before us if we don't evolve and adapt. His gleaming plane symbolizes not only humanity's bright hope for the future, but our innate ability to turn curiosity and imagination into clever technical solutions to difficult problems. This is what makes us curious monkeys magnificent as human beings, and Bertrand Piccard is continuing the family tradition of representing that which is great within us all.

James Cameron, July 2013

Introduction

More than a hundred years after the birth of Auguste Piccard, the first of three generations of explorers, researchers working separately in Israel and the US published near-identical findings. Both teams had been looking at the 11th chromosome of the human genome, on which lies a gene called D4DR. This acts as a receptor of dopamine – the chemical that mediates sensations of pleasure. The middle of the D4DR gene contains a variable repeating sequence that is 48 base pairs in length, repeated like a stutter anything from two to 11 times, but most often between four and seven times. In January 1996, the two separate studies were published, both stating that "novelty-seeking", a defined personality trait, was more common in people with a seven-fold repeat. The scientists hypothesised that a longer D4DR sequence could make some individuals sensitive to changes in dopamine: high levels of dopamine would lead to a more intense feeling of pleasure.

The desire to explore, one of the definitive characteristics of humanity in general, has always been felt more keenly by certain individuals, whether it was called wanderlust, or the "arctic fever" of polar explorers of the early 20th century, or the impulse, as Tennyson wrote in his 1833 poem on Ulysses, the original explorer in the Western tradition, "to seek, to strive, to find and not to yield". Now scientists had found another name, written right into our genetic code: D4DR, the explorer gene.

The first study to question the link between D4DR and novelty-seeking was published 10 months later; a paper published in *Biological Psychiatry*, which analysed all 36 previous studies, said "the strength of evidence for this association remains uncertain." In any case, individual personality traits are too complex to be determined by one gene alone.

D4DR may be as much a metaphor of the genetic age as arctic fever was in an era of widespread infectious disease, or wanderlust in an age when romanticism held sway (neuroscience being the flavour of the decade, a 2012 paper published in *Neuron* found that "explorers", those whose decision-making styles embrace uncertainty, used a specific part of the brain to solve puzzles – their right rostrolateral prefrontal cortex).

As a scientist who counted Marie Curie, Niels Bohr and Albert Einstein among his friends, Auguste Piccard would no doubt have put the explorer gene to the test in the lab. This book does not attempt to do the same, but rather to describe how successive generations of the Piccard family, through their natures and their nurtures, and their relationships with one another, came to be such pioneers. Neil Armstrong, himself no slouch as an explorer, wrote: "Son of Jacques and grand-son of Auguste, Bertrand inherited their explorer genes... There exist few families in the world of exploration who have had a vision more vast, ambitious and creative."

We do not know whether the Piccards carry the D4DR gene; as well as being characterised as explorers, novelty-seekers are fickle, excitable and quick-tempered, none of which applies to this Swiss family of adventurers. Instead, it seems the explorer gene may in fact be a meme – a unit of cultural transmission that, like a gene, replicates and propa-gates itself. The strongest, fittest memes are handed down. The explorer meme means that we can all learn something of the Piccards' spirit and passion for discovery ourselves.

THE
EXPLORER
GENE

Prisoners of the Stratosphere

Auguste Piccard was ten miles high, the first human to enter the stratosphere, in a balloon he had designed and built himself. Writing calculations in his notebook, he was working out whether he would return to earth alive.

Some hours earlier, and a few minutes after take-off from Augsburg at 3.53 on the morning of May 27, 1931, Piccard had heard a whistling sound. An electrical insulator had broken off and the pressurised cabin – the very first of its kind – was leaking air. His assistant Paul Kipfer, with an eye on the pressure gauges, had reported to Piccard: "We are at two and a half miles and there is still an equal pressure inside and outside the cabin." Piccard, dismayed to find the airtight aluminium cabin he had designed was nearly as leaky as a traditional wicker basket, set about patching the hole with a mixture of tow and Vaseline, along with sticking tape, so as to avoid suffocation. Little by little, the whistling grew feebler, until the pair had never been so glad of silence. Piccard had brought a reserve of liquid oxygen. He poured it onto the floor and it evaporated into breathable gas. The problem was solved, for now.

Piccard could observe the stratosphere for the first time in human history: "The beauty of the sky is the most poignant we have seen," he wrote in the logbook, in a neat and tightly packed hand. "It is sombre, dark blue or violet, almost black." But he didn't have long to reflect; Kipfer and Piccard soon made "a very unpleasant discovery". The valve to release hydrogen from the balloon was broken; the rope which controlled it had tangled with a supplementary rope tied on at the moment of departure. If the gas could not escape, the balloon could not descend; it would do so only when the sun grew weaker and the gas within the envelope cooled. Piccard decided to pack up his scientific instruments in case the balloon, as it drew itself out under the sun's rays, pulled open the valve of its own accord and crashed. The two scientists tried again to open the valve, turning the winch using a crank inside the cabin. The cable broke clean off, definitely ending any hope of bringing down the balloon under control. At 9.56 am, six hours after take-off, Piccard noted in his logbook: "We are prisoners of the air."

"I do not know of any case of a balloon not coming down," Piccard reassured Kipfer, "The only question is where, and when." The oxygen reserves would allow the two to remain in the cabin until sunset. But that depended on an airtight cabin. Now, Piccard and Kipfer both felt their ears pop, several times, then heard the whistling once more. The Vaseline had run out through the tow and air was again escaping. The balloon was also starting to drift toward the Adriatic Sea. Piccard and Kipfer could do nothing: they could not turn the cabin, nor could they control the balloon. They would drift aimlessly until they landed.

The sun passed its zenith and the balloon began a slow descent. Piccard, as he invariably did when faced with a problem, started working through the sums in his note-book. The descent was too slow: at this rate, it would take 15 days. By 3 pm, the descent had accelerated, but would still take more than 24 hours. Piccard found himself thinking of Salomon Andrée, a Swedish engineer and civil servant who in 1897 had set out to fly across the North Pole in a hydrogen balloon. He wasn't found until 30 years later, when a Norwegian fishing expedition discovered his remains on a lonely, ice-bound island, along with his observations and photographs; the body had been carried back to Stockholm in a grand procession on October 5, 1930. Piccard, a scientist to the last, wished he could at least make his own observations, but needed to save oxygen: he and Kipfer decided not to make any unnecessary movement. They sat motionless in the cramped, spherical cabin, looking at each other in silence.

Ten miles below, the activity on the ground was as frenetic

The F.N.R.S takes off from Augsburg

as the stratosphere was still. Piccard had been supposed to land at noon. The last sighting of the balloon, a tiny, flashing point of silver, had been at around eight o'clock in the evening; its altitude was estimated at 10,000 feet (3,048 metres). Thousands of spectators had watched the balloon wander aimlessly over the Bavarian–Tyrolean border areas. Two airplanes had taken off from Munich during the afternoon in an attempt to make contact, but were unable to reach the altitude of the balloon and returned. Reports were confused: the balloon was spotted simultaneously north of Innsbruck and south of Garmisch-Partenkirchen, which are 25 miles apart. Nor could anybody tell whether Piccard had even succeeded in penetrating the stratosphere.

Little was known about pressurised cabins and the worst was feared; the *New York Times* reported that "the smallest leak in the cabin would produce immediate unconsciousness and subsequent death." On May 28, Piccard's fate was front-page news, headlined:

PICCARD BALLOON DRIFTS HELPLESSLY
ABOVE ALPS; SCIENTISTS FEARED DEAD.

"Wrapped in silence and mystery, shrouded in the folds of night," Guido Enderis, a reporter, cabled the *New York Times*, "Professor Auguste Piccard's stratosphere balloon is tonight drifting aimlessly over the glaciers of the Tyrolean Alps, apparently out of control and occupied only by the dead."

The European press was no less pessimistic, and even more macabre. *Le Journal*, in a late bulletin, wrote: "The news coming from Berlin this evening a little bit after 2100 leaves no hope of finding the two brave explorers alive, who, risking their lives, have continued to explore the sky. At the present, one should note that M. Piccard and his companion are not accomplished aeronauts, capable of triumphing over the treachery that can assail a sphere at the mercy of the elements, in unknown parts, and that neither of the men would have been even able, if at all, to regulate the speed of the balloon by an appropriate jettisoning of ballast... if the aeronauts are obliged to land in pitch black, the balloon heavy with nocturnal humidity and the natural loss of gas, their fate is already sealed. There will be without doubt two mutilated corpses, crushed, unrecognisable, once the debris of the aircraft is removed."

All the spectators could do was wait. Among those craning their necks up and reading the reports was Piccard's family: his wife Marianne, his four daughters and his nine-year-old son, Jacques.

The Extra Decimal Point

The twins Jean Felix and Auguste Antoine Piccard were born in Basel, next to the Rhine on the borders of Switzerland, Germany and France, on January 28, 1884. Their first act on earth was, reportedly, to save the life of their father Jules, who was lying in his sickbed, victim of an unknown disease. The arrival of twins gave him strength to live again, which does not say much for the two children, Paul and Marie, born before the twins. Jules, considered as good as dead by the doctors, would live nearly another half-century, dying at the age of 93 in 1933.

The twins were born into an old, but modest family; the first recorded trace of a Piccard is in June 1390, a marriage contract between Alexia Peccar de Sechatel and Jean, the son of Perrius de Fortuna, in what is now Jourdillon, in Switzerland. Alexia was the daughter of Memet Peccar (the name suggests a Turkish origin), who owned a house which stood until at least 1882. Many of the early Piccards were ministers, but the family developed a tendency towards novelty, invention and tinkering. Rodolphe Piccard, born in 1807, was a famous miniaturist and painter at the Tsarist court, a creator of schematic drawings for two archaeological digs, on the Bosphorus and Black Sea, and the inventor of an exploding cannon ball. The twins' uncle, Paul Piccard, was a renowned engineer. In 1887, he invented a salt-making device based on thermocompression, which worked on the same principle as the heat pump; brine was brought to the boil in an evaporator using steam generated from boilers; the steam was compressed, further increasing the temperature, and so heating the brine – all as part of a closed circuit. The Piccard apparatus was first used in the salt mines of Bex; its principles are now applied all over the world. Paul Piccard also built the turbines for the first hydroelectric power station in the world, at Niagara Falls, working alongside Nikola Tesla. The plant started producing electricity in 1895 and continued well into the Second World War, and the turbines still stand. Paul's company, Piccard-Pictet, produced high-end motorcars called Pic-Pic, to rival Rolls-Royce and Mercedes, and built the first grand-prix cars with brakes on the front wheels; these cars didn't complete a grand prix, but, maybe thanks to Swiss mountain know-how, won several hill-climbing auto races in the 1910s. During the First World War, the Swiss army bought a large number of Pic-Pics because of their reliability.

Jules Piccard, the father of Jean Felix and Auguste, was a scientist. Born in 1840, he had studied at the Swiss Federal Institute of Technology (Eidgenössische Technische Hochschule Zürich), obtaining a degree in chemical engineering and a doctorate in philosophy; at the age of 28, he was named professor of chemistry at the University of Basel. He was curious about every innovation. He installed the first telephones in Switzerland. Demonstrating the system to his university colleagues, he called his wife Hélène to say that he would be late for lunch. One of the party told the professor: "Yes, my dear Piccard, this experience is amusing, but let me say that this invention, this telephone, has absolutely no future."

The twins were truly identical: the only way their mother could tell them apart was from the fact that Auguste was left-handed, Jean right. They both soon taught themselves to be ambidextrous and made full use of others' confusion. One trick was for Jean Felix to go for a haircut; then

Auguste, with a full head of hair, would walk through the door ten minutes later, demanding a refund.

Encouraged by their father, they turned their inventiveness to more useful pursuits. The twins grew up in a house where discovery, curiosity and research were encouraged. They were both fascinated by the stories of Jules Verne – Auguste was in particular enthralled by Captain Nemo – and they received an education that encouraged them to come up with the science to match Verne's grand fictions. Visiting professors and teachers would spend hours in Jules Piccard's company; he would encourage his children to take part in, or at least to observe, the scientific arguments, and he provided a child's version of a laboratory for them to play with. Jules Piccard loved the outdoors, especially the mountains, as much as the lab, and from an early age took the twins climbing. The two became experts and would maintain that passion the rest of their lives, combining their love of science and nature in spectacular style, making the outdoors their laboratory.

Gas ballooning, invented in France during the 1780s, was a well-established discipline as the Piccards were growing up; the Swiss Army even maintained a balloon corps as part of its defence force. Powered flight was in fact an old concept too – Sir George Cayley, a British engineer, had described the concept of a fixed-wing flying machine with separate systems for lift, propulsion and control in 1799 – but aviation, rather than ballooning, was now the more exciting field (the Wright brothers made their first flight when the Piccard twins were 18). It was clear to the twins that, no matter what the means, man would soon be moving through the air as freely as he crossed land and sea. Aged ten, they began experimenting with hot-air balloons made of paper. The paper wasn't very good, tearing and crumpling in on itself easily, and neither were the balloons: the twins had much to learn about pressures and volumes. But their father encouraged further attempts: "The effort is a most vital part of any experiment," he told them. "Without continued trial and error, you can never hope for success."

Auguste and Jean were fascinated in particular by the experiments of Léon Teisserenc de Bort, a French meteorologist. Meteorology was a young and inexact science: although the United Kingdom Meteorological Office had been created in 1854, it was only in 1904 that Vilhelm Bjerknes, a Norwegian scientist, argued that it should be possible to forecast weather by making calculations based on natural laws. Experiments into the nature of the atmosphere mostly relied upon flimsy kites, which were quite unreliable. De Bort used sounding balloons filled with hydrogen instead: about a metre in diameter on the ground, these expanded greatly as they rose into lower pressure, until they burst. A small parachute would then bring the scientific apparatus back down to earth; an attached label asked its finder to ship it back to de Bort. In 1902, he sent 238 balloons from Trappes, near Versailles, up into the atmosphere. It quickly became apparent that the temperature of the atmosphere ceased to fall, remaining at minus three degrees Celsius, after a certain height: about eight miles (12.9 km). De Bort suggested the atmosphere was divided into two; he called the lower region the troposphere and the upper, the stratosphere. The discovery was not immediately acclaimed as a great breakthrough, perhaps because of meteorology's lowly status, but it had a profound effect on the twins.

Auguste and Jean both excelled at *Oberrealschule* (Swiss secondary education); other pupils accused them of collaborating ("Maybe," the teacher replied, "but I know very well that neither one nor the other would be able to trust in the calculations of his brother without verifying them himself.") In 1905, the twins followed their father and matriculated at the Swiss Federal Institute of Technology. Auguste and Jean between them divvied up the disciplines dearest to their family: physics and chemistry. Auguste had already made his first steps into a career of science a year earlier, when he published his first paper, "New essays on the geotropic sensitivity of root-ends". This proposed that the ends of the roots were sensitive to gravity and accordingly grew downward. Although quite incorrect, the theory was generally admired at the time; Auguste was 20. Jean was also excelling, at a similarly prodigious rate: in 1909, he was named a doctor of science in organic chemistry; he started teaching at the University of Munich and became personal assistant to Adolf von Baeyer, who in 1905 had won the Nobel Prize in Chemistry. In 1916, Jean was offered a prestigious teaching role at the University of Chicago and took it, moving to the US.

Auguste was awarded his degree in mechanical engineering in 1910. Three years later, he was named a doctor of science and he gave his first lecture to the French Academy of Sciences, the institution created by Louis XIV in 1699 (members have included Louis Pasteur, Ivan Pavlov and Francis Crick). Piccard spoke about the co-efficient of the magnetisation of water and of oxygen. Four years later, he wrote his doctoral thesis on the same subject; Albert Einstein was one of his examiners. Between 1915 and 1917, he wrote many remarkable papers. One, a study of extremely low temperatures co-written with Pierre Weis in 1918, explained "the Magnetocaloric Effect" first observed in 1880, and opened the way to research into superconductors. Another, "The hypothesis of the existence of a third simple radioactive body in the uranium group", predicted the existence of a chemical Piccard called "Actinuran". When the element was formally discovered, in 1935 by

Canadian-American physicist Arthur Jeffrey Dempster, it would be called Uranium 235 and prove useful for the manufacture of nuclear weapons.

These research breakthroughs went hand-in-hand with formal academic recognition. In 1917, Auguste Piccard was named a professor at the Institute of Technology. Three years later, at 36 years old, he was awarded the chair of physics, and two years after that he moved to the Free University of Brussels. Piccard had visited it to install a 20-tonne seismograph, the most precise ever invented. This young university, founded in 1884, was poaching talent to compete with its Catholic rival in Louvain and, together with the International Solvay Institute for Physics, founded by Belgian industrialist Ernest Solvay in 1912, was putting together an all-star team of scientists – and money was no object. At the Solvay Institute, Piccard kept company with the great names of his age. A photograph of the October 1927 meeting shows Auguste standing a head taller than anyone else, on the very left of the back row, close to Max Planck, Marie Curie, Albert Einstein, Niels Bohr and Erwin Schrödinger. Piccard of course knew Einstein well from his research, and had a great deal of personal affection for him. He described the German-born physicist as "the most remarkable man I have ever met. He takes a serious and profound interest in the works of other people, listens attentively for hours, asks questions, and talks with great interest, never speaking of his own work, never even referring to it... Anyone who sees and hears him would never guess from his simple manner that he is a man of world renown. However, his appearance is compelling and reveals his genius. Have you noticed his neck and head? His figure expresses extraordinary individuality.

"Every time I meet Albert Einstein, I feel rich and happy, and I always wish I could be with him more."

In 1926, a year before the Solvay Institute photograph, Piccard had gone up in a balloon called *Helvetia*. He was replicating an experiment first run in 1887 by Albert Michelson and Edward Morley in Ohio, which had found that the speed of light did not vary depending on the direction of its measurement, or the movement of Earth in its orbit. Others took this as the first strong evidence that light did not travel through a medium; the lack of evidence for this "luminiferous aether" prompted Einstein to postulate a constant speed of light in 1905. Michelson and Morley had carried out their experiment at ground level; another American physicist, Miller, carrying out the same experiment in 1904, had found that light travelled at a different speed at 5,900 ft high (1,800 m): by Miller's calculations, the speed of light did vary and Einstein was thus mistaken. Piccard did his version of the experiment 14,763 feet up (4,000 m), from June 20 to June 21, then performed two terrestrial tests, and confirmed that light travelled at the same speed. The results, published in 1926, were an important confirmation of the Special Theory of Relativity. Einstein sent a warm letter of thanks to Auguste.

The *Helvetia* experiment was not the first time Auguste Piccard had employed a balloon in the service of science. As a young physicist, he had read all the aeronautical journals he could lay his hands on. "A question was being discussed in them by specialists," he later wrote, "that of the distribution of gas temperatures in the interior of spherical balloons. Now, I did not agree with the published results." Auguste went to the Swiss Aero-Club, which helped him make several ascents, in a basket laden with scientific instruments. "I had in the interior of the balloon, along its vertical axis and also in the neighbourhood of the equator, a dozen electric thermometers, thermo-couples whose cold junctions were in the basket of the balloon. I myself constructed a simple and exact potentiometer and by means of an Einthoven galvanometer I could measure the temperatures of the gas within approximately a tenth of a degree. At the same time I could, by means of a rubber tube, take samples of a gas from different parts of the balloon when it was at different heights and from them determine the density by means of a Bunsen apparatus... These studies familiarised me with the balloon. I did not then think that later they would lead me into the stratosphere." Auguste's scientific method had grown more precise since his and Jean's first experiments as children.

But ballooning for Auguste was not purely an experimental method; it was "the most beautiful of sports, the one which offers man the most pure of pleasures". He had begun ballooning for fun in 1912, during his twenties. The young scientist had gone to Paris, to help with the start of the Gordon Bennett Cup. The millionaire newspaper-owner James Gordon Bennett Jr had established the race in 1906. The rules were simple: fly as far as you could from the launch site. The race continues to this day, and continues to be dangerous: in 2010, an American balloon team took off from the Bristol launch site on September 25 and disappeared five days later, during a storm over the Atlantic. Two months later, a fishing boat recovered the capsule containing the pilots' bodies, off the coast of Italy.

Piccard was fascinated, not so much by the packed crowds that cheered the start of the race, nor the competition itself (he thought organised competition something foolish) but by the state-of-the-art balloons, straining against the ropes that lashed them to the ground. In September 1912, Auguste made his first solo ascent. In 1913, he left from Zurich and looked upon Basel at night. The same year, with Jean, Auguste made a 16-hour balloon flight; they left from Zurich and flew over France and Germany. The twins were measuring the density and pressure of gas inside the balloon, as it fluctuated according to the temperature and pressure of the surrounding air – knowledge that would prove indispensable two decades later. As night fell, they could see they were passing directly over their own house in Basel. They called out to their mother, who could not see them, but who told her doctor that she was hearing voices.

Auguste and Jean then joined the Swiss Army's Lighter-than-Air Service – the balloon corps – in 1915. According to the army, though, the twins were too tall for active service: they were both 6ft 6in with wiry frames, so were employed as civilian advisers instead. In 1923, Auguste was asked to serve his country in another capacity – by racing the Gordon Bennett Cup, to be held in Brussels, in Swiss colours. He accepted, still maintaining his principled opposition to the whole spirit of the competition. And when he lifted off, he remained the prudent scientist, not the risk-taking competitor. The weather conditions were terrible so Auguste decided to land in a beet field, 62 miles (100 km) from the start of the race, near Eindhoven. Five other aeronauts, lacking his good judgment, were killed.

*

Georges Prosper Remi lived in Brussels during the 1920s and 1930s. The young illustrator often came across Auguste Piccard, who was well known in the city. Piccard was "very tall", as Remi would recall in the 1960s. "He had an interminable neck that sprouted from a collar that was much too large." Remi would become better known as Hergé, the creator of *The Adventures of Tintin* comic books, and in his strips he recreated Piccard as Professor Calculus – the archetypal mad professor. "Calculus is a reduced scale Piccard," Hergé said. "I made Calculus a mini-Piccard, otherwise I would have had to enlarge the frames of the cartoon strip."

Calculus was a caricature, a parody of the unworldly scientist, but then so was Auguste himself; Hergé only made real what other people had frequently observed. As *TIME* magazine put it in 1932, Piccard looked "precisely like a cartoonist's idea of a scientist"; the *New York Times* said in 1930, ahead of the stratospheric attempt, that he was "somewhat reminiscent of Jules Verne's hero".

The first thing most people noted about Piccard, as Hergé did, was his spindly height. Auguste would peer down from behind his round, near-sighted spectacles. His forehead was high; his hair receded at the front, but Piccard cut it himself and so let it grow long on the back, and it curled broadly on its ends. He often wore a Basque beret, or, in the summer, a scarecrow hat. Every feature on his owlish face seemed to lead to a point, but his poor sight made him look gentle. His unworldliness was just the manifestation of his near-constant focus on scientific problems. He insisted that his best thoughts came to him not in the laboratory, but on long walks, hands behind back. "He always looked like his head was in the clouds," Olivier Maillard, the brother-in-law of Auguste's son Jacques Piccard, later told Jean-François Rubin, a biologist and author. "But he remembered every last detail." Piccard was always calculating, secure in the belief, common to the age, in the supremacy of scientific technique: everything, if you worked it through well enough, could be explained. His response to any problem was to start inscribing calculations in his notebook, earning him the nickname of "the extra decimal point". His scientific curiosity was wide-ranging – he was even made a member of honour of the "Belgian Committee for the investigation of reportedly paranormal phenomena". Piccard contented himself with very little. "To work, he needed nothing, everything was in his head," his daughter Denise told Rubin. "On his desks, along with the files of his correspondence, next to his table of logarithms, he had his Bible: he would read it, not as a theologian lacking doubt, but with respect, with interest. He often talked, and when I would suggest to him that theology would allow me to rise higher and to descend more deeply than him, he acquiesced smiling. He had within him a sincere humility, like a spirit of childhood, of confidence, of faith."

Although always neatly presented, Piccard didn't care much for physical appearances, eschewing tailored suits in favour of second-hand clothes. He wore the pastelbord collars traditional to Belgium, which he would tear up and throw away after use. The rumour was that his wife filled his pockets with money in the morning, but in fact he carried money in a bag tied around his neck, underneath his shirt, which he wore even in bed. He always had two watches – like all good Swiss, he said. In his waistcoat pocket, he kept a very large slide rule for quick conversions.

On campus, his students loved and admired him, precisely for his wandering mind. One student once came across Piccard on a narrow campus path and stepped aside to let him pass. They began a discussion, which Piccard soon interrupted to ask which direction he had come from. Taken aback, the student replied and pointed to the lecture hall. Piccard, satisfied, concluded: "If I came from there, that means I must have already had lunch," nodded to the student and strolled on. In lectures, Piccard would command the blackboard, sketching mechanical diagrams with chalk in both hands at once, then break off to admonish the students: "The Lord gave you two hands and a brain. Why don't you use them all?" Piccard was known on campus as the "absent-minded professor" – a nickname that the press would later adopt, and use to cast doubt on Piccard's ability to succeed in his adventures. Piccard, "for all his technical virtuosity, seems at times as unworldly as a mediaeval saint," one newspaper later wrote. "His motives are simple and good; his inventions are not aimed at making money or at killing people... Individuals help him in smaller ways. Everyone smiles and wishes him well."

Piccard was a popular lecturer. His halls were usually full and students from other courses and even universities would seek them out: a young German called Wernher von Braun once attended one and, while Piccard talked, made a promise to himself that he would one day send a rocket to the moon. The students were "continually seeking ways of doing him a kindness", according to one newspaper. Noticing that the professor seemed to have only one suit to his name, a student who was the son of a Verviers cloth manufacture took his measurements, wove the cloth himself and begged Piccard to wear the suit he had made. The next day, the professor did, walking to the university in his new suit. His wife, tidying the house, was horrified to find her husband's only pair of trousers hanging over the end of the bed. It was only when she asked another student to check what Auguste was wearing below his shirt that she learned of the brand-new suit. This left her slightly confused, but happy that Auguste had not just forgotten his trousers.

When it came to interests beyond academia, Auguste cared little for the arts. He didn't drink or smoke, in an age when cigarettes were supposed to clear the lungs, and abhorred those habits in others (although he thought smoking the greater sin by far). Piccard liked photography and walking. The love for the outdoors, which his father Jules had inculcated, never left him; Auguste was something of an ecologist before the term was invented. His first scientific publication had been on tree roots and he later published a pamphlet, *The Great Pity of our Alpine*

Flowers, which lamented their disappearance. "The beauties with which the Creator provided our homeland are dear to us; everything related to their existence touches us directly," he wrote. He developed a very close knowledge of landscape he grew up in. "He knew the rocks, the flowers, the glaciers, the summits, almost personally," remembers Denise. "There was an intimate relationship between him and the Alps." One afternoon, he was walking with his son Jacques, still a child, when they came across a small tree that had been uprooted. He took it back to their house, and explained the role of roots, leaves, and branches, then planted the tree in front of the house. Years later, Jacques was happy to see it grow into the most majestic specimen of the neighbourhood. Auguste would contentedly toil in the garden in front of the Piccards' house in Brussels. When a professional gardener trimmed the wisteria a bit too short, Auguste's reaction was like "a day of mourning", according to Denise.

*

Professor Calculus, despite his apparent lack of attention to the non-scientific world, is the only character in the Tintin books to show any attraction to women. Haddock may have been too drunk, and, although a spokesperson for Hergé studios said in 2009 that Tintin was definitely not gay ("very macho in fact," was the statement), one does wonder. Calculus, though, falls in rapture with Bianca Castafiore, for whom he creates a new type of rose through botanical experiments. The green-fingered Auguste Piccard was likewise his own sort of romantic.

Marianne Denis, born in 1895, the ninth of ten children, grew up in Paris. Her father, Ernest Denis, was a professor at the Sorbonne. He specialised in political studies of Germany and Bohemia, and founded and edited the magazine *La*

Nation Tchèque. He was instrumental in the creation of the Czechoslovak state in 1918, working alongside its first president, Thomas Masaryk. The latter described Denis as a "historian of nations and their evolution; he understood us, us and our history, and he was accepted, he, a Frenchman, among the ranks of our national leaders." A statue to Denis was erected near the church of St-Nicolas in Prague in October 1928, some years after Denis's death; on the evening of April 20, 1940, German occupiers tore it down.

Denis was stern and unyielding, especially in matters of honour and morality. He did not immediately take to the young Auguste Piccard, who, in spite of otherwise excellent recommendations, had made the unforgivable error of not being French. Still, he allowed Auguste to marry Marianne, on May 26, 1920, on condition that the couple's first child was born in France. Had the baby been a boy, he would have been able to serve in the French army; two years after the end of the Great War, Denis was seeking to defend France any way that he could. The baby was born in 1921 – a girl, whom they called Denise to honour Marianne's family name (she would, in 1960, become one of the first female vicars ordained in Switzerland). Jacques was born a year later, in Brussels. He wasn't therefore bound by his grandfather's vow, but still ended up fighting for the liberation of France in 1944. In 1924, Marianne was born; the year after, Hélène (they would become a nurse and librarian respectively). Geneviève, born in 1931, eventually married an Italian count.

As we shall see, Marianne's care enabled her husband's (literal) flights of fancy; Auguste would not have achieved so much without her. When he was decorated by the king of Belgium, so was she, for courageously putting up with such a husband. According to her son Jacques, she "never reproached my father for putting himself in danger. She always supported him. She obviously had a very limited material role, but brought support of a moral and mental kind."

Auguste raised his children in a house much like the one he himself had grown up in. "It is all high thinking and poor living in that house," one newspaper report said. He encouraged scientific enquiry in his children just as his own father had done. On winter nights, he took Denise and Jacques to the roof of his university to observe the stars. His explanation of how spaghetti was cooked made his children think that they were "eating convection currents". Bewildering electrical circuits ran through the house; light was refracted throughout by prisms. Holidays were invariably spent in the mountains. Auguste gave his children a strict education, but he was attentive and caring, explaining the principles of nature while they sat on his knees. On the children's birthdays, Auguste would inflate balloons, which, let loose, would crowd the ceiling. "He was like a magician," Jacques said. "Who does not dream of having a father like that? We were overwhelmed. I don't even remember him once using a calculator."

*

In 1926, Jean returned from America for a family gathering and Auguste confided a plan to his twin. Auguste had just proven the constancy of the speed of light. He wanted to study cosmic rays, which were little understood at the time. Henri Becquerel had discovered radioactivity in 1896; in 1906, Theodor Wolf had developed an electrometer, a device to measure radiation, and taken it to the top of the Eiffel Tower, where he had found higher levels of radiation than at ground level. Subsequent experiments, by Victor Hess and Robert Millikan, had attached electrometers to free balloons, a similar method to that used by De Bort to discover the stratosphere; Hess had concluded that "The results of my observation are best explained by the assumption that a radiation of very great penetrating power enters our atmosphere from above." Hess won a Nobel prize for his work. Millikan later coined the term "cosmic rays", to distinguish this sort of external radiation from that which comes from the earth itself.

The atmosphere, which absorbed many of these cosmic rays, made such studies difficult: scientists could not observe their experiments directly, only wait for their balloons to return to earth. Auguste's logic was simple: all he had to do was study the rays where there was no atmosphere. "A generation had laboured to devise automatic instruments for recording pressure, temperature and humidity," he later wrote. "But the measurement of cosmic rays was a delicate operation very different in nature, and could not be effected at the time with the necessary precision by these automatic instruments. This is why I decided to ascend myself to 10 miles."

The fact that no man had been there before, let alone with a laboratory, and that most scientists assumed it was impossible for a human to survive in the upper regions, was incidental.

"I had thus to construct a particularly large and light balloon, so that it could carry observers and instruments," wrote Piccard. He began making calculations.

Lighter than Air

On September 19, 1783, Louis XVI and Marie Antoinette watched a hot-air balloon launch from the front courtyard of the Palace of Versailles. Three cannon shots had served as a count-down to take off. The balloon's pilots were a duck, a rooster and a sheep, called Montauciel ("climb to the sky"). The sheep was chosen as a reasonable approximation of human physiology. The duck, an animal used to altitude, was included as a control to determine the effects of travelling in a balloon. The rooster was a further control, as a duck-sized animal unused to altitude. The sky-blue balloon, called the *Aérostat Réveillon* and decorated with golden suns, royal insignia and signs of the zodiac, flew for eight minutes, travelling roughly two miles (3.2 km) at 1,500 ft (460 m), before landing. Its crew was mainly unharmed; one of the cockerel's wings was slightly hurt, but the duck was fine and Montauciel the sheep was found grazing quite calmly on some nearby grass. It later emerged that the cock's injuries were not caused by the flight: several witnesses said they had seen Montauciel kicking the rooster before take-off.

The *Aérostat Réveillon* was the first "manned" flight in aviation history, but ballooning had a long tradition. Among the inventions attributed to Zhuge Liang, a chancellor of the state of Hu Shan during the Three Kingdoms period in China who reportedly created the landmine, the wheelbarrow and the repeating crossbow, was an early type of hot-air balloon: an airborne lantern used for signalling – or perhaps the delivery of love letters. As Richard Holmes notes in his recent book *Falling Upwards: How We Took to the Air*, "Peruvian funeral rituals involved sending corpses out over the Pacific by hot-air balloon." Some have speculated that the Nazca lines – the meticulous carvings that stretch over miles in Southern Peru – were planned using balloons (that or flying saucers).

But the first recorded balloon flight would not take place for another millennium. That it took so long is surprising, given that the technology required to build a hot-air balloon is not very advanced – certainly within the capabilities of those who lived in ancient Rome, Peru in the fifth century AD or Renaissance Italy (Leonardo Da Vinci completely overthought human flight with his diagrams for helicopters) – and that the insight which prompted the Montgolfier brothers was reportedly so mundane. Myth has it that Joseph Montgolfier's – or perhaps his wife's – blouse caught fire and floated up the chimney, thus prompting the dawn of aviation. In fact, Montgolfier had been playing close attention to the experiments of Henry Cavendish and Joseph Priestley, who had discovered "different kinds of air", as LTC Rolt relates in his brilliant history of the early days of ballooning, *The Aeronauts*, since republished as *The Balloonists*. Montgolfier himself said that one evening he was watching a fire, pondering how the French might seize Gibraltar from the British. Repeated assaults by land and sea had proved in vain, but Montgolfier wondered if the air that lifted the embers from the fire could also lift French soldiers over British defences: "a super-human means of introducing our soldiers into this impregnable fortress… right above the heads of the English". He had no conception that heated air, being lighter than the surrounding cooler air, rose; instead, he hypothesised that the smoke contained a special vapour, which he quickly named Montgolfier gas. His hypothesis was that different materials produced different lifting gases: the perfect recipe, which he later concocted during an experiment in front of the King and Queen, was burning straw, rotten meat and old shoes. According to one account, "the noxious smell thus produced obliged them to retire at once."

Joseph's first experiment was to fill a paper bag with steam, which resulted in a soggy paper bag. But in November 1782, he a built a small, one-metre-cubed frame out of thin wood, covering the sides and top with taffeta cloth. He lit a fire underneath it and the prototype quickly lifted off, hitting the ceiling. Joseph wrote a letter to his brother Etienne, the fifteenth child of the family: "Get in a supply of taffeta and of cordage, quickly, and you will see one of the most astonishing sights in the world." On December 14 the same year, the brothers released a device three times the size of that first Montgolfier balloon. It rose so quickly that the brothers lost sight of it, and the aircraft drifted for 1.2 miles.

The brothers gave the first public display of a larger craft in Annonay, in the French Alps, on June 4, 1783. The flight lasted ten minutes, covered a distance of a mile and reached an altitude of 6,560 ft (2,000 metres). They teamed up with a wallpaper manufacturer, Jean-Baptiste Réveillon, who created the animal-crewed balloon which flew that September in Versailles. Manned flights followed, in October 1783; Etienne Montgolfier may have been the first human to lift off earth in a test flight (accounts differ), but Jean-François Pilâtre de Rozier, a scientist who worked with the Montgolfiers, was officially the first human to fly a balloon. Two years later, he would be the first human to be killed in one.

Simultaneous invention is common in science – historians call these events "multiples"; a study in 1922 identified 148 major scientific discoveries that had been made almost simultaneously. The Montgolfier brothers won the credit, but at the same time, in the same city, Jacques Charles was experimenting with hydrogen. His approach was more rigorous, and more technologically advanced, than that of the Montgolfiers. A scientist, he had studied the work of Robert Boyle, who had discovered hydrogen 100 years earlier. Charles thought hydrogen could be a suitable lifting agent for balloons and set about making a prototype. The principle of a hydrogen balloon was the same as that of a hot-air balloon: a gas sufficiently lighter than air should be able to bear a load into the sky. In practice, hydrogen balloons would prove to have much greater lift, and be able to fly longer, than hot-air balloons, although with less control over altitude. Along with the Robert brothers, Charles invented the airtight gasbag, by dissolving rubber in a solution of turpentine, varnishing silk sheets and stitching them into an envelope. They used alternating strips of red and white silk, creating the particular balloon style that persists to this day, despite the attractiveness of the Montgolfiers' more idiosyncratic designs.

Charles launched his hydrogen balloon, unmanned, on August 26, 1783, less than a year after the first Montgolfier experiments. Benjamin Franklin (who thought balloons might have some military application and would later patent the balloon fridge – an icebox taken up to high altitude – "anchored in the Air" – and thus kept cool) was among the Parisian crowd looking on, which was by this stage becoming quite au fait with flying machines. The villagers of Gonesse, where the 35-cubic-metre sphere of rubberised silk landed, were, however, not, and set upon the craft with pitchforks and knives. A month later, the French government issued a notice advising the general public that balloons were "far from an alarming phenomenon" and generally harmless. On December 1, 1783,

Charles, with his assistant Nicolas-Louis Robert, made the first manned hydrogen-filled balloon flight – ten days after the first manned Montgolfier flight – in front of a crowd of 400,000, among them, Joseph Montgolfier. As the pilots took off, Charles turned to Robert and said: "I'm finished with Earth. From now on our place is in the sky!"

"Ballomania" quickly gripped populations on the continent and across the Channel as hordes of aeronauts took to the sky – in December 1784, Horace Walpole wrote in a letter that "This enormous capital [London], that must have some occupation, is most innocently amused with those philosophic playthings, air-balloons... half-a-million of people that impassion themselves for any object are always more childish than children... "Walpole took a rather dim view of balloon demonstrations, labelling them "a mere job for getting money from gaping fools" and chiding Vincenzo Lunardi, a balloonist who had won fame in England in 1784, not for risking his own life, which Walpole didn't mind, but for that of the cat he took up with him. Walpole wasn't the only British curmudgeon: when George III offered funds to the Royal Society to finance balloon flights, its president Joseph Banks declined, saying that "no good whatever could result from them"; in 1832, the poet Percy Bysshe Shelley felt compelled to write "A Defence of Ballooning". Even in 1851, a baffled foreign newspaper correspondent could still report that "a sort of balloon mania has been raging in Paris for months... The Parisians seem as tickled with each repetition of the spectacle, as though aero-navigation were a novelty." But even 150 years on today, balloons have lost little of their romance.

The principles of Charles's hydrogen design would dominate ballooning for the next 200 years. There were innovations. Pilatre de Rozier invented the hybrid hot-air and hydrogen balloon, combining the self-regulating nature of

Montgolfière with the greater lifting power of the Charlière (as the different designs of the Montgolfiers and Charles were known). His plan was to fly it over the Channel, but he had grave reservations about the design: he was "certain of meeting with death". He was correct. Shortly after take-off, the balloon exploded, killing de Rozier.

Although several balloons saw military action, both in Europe and the US, and new altitude records were set, the hydrogen balloon itself had not changed much over 150 years, when Auguste Piccard turned his attention to it. He secured 500,000 Belgian Francs (around £130,000 today) from the *Fonds National de la Recherche Scientifique*, an institution created by King Albert of Belgium in 1928 and funded by the Solvay family with 100 million francs. Showing a pioneering sensibility towards sponsorship and marketing that was ahead of its time, but natural to three generations of Piccards, Auguste named his balloon the *F.N.R.S.*

To observe his cosmic rays, Piccard estimated that he would need to go up about ten miles. No such flight had ever been undertaken. The sounding balloons pioneered by De Bort and studied by Auguste as a child were still in use; a balloon sent up from Hamburg had recently reached nearly twenty-two miles. When it was retrieved, its instruments showed that the temperature there was about minus 50 degrees celsius and that the air pressure was about $1/250^{th}$ that of the atmosphere at sea level. Piccard called the stratosphere the "region of perpetual good weather, eternal peace", but the environment at that altitude was an impossible one for humans to live in, using existing technology. Today, flying in the very low levels of the stratosphere in commercial airliners is routine, and comfortable enough to pass the time watching films and drinking bloody marys (the reduced pressure in airplane cabins affects the taste buds, making tomato juice much more palatable – and thus much more popular – than it is on the ground). But at the beginning of the twentieth century, to venture into the sky was a huge risk, and it was often lethal. Piccard's *F.N.R.S.* was experimental and high-tech, but may have seemed slightly old-fashioned nonetheless. The pioneering powered flights of Lindbergh and Earheart had delighted the public during the 1920s; Piccard was aware that he was fighting the tide of popular interest: "The free balloon conquered the troposphere, where it reigned sovereign for a century and a half," he wrote. "Then, competition came in the form of the airplane. The world's interest turned more and more to heavier-than-air, which was perfected to such a point that it could, in 1930 beat every altitude record. That's when the balloon made a great effort. It metamorphosed itself to conquer the stratosphere."

Several stratospheric attempts had already been made. On September 5, 1862, English balloonist Henry Tracey Coxwell and meteorologist James Glaisher rose to 3,900 ft (11,887 m) before they lost consciousness. Glaisher became hypoxic – oxygen-deprived – and thus insensible; Coxwell, his hands frost-bitten, was forced to use his teeth to open the gas valve and prompt a rapid descent back to earth. In April 1875, a French team reached 28,215 ft (8,600 m), but two crew members died from breathing the thin air. The third survived but became deaf. The most technologically advanced attempt before Piccard's was a US Army Air Corps balloon in 1927. Captain Hawthorne C. Gray flew a 1,900 cubic metres single-ply, rubberised silk envelope. On his first flight, he set a US altitude record of 29,000 ft (8,839 ft.) but passed out when his oxygen equipment froze; luckily, the balloon descended of its own accord. On his second attempt, on May 4, he reached 42,470 ft (12,945 m), but the record was discounted, as Gray was forced to parachute from the gondola to save himself after the gas valve became jammed in the open position, causing the balloon to fall too fast. His third attempt into the stratosphere, on November 27 the same year, was a grim success. Gray reached the same altitude as his previous flight and stayed inside the gondola, testing high-altitude oxygen systems and scientific equipment. He successfully landed the balloon, but was found dead inside the open gondola. The official report noted "no marks or violence of a crash on his body"; the last entry in his logbook, recorded in jerky handwriting, was to say he had reached 40,000 feet.

Piccard understood he would have to recreate the conditions of a breathable atmosphere ten miles high. The percentage of oxygen in the stratosphere is more or less the same as at sea level. But the low air pressure makes it difficult for oxygen to pass through selectively permeable lung membranes into the blood. This can lead to vomiting, headaches, distorted vision and a blunt inability to think; in the most extreme cases, like that of Captain Gray, it causes haemorrhaging in the lungs, heart failure and an undesirable accumulation of fluid around the brain, leading to death. Go too high in the stratosphere, and with a low enough air pressure, the body's heat will be sufficient to boil its blood. Therefore Piccard's balloon basket would not be a basket at all, but a hermetically sealed cabin – completely water- and air-tight, and supplied with tanks of oxygen. This pressurised cabin, the first of its kind, would allow Auguste not only to survive, but also to conduct his scientific experiments in relative comfort. It was not without its risks, however. As *Popular Mechanics* noted before the attempt, "... such a cabin is perfectly safe: but if it leaks, it at once becomes a death chamber." Many at the time thought that exposure to the thin air of the stratosphere led to instant death, rather than the drawn-out descent into hypoxia, and many questioned the feasibility of the cabin: "The specialists of the day considered my suggestion as unrealisable," Piccard later wrote, in an account of his stratospheric ascents. "But the single objection that they were able to make was that up till then no one had ever done it. How often have I heard reasoning of this sort! But it is just the function of the engineer to place his reliance upon theory when creating something new. If I had been an aviator I should perhaps have constructed, at the beginning, a stratospheric aeroplane. But being an aeronaut I plunged into the construction of a balloon. It was besides a relatively simple thing to suspend an airtight cabin to the free balloon." Simple, but as Piccard himself noted, with typical accuracy and self-detachment: "Our lives depend upon the airtightness and the strength of this cabin."

Piccard's chamber was spherical, since this shape offered the maximum volume for the smallest surface area. The cabin was 2.1 metres in diameter, which Piccard reckoned adequate: "Two observers, surrounded by their instruments, will be perfectly comfortable here, surveying the outside world through two round portholes of a convenient diameter" (8 cm being Piccard's convenience). The sphere had to be strong enough to resist its own internal pressure when the outside pressure would be no more than one-tenth of an atmosphere; otherwise it would explode. Piccard chose aluminium 3.5 millimetres thick; to avoid the windows shattering due to the different pressures prevailing on the two faces, he used double-glazing: two panes of glass, each 0.7 mm thick, separated by a thin layer of air which would act as an insulator. These windows "offer no chance of breakage, even when obliged to sustain a difference in pressure of nine-tenths of an atmosphere." (Nine years later, Piccard would construct portholes strong enough to resist a pressure of 600 atmospheres – underwater.) Half the cabin was painted black, the other half white: a mechanism – a small electric motor turning a propeller – would slowly and constantly turn the cabin in the sun to regulate its temperature. Only the occupants' feet would get cold, Piccard joked, as no rays could reach the underside of the gondola.

The cabin was built in Liège, at the factories of George L'Hoir, a Belgian industrialist. The factory made metal kegs for storing pressurised beer, among other things. Piccard gave L'Hoir the plans for his gondola without telling him much: when it was finished, L'Hoir told the professor that it was "rather unconventional for a beer barrel". Piccard himself closely supervised the construction; black-and-white film footage shows him wandering around the metalworks, peering and craning, as molten ore flows into vast containers. The process was nearly faultless, save for the manholes. There were to be two of these, 46 cm in diameter, and circular, rather than the more common oval. Circular covers would be more airtight, and would suit the spherical form of the cabin better. Piccard had ordered that the covers be put inside the cabin before the last sheet of aluminium was welded. A worker neglected the order, perhaps, according to Piccard, deliberately. "For him, a man of action, only practical experience counted. He was wary of theory and was not going to let anyone impose upon him; still less a university professor whose reasonings were abstract." If Piccard was too condescending, it was perhaps understandable: he did stand to lose his life. He pointed out that the hatches would not now fit in; the worker tried to force them, "like a child trying to push a saucepan lid into the saucepan". The next time Piccard returned to the factory, the hatches were inside the cabin. Auguste never worked out how they did it.

The cabin was fitted with a Dräger apparatus, which would supply oxygen and, more importantly, remove carbon dioxide (avoiding too much carbon dioxide would become something of a family obsession for the three generations of Piccards). It released a thin but rapid stream of oxygen, from a steel cylinder of the gas compressed to 200 atmospheres. The oxygen, run through an injector, would be mixed with the air already in the cabin, and this mixture would be blown through a wide tube containing an alkali, potassium hydroxide, which absorbs carbon dioxide from the air to form potassium carbonate. Each minute the Dräger apparatus would produce just over two litres of oxygen and blow 80 litres of air through the alkali, giving 82 litres of fresh air every minute. In addition Piccard would keep some oxygen in reserve tanks. The cabin also held two parachutes and the scientific equipment: an electrometer, for measuring the electricity in the upper air, and a potential difference meter.

Because the balloon would use hydrogen rather than hot air, ballast would be crucial in controlling the rate of ascent and descent. In an open-air gondola, the pilot can throw extra weight from his or her basket. This was impossible to do in the *F.N.R.S.* without compromising the airtight seal. Piccard drew inspiration from a childhood memory of the circus. "One day, I was taken to visit a menagerie," he wrote. "In one of the cages was a lion and a lion-tamer. How would the tamer get out without the lion being able to follow him? It was a revelation for the little lad that I then was: the tamer went into a little adjoining cage through a door which he closed behind him: only after this did he open a second door which gave him access to the outside: at no time were the two doors open at once and the beast had not been able to get out." Forty years later, Piccard had not forgotten the scene. "The tamer was now the ballast, which had to get out of the cabin without allowing the lion, that is, the air, to follow it."

Auguste Piccard and his team

Piccard designed a container, with two taps. Using a funnel, he would pour the ballast, composed of lead shot, into the first tap. Then, with that tap closed, the other tap would be opened and the ballast poured into the sky, onto the ground below. Piccard had chosen lead as his ballast since the metal was denser than sand or water. The latter substances were the only materials permitted by international regulations, but there was no room for sandbags or watertanks in the cabin. Lead took up less space, but would have to be accepted by the authorities; Piccard was also eager not to injure any individuals unlucky enough to be wandering ten miles below the *F.N.R.S*, so he chose a very fine-grain lead shot. To prove its safety, he stood beneath the large chimney of the University of Brussels. An assistant, furnished with several buckets of different grains of lead 165 ft (50 m) up at the top of the chimney, poured the lead onto Piccard's head. The professor emerged unharmed, if sooty. Still, the regulators wouldn't budge: ballast had to be sand or water, or there would be no flight. Auguste, "to cut all discussion short", called his ballast "lead-sand". "This explanation aroused no objection," he wrote. "However, by definition, sand is a non-metallic substance and nobody has ever seen lead sand."

The balloon itself was constructed in Augsburg, by the Reidinger company. A huge gas-bag was needed to lift the weight of the gondola and its contents – about 1,000 kg all told – into the stratosphere. Piccard made his calculations, determining that the balloon should have a volume of 14,130 cubic metres and a diameter of 30 metres. This led to one of the main difficulties in the construction of a stratospheric balloon. A balloon of this huge volume (most modern hot-air balloons have a volume of around 2,800 cubic metres), completely inflated with hydrogen, would have, at take-off, a static lift of nearly 16 tonnes. To resist this force, and so prevent the balloon soaring away from the cabin and hurtling into the heavens, the materials and net would have to be extremely strong, which would make them heavier. But at ten miles high, a cubic metre of hydrogen can bear only one tenth of the weight it can at sea-level: the balloon would never reach the stratosphere. To keep the materials light, then, Piccard decided only to part-inflate the balloon with hydrogen, to a fifth of its maximum volume. During the ascent, the gas would expand as atmospheric pressure decreased. Only in the stratosphere would the envelope of the *F.N.R.S.* take its final, spherical form.

This presented Piccard with another design challenge. When conventional balloons were rigged, the envelope was spread out over the ground and a net thrown over the top.

The gas was introduced and the envelope would dilate, lift off the ground and bob up the net, which was held by bags of ballast. As the balloon grew and grew in volume, the bags were moved from the mesh lower down. The main concern of the riggers was to make sure that the folds in the expanding envelope open out completely, without being caught in the folds of the net. When the envelope was fully inflated, the ropes attached to the net were tied to the hoop of the gondola and the balloon was ready to go.

The same method would not work for the *F.N.R.S.* Only the upper portion of the envelope would contain gas; the rest of the envelope would remain empty, hanging in large, loose folds, which would gradually fill during the ascent. Piccard was unsure how to avoid the accidents that would arise from folds snagged in the net. "We could not count upon a procession of guardian angels to release the folds during the ascent"; Auguste wrote, "and as we could not give up the envelope, we were obliged instead to give up the net." Instead, a heavy rubber belt was sewn to the gasbag three quarters of the way down from the bottom of the balloon; the suspension cords holding the aluminium cabin were attached directly to this belt. To hold the balloon fast prior to ascent, another wide belt was sewn around the circumference of the gasbag, a third of the way down from the top of the balloon, and 32 double ropes attached to that belt held the balloon down to the ground.

Reidinger made the envelope using two layers of high-quality cotton, with a middle band of rubber that weighed 1.6 kg per square metre, and dyed the fabric with chloramine yellow, giving the state-of-the-art balloon a jaundiced look; the colour was chosen to absorb some of the blue, violet and ultraviolet rays of the sun. Piccard estimated that the metal of the gondola would be sufficient protection against the ultraviolet rays, but he speculated that gamma rays might tan his face and hands.

On Friday, September 5 1930, Piccard brought the gondola to Augsburg on a truck that travelled at ten miles per hour all the way from Belgium. The globe was attached to the balloon and plans were made to fly on the first quiet day after Tuesday. The *F.N.R.S* was complete, the largest balloon ever built, ready to shoot for the stratosphere.

Piccard would fly with Dr Paul Kipfer. A Belgian born in Switzerland, Kipfer was a smiling young man of 25 who proclaimed he did not feel nervous at all about the flight. The *F.N.R.S.* would be his first-ever balloon ascent.

But having conquered all the challenges of design, Piccard was faced with another, more intractable problem: Bavarian bureaucracy. He had chosen Augsburg as the point of departure because it was where the balloon had been made, as well as having the other distinct advantage, in Piccard's eyes, "of being distant from the sea in any direction". Balloons, though, like any vehicle, were subject to regulations and the extremely experimental *F.N.R.S* complied with nearly none of them: the absence of a net and the extreme lightness of the construction materials were particular problems. ("An administration can make no exceptions, above all when a foreign professor is in question!") The Germans refused Piccard a certificate of airworthiness, as his aircraft was "of a type never tried before and therefore no evidence of its reliability was available". Piccard, with his usual elegant thinking, applied to his native Switzerland for the permit; international agreements allowed a Swiss aeronaut to leave Germany with just such a certificate. Bern gave the authorisation, on two conditions: that the trip was made at the risk of the aeronauts, and that Piccard and his assistant wear helmets. Piccard complied, but his design for a new type of headgear hardly matched the high-tech standard of the *F.N.R.S.,* and showed that he perhaps did not take the officials' request very seriously: he and Kipfer would wear wicker baskets turned-upside down and padded with cushions. As soon as the hatch was shut, they removed the helmets, and used the baskets as extra storage and the cushions as extra padding for their seats. "In case of a sea landing," Piccard drily noted, "the cushions, with their kapok filling, will serve as a life-vest."

With wicker helmets on, the pair looked ridiculous. But they were ready to go up.

Piccard and Kipfer with their "helmets"
– also useful as lifejackets or seats.

Up

E arly on the morning of September 14, 1930, the yellow, rubberised gasbag was inflated for the first time. The F.N.R.S. was soon straining at its anchor lines, ready to soar 10 miles into the stratosphere. Auguste Piccard kissed his wife and children, waved to the crowd which numbered in the thousands, and followed Kipfer into the globular gondola. Piccard pulled shut the manhole and screwed it fast to make the cabin airtight; he and Kipfer checked the oxygen supply, the Dräger apparatus and the scientific equipment. Through a porthole, Piccard gave the signal to cast off and the ropes were released. The balloon remained exactly where it was.

Some said Piccard's calculations were wrong: that the 2,200 cubic metres of hydrogen in the gasbag – about a seventh of the total volume – were not enough to lift the balloon and cabin. That, or the preparation – longer than anticipated – had allowed the gas to cool too much. The wind picked up and batted about the yellow gasbag dangerously, damaging some of the scientific instruments and tearing a small hole in the envelope. Three hours after the scheduled launch time, the order was given to abandon the flight. The gas was let out and the balloon, nearly 50 metres tall, slowly slumped back down to the ground. "The crowd seemed greatly disappointed when the balloon failed to rise," the *New York Times* reported. Piccard noted with understatement: "I, too, was disappointed."

"Had I been able to get away an hour earlier," he told journalists afterwards, "everything would have been all right.

"The sudden down-pressing wind confronted me with a dilemma: Either of throwing off ballast, or not starting. Had I thrown off ballast I could not have risen to the height desired. I therefore preferred not to start.

"When I try again it will be only during a long and continued period of high pressure, even if I must wait until early winter."

Piccard was forced to wait longer than that, until May the next year, and put up with public scepticism on a number of different fronts. Supporters of Piccard in Brussels and Paris claimed his Zurich associates were turning his scientific adventure into a business matter by selling exclusive contracts where possible. Others loudly queried Piccard's technical methodology. Asmus Hansen, a German aviator and engineer, declared that Piccard would have trouble landing and predicted that the "abnormal extension" (the expanding volume of the hydrogen) of the balloon in the stratosphere would lead to entanglement of the line operating the safety valve. Hansen's prediction was startlingly and horribly accurate, but he had his own reason to talk down the *F.N.R.S.* He was working on a rival project, a stratospheric airplane being made at the Junkers works at Dessau. Likewise, members of the German Society for Scientific Research, which was sponsoring the Hansen project, suggested that Piccard's plans would offer no significance for future stratospheric travel, as his experiments dealt only with theoretical physics and the nature of cosmic rays, rather than the practical engineering concerns: his approach was too scientific. But then, for others, Piccard's approach wasn't scientific enough: some scientists argued that the nature of cosmic rays was already known; that there was no question of them having an effect on passengers protected by cabin walls, given that the atmosphere surround Earth weakens them; that he had not revealed the specifics of his scientific programme; and that he did not anyway have the scientific equipment suitable to make these studies that he had not specified. Nor had Piccard asked the help of other researchers, such as the physicist Erich Regener, who had developed self-recording electroscopes to measure cosmic rays at altitude and would later help create the V2 rocket, and the German meteorologist Hugo Hersell, who had investigated the characteristics of the stratosphere. The final (and just as inconsistent) line of argument from the German scientists ran that, although Piccard might help ascertain certain theories, clarifying interesting problems and so on, to laymen his observations would be no more interesting than the results of experiments carried out every day in the laboratory by hardworking, less glory-seeking scientists who, unlike Piccard, knew their place. In summary, Piccard's flight could not work; if it did, it was too focused on theoretical physics anyway; in fact, it was not sufficiently focused on theoretical physics; and his science was, anyway, too scientific and of no interest to the layman, and thus should not be attempted.

Others simply thought Piccard reckless. The *New York Times* reported that some believed it was "not soundly organized from a technical viewpoint". "It is not my intention to commit suicide," Piccard publicly responded. "I have a wife and children. The only danger would be from an explosion of the balloon, due to changing atmospheric pressure, but the aluminium cabinet will harden in the severe cold of an altitude of 50,000 feet [15,240 m]. As for landing, our car can stand severe bumps without damage." He was a scientist, not a daredevil: "the modern scientific seeker should not cast himself foremost into these perils," he wrote. "The sport of scientists consists in utilising all he knows, in foreseeing all the dangers, in studying every detail with profound attention, in always using the admirable instrument of mathematical analysis wherever it can shed its magic light upon his work." But Piccard hadn't foreseen all the dangers; he hadn't studied every detail.

For now he ignored the criticisms. Despite the long winter of waiting, Piccard remained intent: the *New York Times* wrote that "Professor Piccard shows no signs of abandoning the project and the obstacles are seemingly merely increasing his determination."

Finally, on May 26, 1931, the weather forecasts were favourable. At 11 pm that night, the filling of the gasbag began, this time roughly 2,800 cubic metres of hydrogen were pumped in. The next morning, the large balloon stood 80 metres tall once more. Underneath, the gondola hung from the hoop, "relatively toylike in size", *Popular Mechanics* recorded.

The flight had been designated CH 113, a reference to the fact that this would be Piccard's thirteenth balloon flight. To the journalists who pointed out the portent, Piccard replied by quoting his friend Einstein: "God does not play dice." Once more, though, the wind rose again. The situation became chaotic, and the wind knocked the cabin off its lorry, putting it, according to Piccard, "slightly out of shape". He and Kipfer would notice the consequences of this later in the flight, but for now, Piccard had to take the decision: stay or go.

Piccard and Kipfer entered the cabin and closed the manhole behind them. The balloon looked like an inverted teardrop. The wind increased and the ground crew attached another rope to the hoop, without informing the pilots.

At 3.57 am, Kipfer looked out of the manhole and noticed that a factory chimney was passing beneath them. The assistants had let go of the balloon two minutes earlier, without giving the signal of departure. The most historic balloon flight since de Rozier's trip in the Montgolfiers' balloon had begun in a similarly haphazard fashion.

The *F.N.R.S.* bounded up into the pale sky; "the two men

Auguste addresses the press ahead of launch

hitched their chariot to a star," *Popular Mechanics* wrote. The balloon soon reached 10,000 feet (3,048 m), then veered southwest; 25 minutes after take-off, the balloon had reached 50,000 feet. At 4.45 am, the *F.N.R.S.* was once more directly over Augsburg, apparently nearly in the stratosphere, and a strong wind was carrying it due west. The *New York Times* reported: "It is expected that the scientists will land this afternoon somewhere between Freiburg and Basel."

*

Inside the cabin, the ascent had been less serene. "We went up very quickly," noted Piccard in his logbook. A few minutes after launch, Piccard noticed that the insulator of the electric sounder going through the wall had been broken when the gondola was batted off its transport. The flight was only minutes old but it was already in trouble. "The air – our precious air – was rushing out, whistling through the hole." Piccard went to work fixing it, with his mixture of Vaseline and tow. "If we don't become airtight immediately," he told Kipfer as they reached two and a half miles high, "we must pull the valve and land, if we don't want to suffocate." Piccard didn't yet know the valve was blocked, by the rope attached just before take-off.

Little by little, Piccard plugged the large hole and the pilots were able to relax. At 4.25 am, Piccard asked Kipfer their altitude: 51,200 ft, he replied. In less than half an hour, the *F.N.R.S.* had gone up nine miles (14.5 km). The balloon, which had looked like a dried pear at the point of departure, was now fully spherical. "At last, here we are in the stratosphere!" Piccard said.

For the first time, humans could see the curvature of the planet they lived on. The pilots took it in. Below, stretched a field of vision of 246,000 square miles (637,137 square kilometres) - more than the size of France. But the earth was veiled by the troposphere, which is much less transparent than the stratosphere. "At the horizon, we perceive the confines of the two zones, as if drawn with a ruler," Piccard wrote in his log. "If one looks obliquely across the troposphere, the Earth, so distant, is invisible: there is nothing to be seen but fog. But the more the glance is directed downwards, the more visible is the Earth. Beneath us is the Bavarian plain. But, even if we look vertically down, the picture is blurred as in a bad photograph. There is, in fact, between us and the Earth, nine-tenths of an atmosphere, almost as much as if, at sea-level, we were looking at the moon.

"Alone, the mountains emerge from the foggiest regions of the troposphere. At first hidden by clouds, they reveal themselves bit by bit: a summit, then another: at last, all the snowy chains of the Bavarian Alps and the Tyrol, which we are approaching gradually." The Alpine scenery was "overwhelmingly grand". The lower sky itself looked like an upturned, illuminated disc. The corners of that disc had a copper tinge, as the sun came up to meet the *F.N.R.S.*, the same colour as the setting sun throws on clouds. The sky itself was more bleak. It was, quite simply, "blue space".

This was a moment of calm and of reflection for the two pilots, and it would be their last of the voyage. Shortly after he wrote the description of the stratosphere in his logbook, Piccard discovered the valve was jammed; then that the hole he had patched up had reappeared, bleeding oxygen once more. The programme had factored for landing about midday. Piccard, wanting a margin of error, had brought enough oxygen to last until sunset – provided the cabin was airtight. The balloon was also starting to drift, towards the Adriatic, a sea landing that would have been disastrous: the gondola was liable to sink. Piccard could not be exactly sure of the balloon's position – "the view was too often obstructed by clouds to permit us to follow our course on map. It would not have helped much anyway. We could do nothing about it and all we could do was to await the turn of events."

Events were not done yet. In another "stroke of ill-luck", one of the large mercury barometers broke as the balloon lurched, blown by a stratospheric wind. The liquid metal flowed to the bottom of the cabin. Mercury rapidly eats away at aluminium: it is today not allowed onboard most aircraft for this reason. Piccard and Kipfer wished they had a vacuum cleaner, before Piccard realised that "never had a physicist at his disposal more vacuum than we... The whole stratosphere was at our disposal." They connected a rubber tube with a tap which led outside, and sucked up the mercury, with this stratospheric hoover.

The two pilots continued to wait for the balloon to descend with quiet endurance. Having taken off at sunrise, they had been flying at high speed through regions where the temperature was between minus 50 and minus 75 degrees celsius. "The walls of the cabin were then very cold and its interior was rapidly covered by a good layer of frost," Piccard noted. "It was as if we were in a drop of crystal." If the situation had persisted, Piccard and Kipfer would have suffered, but the risen sun created a different problem. In the stratosphere, its power is twice that at sea level. The sun heated the cabin, at first pleasantly, and the frost dropped off. "It began to snow in our cabin."

Slowly, unrelentingly, the temperature rose. The motor designed to turn the cabin had also been jammed by the rope attached at take-off; the whole morning, the black, heat-absorbent side of the globe had been facing the sun, holding its heat. "70 degrees F [21.1 C] was very pleasant. 85 was bearable. But over 100 [37.8 C] was too much!" The two huddled down low in the sphere, the coldest part of the cabin, where Piccard had said his feet would be kept cool, but they began to feel thirsty. Piccard had asked for two big bottles of water to be supplied: they found only one small one. There was condensation beneath the flooring, and enough of it to sip, but dust, oil and mercury made it undrinkable. Kipfer found a spring of sorts: distilled water flowed along the wall, on the shady side of the gondola. There was not much of it, but the two scientists wet their tongues with it occasionally. Piccard found a better method: when he poured liquid oxygen into an aluminium cup and waited for the oxygen to evaporate, a thick layer of frost formed around the outside. This cold ice also burned to the touch.

During the afternoon, the cabin rotated, showing its bright side to the sun and reflecting some of its rays. By two o'clock, the balloon had begun to lose altitude. Piccard, scribbling in his notebook, calculated that at this speed it would take them 15 days to descend. He and Kipfer continued to sit in silence, not moving. By 3 pm, the speed of descent was more marked. "It would still take twenty-four hours at this rate to land. All the same the descent is getting faster: that is the essential thing." Still, at 6 pm, the *F.N.R.S.* was still in the stratosphere, now crossing the Bavarian Alps. The sun was setting. "The balloon, now colder, descends faster and faster." At 8 pm, the balloon was seven and a half miles high – finally out of the stratosphere. Piccard and Kipfer knew this by the fog they could now see on the distant horizon. Below, those on the ground of the valley of the River Inn saw a little moon, a tiny crescent, which had a halo: the *F.N.R.S.*, still reflecting the sun's rays, was brilliantly illuminated against the dark sky, the celestial chariot hitched now to a falling star. The observers took the balloon for a heavenly body.

The sun set and darkness fell. The balloon went down faster and faster. Piccard and Kipfer were wary of throwing out too much ballast in order to slow their descent. If more than necessary were ejected, the balloon would climb again to its position of equilibrium. As he jettisoned the lead-sand, Piccard had to be extremely careful "not to jump at once back to ten miles up". And as for their unstable, rapid rate of descent, well, it "was just unfortunate if the landing proved a little rough."

Piccard now used the tap which led outside the gondola to let some of the cabin air out and so decrease the internal pressure, so that they could open the manholes as soon as possible. Kipfer watched the barometers. At 15,000 ft (4,572 m) he told Piccard they had equal pressures within and without. They immediately opened the manholes and put out their heads: they felt the open air for the first time in 17 hours. Despite the real risk of death by a variety of methods, Piccard was nonetheless able to ignore his own concerns, and he looked about him: "Above us, the starry sky. Beneath, the high mountains, snow and rocks. The moonlight was magnificent. Two little clouds were lighted up from second to second by stormy discharges: but we saw no lightning nor heard any thunder. To be ready for anything, we prepared our parachutes.

"A glance towards the horizon: it still formed a straight line. But soon gloomy silhouettes emerged: mountains. We were already lower than the highest peaks. Things were going to happen fast."

The *F.N.R.S.* was in the high mountains, near a pass covered with ice. South of the balloon, the peaks led down directly to the plain and the promise of a soft landing, but the aerostat was drifting north. Because of the danger of climbing rapidly to ten miles high with the manholes open, the pair did not jettison any ballast. The only way they could manoeuvre was by pulling the ripping panel, which would empty the balloon of gas almost immediately. Piccard held the strap to open the panel in his hand. He took good care not to do it: the craggy, jutting terrain beneath was not suitable for a landing. The balloon bounced and flew over a glacier. "It was a maze of crevasses," but they were unable to change direction. Straight on. The two glimpsed the lights of a village, and Piccard flashed a signal with his torch. There was no response. The village disappeared from view, hidden in the dark of the valley.

The *F.N.R.S.* closed on the flats of the glacier. "Now was the moment!" Piccard pulled the strap of the ripping panel; the balloon started to empty. The gondola touched the ice, rolled, then skidded on, and eventually came to a rest. "The envelope was floating above us. The wind was so light that at every moment it threatened to fall on the cabin: then it leant over and lay down on the glacier: the opened ripping panel being underneath, it emptied only very slowly. A glance into the dark cabin showed me a heap of strange objects: 400 lb [181 kg] of instruments, 750 bags of small shot, all scattered about upside down. And underneath, Kipfer, who was slowly picking his way out towards the top." Piccard had returned safely to earth. In the oxygen tanks, there was an hour's supply left.

Piccard and Kipfer knew they had landed at an altitude of 8,700 feet (2,652 m), but they had no idea where. They would have to spend the night on the mountain in any case. "We bivouacked where we were," Piccard later wrote. "The place would have been fairyland if it had not been so cold!" They were hungry but lacked food. They collected the discarded orange skins still in the gondola and rubbed them into the ice. "This is the most delicious drink I ever had in my life, Paul," Piccard said. Kipfer agreed. They wrapped themselves in the balloon material as thickly as they could, huddled together and tried to sleep. Piccard woke throughout the night, mistaking the sound of a nearby waterfall for the whistling of the air leak that had nearly killed them.

The night was extremely cold and uncomfortable for the pair. "At dawn, from aeronauts we became alpinists." Piccard's childhood spent in the Alps would prove more useful than any calculation now. The two pilots didn't know if they had been spotted on the way down and thought it foolhardy to wait to be discovered. Piccard cut some ropes from the balloon, and they linked themselves with a double rope. The professor tested the snow at every step with a bamboo stick salvaged from the rigging of the balloon. Slowly, they reached the edge of the glacier on which they had landed. They sought a way down across the rocks, and descended towards the valley.

After six hours of walking, halfway down the glacier, Piccard and Kipfer saw a group of mountaineers. They waved, wildly, but the rescue party trudged past in the distance. The group, led by Falkner, a ski-champion of

Obergurgl in Austria, was on the way to recover the scientists' bodies; like everyone else, they assumed the aeronauts had landed dead. When they reached the *F.N.R.S.*, though, they found no corpses. They quickly realised that the two men they had seen on the way up, whom they had taken for mountaineers, must have been the pilots. They retraced their steps and caught up with Piccard and Kipfer; Falkner told a surprised Piccard that everyone had given them up for dead.

Falkner and his team escorted the pair down to Gurgl. The first thing Piccard did when he reached the village was to send a telegram. The message, to his wife, was brief:

AFTER A LONG DIFFICULT TRIP KIPFER AND
I HAVE LANDED. WE REACHED THE HEIGHT
WE DESIRED. ALL MY LOVE.

Back Down to Earth

Obergurgl was a small village, the highest in Austria, of a few hundred inhabitants and about 20 farms. The largest buildings were a church and two modest hotels, run by the son of a mountain guide who, against the advice of everyone, had built two high-altitude guest-houses. Obergurgl now, briefly, found itself the most famous place in the world, occupied by newspaper reporters from scores of countries. The single telephone line between the village and Vienna was constantly engaged. Every conceivable source of news in southern Germany and western Austria – newspaper offices, airports and police headquarters – was ringing with the sound of telephones, enquiries about the "obscure Belgian university professor", as *Popular Science* described Piccard. One "fat and weary police official in Munich" said: "I don't believe there is a single Bavarian who has not called up and asked about that cursed professor."

Piccard's flight was a sensation, reported throughout the globe. The first account, a telegram from Piccard himself, was typically concise: "We ascended into the stratosphere because we wished to be assured that the cosmic rays at that height were ten times as powerful as on reaching the earth after passing through the atmosphere." He sent another message, to Riedinger, the builder of the F.N.R.S. (who had also assumed Piccard to be dead and was blaming himself): "the balloon was so well constructed I couldn't come down any sooner."

Piccard holed up at the Hotel Edelweiss; the night before, Angelus Scheiber, the innkeeper, had watched the balloon for several hours as it sank down. He had taken accurate bearings and dispatched the rescue party. The professor, who "seemed considerably exhausted and very pale", took some hot tea after he arrived. He told the innkeeper that the world now seemed "a strange place" although he had been away from it only 16 hours. He then retired to bed. At 3 am, Piccard was woken by a reporter from the *New York Times*, who had himself nearly crashed a plane trying to follow the balloon. He had landed and then trekked with a guide through the night to Obergurgl, for a "nightshirt interview" (the reporter said that it might have seemed "extreme cruelty" to do so, but that Piccard forgave him the next morning). After answering a few questions, Piccard was allowed to go back to sleep.

*

"Apart from the cold, we did not suffer any great inconvenience," Piccard told the press pack the next day, not entirely truthfully. The yellow heap of the *F.N.R.S.* could be seen from the village, on the grey of the glacier above. Dressed in a rough, homespun suit with an open-neck shirt he batted away questions and "scrambled crags to escape the crowds of newspapermen".

"There was nothing much, however, to see apart from blue space," Piccard said initially. "The Earth was somewhere beneath us and atmospheric conditions at that time were against our seeing it.

"We were busy with our observations for some time and then began to think about getting down again. We had already been up longer than we expected. We had to be careful not to release too much gas, otherwise we would have descended like a stone. The balloon obliged us by lowering itself almost of its own accord to about 4,000 metres [13,123 feet], but then the expansion of the gas, owing to the warmer atmosphere in the afternoon sunlight – it was cool in the morning when we left – checked our descent.

"We were afraid to let any more gas go for as night time approached, the air would cool, the gas contract and the balloon sink, and we were not certain where it would fall. We wanted to choose our own landing ground at that moment [when] we were over the inhospitable Alps.

"The hours passed all too slowly for us. We were held poised, it seemed immovably, above the sharp points of snow-capped peaks and precipitous-looking glaciers. Slowly we sank down and, by a stroke of good fortune, when the gondola finally touched it was on the soft snow covering a flat ice field.

"We are happy to have served science and I believe our observations will certainly prove valuable. I can only say that I firmly believe our endeavours have been crowned by success and I am determined to continue my researches by balloon in high altitudes."

Piccard's account of the flight was unsensational, either because of his nature, or because he wanted to downplay the dangers he had faced to head off any charges of reck-lessness. The rapid initial ascent of the F.N.R.S. was only "rather annoying", because it "interfered with our plans to take samples of air at varying heights, the violence of the jerks upsetting all our appliances till we reached stability at 15,000 metres [49,213 ft]." Licking the condensed moisture from the walls of the gondola was merely "a great relief". The temperature of 40.6 degrees celsius was "unpleasant because it interfered with our work". Reporters pressed Piccard on why he had not made an earlier landing. Piccard admitted the failure of the valve. The next question was whether, along with the leak in the airtight cabin, the pair had ever abandoned hope. "No," Piccard replied gently.

"We just repaired the hole as best we could. It is a scientific fact that gas condenses and balloons shrink when the sun sets. We just trusted that the science was as true in the stratosphere as on earth, and so it proved to be." To the question "what did the world look like from such a height?", Piccard gave the first description of the earth from above: "We really had little time to pay attention to the world, once we had left," he said. "We were absorbed in the affairs of the stratosphere, but first of all, details disappeared and the world became flat and colourless. Then, as we rose above the blue sky, we saw the world through it in a fairylike bluish haze of extraordinary beauty." (He later wrote, modestly, that "Physicists cannot explain very well this colour of the stratosphere.") The night spent exposed on the open glacier was "uncomfortable"; the trek down to life and civilisation "was a beautiful walk".

Most important for Piccard was not the view from the top, but the scientific contribution of his balloon flight. "I have also given proof that it is possible to fly in the stratosphere in a sealed cabin, a fact of peculiar value to airships, as it is possible to fly great distances infinitely quicker than through the earth's atmosphere. I called attention to such a possibility earlier. Only recently I learned the Junkers works in Germany were experimenting with the construction of airplanes for flights through the stratosphere."

Experimental physics and cosmic rays had taken Piccard up, and given him the most satisfaction. "There is no doubt whatever," he said, "that we reached the stratosphere and that our observations will reveal something of importance in connection with the radioactivity of the stars and the variation of the strength of this radioactivity at various heights. The radioactivity of the stars is one of the most important factors when considering the problem of the transmission of light in the universe and my flight may in the end prove to be a modest step toward the solution of this problem." A few days later the president of the Swiss Aero Club, Colonel Messner, welcomed Piccard and Kipfer in Zurich. He said that he hoped their altitude record would last for many years. Piccard contradicted him: "It will be a fine day for me," he said, "when other stratospheric balloons follow me and reach altitudes greater than mine. My aim is not to beat and above all not to maintain records, but to open a new domain to scientific research and to aerial navigation."

Privately, Piccard was overjoyed with the flight. He wrote in his journal: "I have succeeded in my dream of being the Columbus of the stratosphere."

*

Auguste Piccard was "the only person in the world who declines to see anything but a mildly interesting establishment of scientific theories," according to the *Times*. The professor saw nothing especially important about entering the stratosphere. The press did: he was the "first human being who may be said to have left this world for sixteen hours and returned to it alive". They dubbed him "the Columbus of space", echoing the professor's own, private comparison. Piccard, no longer an obscure professor but an international celebrity on the level of Charles Lindbergh, quickly became used to the attention: "It seemed nonsensical when I started," he said. "People want my photograph. My laboratory life did not accustom me to such things. Now I begin to realise that strangers are quite interested."

The two aeronauts left Obergurgl in a car decked with laurels and mountain evergreens. Their journey to Innsbruck was a triumphal procession: every village and town on the route turned out in force, while local musicians played. Accolades were thrown at Piccard: the French made him a commander in the Legion of Honour; the Belgians gave him the Order of Leopold. On the other side of the Atlantic, Auguste's brother Jean was also finding that strangers were "quite interested". Reporters swarmed around him: Jean, working as a consulting engineer in Wilmington, Delaware, asked for his reaction to his brother's death during the flight, had told them that if Auguste really were dead, he would know it. Now his safe return had been confirmed, he was just as modest as his twin. "I was sure Auguste would not fail. He is a very experienced balloonist. I had every confidence in his ability to return safely, just as I knew he would reach the stratosphere. I also knew that if it *had* come down in the afternoon, as was reported, there must have been some guiding hand to bring it to earth.

"My twin brother, Auguste, first discussed this proposed flight with me in 1926. He wanted to go to the great height, not to establish an altitude record, but to determine, if possible, the action of the cosmic rays, their quality and intensity at different altitudes. Just what the eventual uses of the properties of cosmic rays will be, we cannot say, any more than Benjamin Franklin could foresee the eventual uses of electricity." Jean made no mention of his own plan to go even higher into the stratosphere.

Piccard, now famous, was subject to a public scrutiny for which he was quite unprepared. A few days after the *New York Times* extolled Auguste's achievements on the front page, it published an editorial on May 30, 1931, asking: "Now that the world has heaved its sigh of relief at the almost miraculous descent to safety of Professor Piccard and his assistant, Dr Kipfer, who can fail to wonder whether their elaborate effort was worth the risk." It continued: "there is every reason to doubt the scientific value of the most skilfully conducted balloon voyage to a height of ten miles." The *Times* said that meteorological sounding balloons were quite adequate and doubted whether Piccard's study of cosmic rays, on which "he lays so much stress", could not have been carried out by this method instead. Continuing its tone of condescension, the paper finally invoked Shakespeare. "It seems then that our knowledge of 'this most excellent canopy, the air,' as Hamlet called it; 'this brave o'erhanging firmament', this 'majestical roof', has not been greatly advanced by one of the most picturesque and daring attempts ever made to penetrate it."

Piccard was irked by the criticism, not just in the *Times*, but throughout the press. "In the months that followed [the ascent], although we reached the altitude we aimed at, our enterprise was called foolhardy, partly because the valve rope became jammed: if we are safe and sound, it appears, it is a miracle. My spherical balloon had a bad press: I had no emulator, at least at the beginning." Perhaps stratospheric ballooning was better given up for now: his wife Marianne made him promise never again to make an ascent. Directly after, he declared: "I made this flight because I had agreed to do so, but I cannot expose my wife and children to another such period of mental distress."

Others were of the same opinion. Among the many telegrams he received after the flight, Auguste's favourite, for its "affectionate human sensitiveness", was from Albert Einstein: "You must never go up yourself again. Think of your wife and children."

Indeed, at the house of a famous Viennese physicist that autumn, near the Wienerwald, when Piccard was relating his ascent ("he merely seemed to be describing a little walk into the country," wrote one attendee), Einstein, although full of affectionate enthusiasm, begged Piccard not to go again. Piccard retorted: "But the thing is so simple. One need only make the cabin very thick and nothing can happen, nothing whatever." "Yes, as long as the cabin holds," Einstein said back, "and everything else goes smoothly. But you have promised not to fly into the stratosphere any more." And he repeated: "Think of your family."

"I shall certainly not make the next flight myself," Piccard replied.

Only a year later, on August 18, 1932, Piccard climbed into the cabin of the *F.N.R.S.*, ready for another ascent into the stratosphere. He had won round Marianne over the preceding months. And he simply did not tell Einstein.

*

The months before the second flight had been full of preparation; now Piccard was "ready to pop with excitement," as *TIME* wryly observed. Piccard had paid particular attention to the working of the valve at the top of the gasbag, which had nearly cost him and Kipfer their lives during the first flight. He constructed a brand-new gondola: the top was painted white, to shield the pilots from the sun above them, the bottom black, to keep heat when it set. This time extra clothing would be packed. The portholes were bigger, and offered a clear view of the gasbag above, so that the pilots could check the valves were unimpaired. Piccard also made sure that none of the ground crew did anything without his permission: small mistakes led to large disasters, and Auguste had not forgotten the extra rope that had ensnared the valve cord, nor that they had been sent into the sky with no signal being given. King Albert of Belgium, who had been delighted at the success of Piccard's first flight, took a keen interest in the preparations. He and his wife, Queen Elizabeth, visited the factory. Piccard showed the royal couple around; the king crawled through the small porthole to inspect the instruments.

Paul Kipfer, although keen to fly, had been forbidden by his father from returning to the stratosphere, so a new assistant, Max Cosyns, a 26-year-old Belgian, took his place. Cosyns had less sang-froid than either Piccard or Kipfer (who was still assisting with preparations): the day before the ascent, he showed signs of worry. Piccard had decided to take off from the Dübendorf airfield at Zurich. Two weeks before launch, more than 100 foreign reporters gathered there, sceptical as to whether Piccard could pull it off. No one wanted a disaster, but they certainly wanted to be there if one happened. The journalists readied planes and cars to follow the balloon in the sky and on the ground. King Albert himself drove the 60 kilometres from Lucerne to see the take-off incognito. 300 special police and army guards stood by to control the crowd of thousands that had assembled to watch.

Early in August, the weather seemed favourable and the balloon was spread out in the sunshine, ready for inflation. A little while later, the director of the Belgian Meteorological Institute rang Piccard from Brussels. He warned him that thunderstorms were expected over central Europe during the night. Piccard didn't hesitate and, with not a cloud in the sky, cancelled the flight. The press complained, loudly, and even the ground crew was mystified, but shortly afterwards a violent thunderstorm broke out and the relatively young science of meteorology gained some new prestige. Piccard said "beautiful weather is not enough" and told the press that he had promised his wife that he would do nothing foolish.

On August 17, the weather was good. During a still, windless night, the F.N.R.S. was inflated. Piccard embraced his wife and his four oldest children; his youngest had been born a few months before. At 5.06 am the next day, August 18, the two scientists boarded the gondola. Piccard leaned out of the hatch and gave the signal to cast off,

"Let go everything!" he cried, then, with a flourish, kissed Marianne's hand. The balloon rose silently into the air and the crowd roared; Piccard stayed hanging out of his hatch for a while, a broad smile on his narrow face and shouting out "Au revoir, Marianne! Au revoir, mes enfants! Au 'voir!", before pulling his head in to the gondola, like a turtle drawing back into his shell. Soon the balloon was a tiny speck in the early-morning sky. The planes took off in pursuit, and the crowd dispersed.

Auguste Piccard opened his notebook. "5.15 am Thursday. We are off, and the earth drops away from us. The balloon is not climbing as we wished, so we have jettisoned some ballast. I closed the hatch at about 1,700 feet [518 m]. Everything going well. Light wind."

"We ascended without knowing the direction we were heading." This time, Piccard intended to keep his captain's log meticulously. He had plenty of time to do so: "What can I say about the ascent?" he later wrote. "Everything went smoothly according to our plan, like a laboratory experiment prepared with minute care." Piccard conducted his experiments; he discovered that a particular gamma radiation, which according to one hypothesis should have been intense at the high altitude, did not exist. He also made the first radio broadcast from the stratosphere, saying that "All is going well. Observation good." There was more time to enjoy the trip on this occasion, and to reflect: "My emotional reactions on the flight make me feel sure of the pleasures which are ahead for strato tourists of the future. After we had been up some time, I could not resist the temptation of stopping my work in order to admire the beauties that lay beneath us." In his notebook, Piccard waxed slightly more lyrical than was his custom. The cosmic ray counters "make noises reminiscent of rain falling on the roof of a hut" (A comment that prompted *TIME* to call the professor "a mild hyperbolist", but the publication had misunderstood, thinking that Piccard was suggesting the cosmic rays themselves made a patter as they struck the sphere); "The view is grandiose. It is almost beyond our conception. There is Glarnisch. And also below us are the Silberhorn and Eastern Alps which I, as a young moun-taineer, climbed 15 years ago. Never, then, did I dream of this"; "Italy is a gracious land, spread there beneath us." Piccard and Cosyns drank hot milk and ate chocolate, and realised they had forgotten their passports. At 12 pm, they released the first hydrogen from the balloon, having gone slightly higher than the first flight, and began their descent. Piccard later said: "We could have gone higher, but it was not necessary to do so."

The balloon was sighted from the ground at 3 pm drifting over Lake Garda. A small seaplane, piloted by Colonel Bernasconi, of the Italian Air Force, took off and made contact, staying within a safe distance. On the ground, in Sargan, Paul Kipfer was training his telescope on the balloon. Several hours passed before his group realised they were looking at the planet Venus.

Twelve hours after lift-off, the *F.N.R.S.* landed awkwardly, at 5 pm; the gondola rolled for a few minutes down a plain: Cosysns and Piccard "were jumbled up with our instru-ments". The two aeronauts clambered out. Slightly dizzied by the change from freezing to hot, they staggered, sat down, and opened a can of peaches. Then they ate some bananas offered to them by the villagers who had come to meet the balloon. Thus restored, they made for the village. "Where is a telephone?" Piccard asked. "I want to call my wife." He did (she had earlier received another call, from Queen Elizabeth, letting her know that Auguste had landed safely), then drove into Desenzano, where he ate and slept, declining interviews with a brusque: "Too tired. Too tired.

See me tomorrow." It was an uneventful conclusion to an uneventful day: "In summing up," Piccard said, "I may say ours was not a spectacular flight, for we rose from the earth as lightly as a feather and bumped only once when we came down." Piccard had seen the results of reporting the drama of his first flight, so this time emphasised the opposite: "the ascent was almost boring because of its scheduled uniformity."

A day later, he was "again the wispy, high-collared Marco Polo, bubbling over with tales of wonders" (*TIME*) and more grandiloquent: "A visit to the stratosphere, which is a world apart, is delightful beyond description. . . . No storms, no ice, no snow. The temperature is always between 50° and 60° below zero Centigrade. The winds always blow horizontally when they blow at all. Consequently they will not affect future travelers, who, I believe, will be crossing from Paris to New York in six hours in the near future..."

That night, Italo Balbo, a fat-cheeked, goatee-bearded man who was Air Marshal of the Italian Airforce and a Blackshirt, drove to Desenzano. He had organised a gala dinner that evening in Venice: would Auguste attend? The professor thanked Balbo, but said he had nothing to wear, and should return to Belgium. This did not discourage Balbo, who sent assistants to find evening dress for Piccard. Two hours later, none of the tuxedos they had found could fit the lanky professor, whose spindly stature defied the transalpine tailors. Balbo declared that this was no problem, bundled the professor into his car and drove the two hours to the party on the Lido, where all the guests were in evening dress, save for the Air Marshal and Piccard, in his rough wool suit. Piccard eventually made it back to Belgium and Marianne. Later that year, the Belgian government issued postage stamps in Piccard's honour. They sold out quickly and collectors had only one complaint: "many Belgians feel that the head of Professor Piccard should have been shown on the stamp, instead of a picture of his balloon."

Piccard was happier with the scientific results of his work than another altitude record: during the first flight he had been too busy avoiding death to run proper experiments, but this time, he had useful data about his beloved cosmic rays. He still had no idea what they actually were, but now he knew where they came from. In the higher altitudes, he and Cosyns had found that the level of cosmic rays did not increase as they had expected – a finding confirmed that summer by Professor Regener, who had sent up recording balloons. This led Piccard to form two hypotheses: first, that "cosmic radiation does not come from cosmic space, as we had at first believed, but is produced in the upper-most strata of the earth's atmosphere"; second, that the "hard and most penetrating portions of cosmic radiation do come from cosmic space, but the softer, strongly ionized components are a sort of secondary radiation produced by the impact of the hard rays on the air molecules." Piccard was nearly right, but cosmic rays (most of which we now know to be protons, positively charged subatomic par-ticles, or hydrogen nuclei) do, in fact, come from cosmic space. When they arrive and enter the earth's atmosphere, they collide with mainly oxygen and nitrogen molecules to produce an "air shower" – a cascade of billions of lighter particles; the Earth also has its own natural background radiation (of which cosmic rays form ten to 15 per cent). Piccard observed that cosmic radiation did not come from any particular direction; we know today that cosmic rays come from a wide variety of sources: processes on the sun, other stars, and other, still unknown effects on the edges of the observable universe. We should not be surprised that Piccard's findings tally so well with what modern science tells us; his efforts were an important part of establishing that modern science. Piccard concluded his results: "To physicists like myself and my colleagues, Cosyns and Kipfer, it is a sublime feeling to know that we are approaching a solution and that we may soon peer behind the veil of mysteries. Whatever our future discoveries may be, wherever our quest may lead, it is certain that there will be great strides forward in the near future.

"And perhaps not only for pure science – and this will interest the lay reader – but in the direction of technical knowledge and progress will the revealing of cosmic phenomena be important. I am thinking, not dreaming, of the cheap power of the future, the harnessing of the infinite energies of atoms and molecules that lie all around us.

"Even though this may be reserved for future generations, it is no longer a dream but in the realm of physical realities."

The *F.N.R.S.* ushered in a new era in another way, by proving stratospheric air travel safe. The airtight cabin (despite the efforts of Junkers, Piccard's was still the only one in the world) acquired full civic rights in ballooning and aviation. Years after Auguste died, Jacques remarked that: "I never step across the threshold of a modern airplane's cabin without remembering that my father invented the first one."

Marianne extracted another promise from Auguste that he would not fly again. This time, he kept it. The *F.N.R.S.* made one more flight, two years later to the very day on August 18, 1934, when Cosyns and an assistant once more rose into the stratosphere, to establish that the Ardennes were continuous with the mountains of Yugoslavia. After that, when the balloon wore down, and the rubberised fabric began to crack and split, Cosyns and Piccard attempted to turn the state-of-the-art balloon into the original Montgolfier hot-air design. But the balloon was too slender and its neck too narrow for proper control: on its first ascent, a sudden wind drove back the *F.N.R.S.* The envelope caught fire and was destroyed in a few seconds by the flames. Piccard and Cosyns leapt out of the gondola and jumped the few metres down to safety, narrowly escaping death. The balloon, worth $10,000 according to Piccard (about $2 million now), was uninsured. The Swiss government banned any similar, future experiments, despite the fact that there was no balloon with which to conduct them.

Max Cosyns went to work on his own stratospheric balloon, in the laboratory of Solbosch University. On August 11, 1933, a workman was killed when the gondola, made of magnesium rather than aluminium, exploded during a pressure test. On August 18, 1934, he rose to 52,952 ft (16,1140 m) and carried out more experiments on cosmic rays. During the Second World War, he joined the resistance, and was captured and tortured, then imprisoned at Dachau. But he would survive to work with Piccard on his next grand project.

Piccard had made balloons fashionable again, and other aviators made attempts using aircraft much larger than the *F.N.R.S.* The Soviets built two balloons. The first, the turnip-shaped *USSR-1*, developed by the Air Force, made an unofficial altitude record of 62,336 ft (19,000 m) on September 30, 1933. The second, the hydrogen-filled *Osoaviakhim-1*, made its maiden flight on January 30, 1934, with the approval of Stalin, even though it was known to have technical flaws. It ascended to 72,178 ft (22,000 metres) over seven hours. But the balloon stayed too long in the stratosphere and its gas valve failed. Overheated by the sunlight, *Osoaviakhim-1* vented too much lifting gas. When it descended below 39,370 ft (12,000 m), the reduced gas cooled and the balloon lost buoyancy. It plummeted down, breaking up in the air: 6,560 ft up, the gondola separated from the balloon. The three crew members, likely knocked out by the extreme g-force, were instantly killed on impact at 4.23 pm. Among them was Andrey Vasenko, who, inspired by Piccard, had designed the balloon, although not with the same rigour. The skull of Pavel Fedoseenko, the pilot, disintegrated completely, after smashing on one of the glass portholes. After this catastrophe, the *USSR-1* was retrofitted with parachutes, and flew again in 1935 as the *USSR-1 Bis*. Again, a faulty valve led to peril: two crew members bailed out with parachutes, but the pilot managed a crippled soft landing.

Hitler's Germany sent up a huge sub-stratospheric balloon, the *Bartsch von Segsfeld*, which had a volume of 9,500 cubic metres, aiming to reach an altitude of 32,800 ft (10,000 m), study cosmic rays and further the glory of the Reich. A crew of two, meteorologist Dr Hermann Masuch and pilot Martin Schrenck, took off in May 1934, from Bitterfeld, with enough oxygen for four hours. Nothing was seen of them until the Soviet government announced it had found the balloon 22 miles east of Sedesh. Masuch lay dead in the wreckage. The body of Schrenck was found nine miles further east.

The Americans had better luck. On November 20, 1933, the *Century of Progress* reached 61,000 ft (18,592 m). (As we shall see, the US team had something the other balloon makers did not: a Piccard. Jean Piccard had supervised the construction). In July 1934, another US balloon, the *Explorer,* made its way up, but the attempt was abandoned at 63,000 feet, when the crew discovered a large rip in the canopy balloon. They descended quickly, but inside the gondola the pilots could hear the fabric tearing. At 4,920 ft (1,500 m), the hydrogen that remained in the gasbag exploded, sending the cabin plummeting down. The pilots abandoned the balloon, relying on their personal parachutes. As the last man out, Major Kepner, cleared the hatch, the balloon exploded and the capsule plunged to the earth. The crew landed safely; Kepner deployed his parachute only 500 feet above the ground and was said to have landed with a large thud in a cornfield. The *Explorer II* was more successful, reaching 72,395 ft (22,066 m) – an altitude record which would stand for the next 21 years. The Polish also built a balloon, *The Star of Poland*, but in October 1938 it caught fire less than 100 ft off the ground, luckily with no loss of life; the gondola was saved, a new gasbag made, but the rescheduled flight was permanently postponed by the Nazi invasion of Poland.

The various Soviet, German and American attempts, made with the vast financial and technical available to superpowers, showed just how incredible it was that Auguste Piccard had devised, funded and flown a stratospheric balloon on his own initiative. They also showed how lucky he was to be alive.

The Piccards in America

One Sunday afternoon early in 1933, a commuter returning home on the Baltimore train from New York recognised the Piccard twins sitting opposite him. They were speaking in very technical French, which was difficult to understand, but the conversation lagged when the train reached Philadelphia. Jean, who lived in America, picked up the comic section of the *Herald Tribune* and began narrating the popular *Mr and Mrs* comic strip to his brother. He went slowly through it in English. Auguste didn't laugh or even say anything, but sat there quiet. Jean finished his narration and the two stayed silent until Wilmington, where they got off. A reporter had accompanied the two, and wrote up the idiosyncratic and uneventful tale in full for the *New Yorker*.

America found Auguste fascinating and odd. American aviation pioneers had square jaws and thrusting chests (the male ones at least); Piccard had "the appearance of a poet". A rumour, widely reported in the press, had preceded his arrival: that he had kidnapped a vicious dog belonging to a neighbour in Lausanne and extracted its teeth, explaining to the astonished owner that: "I looked up my legal rights and found that I was justified." When Piccard arrived on January 12, 1933, on the French liner *Champlain*, the professor was met with noisy protests from animal lovers. Piccard said he had in fact pulled the thorns off some dog rose bushes (*Rosa canina*, common to Europe), so that his children would not scratch themselves. This was an unconvincing explanation. Piccard's friend, biographer and translator, Sylvester Dorian, who acted as his public relations guru for the visit, hastily and bizarrely explained: "He loves animals, and at home often plays with my pet raccoon." Dorian said that the US press had misinterpreted fact. What had really happened was that at an event at the Aero Club in Paris, Dorian had talked about this fierce dog to journalists, and mentioned that Piccard was wary of it biting his children while he was away. The dog had attacked several people, biting a piece of the calf out of one unfortunate man's leg, and Dorian said that Piccard had "seriously contemplated" pulling the dog's teeth. "He did not do so however," Dorian now said. "I can assure you he is one of the most gentle men in the world."

One feels for Dorian: Piccard did not make things easy for his publicist. The professor had made headlines in the November before his visit, announcing that he planned to see the native Americans, buffalos and Yellowstone Park and saying: "My heart has always gone out to this vanishing race of red men. They are now almost obliterated from the vast continent they formerly occupied exclusively." There was another rumour, that Piccard had "invented a rocket", which could travel through the stratosphere at "five kilometres [3.1 miles] per second". The astonishing Piccard rocket would thus transport post and passengers across the Atlantic in less than half an hour, or so the American journalists (mis)reported. Indeed, Piccard's final cry before boarding the liner to New York was: "Of the stratosphere I am not afraid. But what those journalists will do to me ...!" Marianne and two children waved him off towards the Atlantic. The last they saw of him was "his long arms gyrating, the wind blowing his wild hair crazily" (*TIME*).

When the *Champlain* dropped anchor in New York bay, and the government cutter carrying custom officials and journalists came alongside, Piccard was nowhere to be found. He had gone to the bridge with the Captain, Victor Barthelemy, to try and catch sight of his twin brother, who was waiting on the French line dock at West Fifteenth Street. Auguste eventually made his way to the dining room where the reporters were assembled. They saw only a glimpse of the professor, as he looked in through the doorway and suddenly turned tail down the corridor. Piccard refused to attend the first press conference as the journalists were all smoking, "a dirty habit that should be banned from America by the government, instead of moderate alcoholic drinking". When portholes in the liner had been opened to clear the fug, he allowed for a brief interview, "during all of which he appeared impatient," according to the *Times*. Piccard frankly admitted to his interviewers that he did not know what cosmic rays were. Asked about his unbelievably fast rocket, Piccard replied that he had no rocket and was not ready to make any further announcement about his researches into this subject; he did believe, however, that planes would use the stratosphere to travel at 500 miles per hour (805 km/h), even "if it might not be possible this year, or even in ten years." Dorian, with an eye on the headlines, intervened, saying that Piccard's work in the field was progressing rapidly (perhaps giving away the origins of the original rumour). The scientist did expound about his personal philosophy, though. One journalist asked: "Do you believe, as many others do, that science will be the ultimate salvation of the world?" Piccard paused a moment. "No," he replied. "Science will never do it, not alone. The salvation, as you say, of the world, cannot lie in science alone." Pressed on what other things might lead to salvation, he said: "Well, religion for one, and work in other fields. But you must know that if I could stand here in this hallway and give you an adequate reply to this I would be more than a physicist."

Auguste had an addendum for the New York reporters though: "Well, for one thing, the customs, or as you call them, the tariffs, are making a good part of trouble in this world." With that undiplomatic addition, Piccard disembarked and was driven to the St Moritz hotel. The first few nights were spent, uncomplainingly, on various beds that were too small for him, until a divan with neither head nor foot was brought in. One day Piccard went to a barbershop near Grand Central station to get a shave. The barber, taking in his appearance, asked him quite seriously whether he had come to New York alone, or with a troupe of travelling performers.

After this shaky start, Piccard was entertained at the homes of aviation's great and good in New York – as the *New Yorker* described it, the "young adventurer scientist set". At the house of Amelia Earhart, the first woman to fly across the Atlantic, he met Charles Lindbergh, the first person to do the same. The two aviation pioneers were heroes of Auguste's and before he left Belgium he had described them as two good reasons to visit America. "You are a great aeronaut," Piccard told Lindbergh. "I am a mere balloonist, studying penetrating radiations. Our territories almost touch, but they are not the same." They swapped stories – Lindbergh described his recent trip to China, and how he had not seen one child smiling during his time there. Piccard remarked that it would be difficult to tell, as the Chinese "are adept at masking their emotions". He used the slide rule he always carried with him, to convert kilometres into miles during the lunch; during a state banquet in Brussels the year before, he had openly used the rule to check the accuracy of statements being made. Piccard admitted that the only American book he had read was *Huckleberry Finn*. He told the party that he was sure that rocket travel would soon be practical. "In fact," wrote the *New Yorker*, "the problem of crossing from New York to Paris via the stratosphere in six hours has already been solved so far as he is concerned and he's working on more advanced rocketeering problems." (That the quotes made the papers caused a row between George Putnam, Earheart's husband, and Lindbergh, who thought the dinner was private; Dorian later admitted selling the story to the press for $40.) Roy Chapman Andrews, an explorer who had led expeditions through the Gobi desert and was the first to discover dinosaur eggs, asked the professor what he thought of the buildings in New York. Piccard said they weren't much beside the Alps. Another explorer, Admiral Richard Byrd, the first person to reach the South Pole by air, took out a pipe and made as if to light it. Piccard frowned fiercely and a member of the committee had to scurry down the speakers' table and tell the Admiral that the guest of honour had come only on the understanding that there would be no smoking; Byrd sucked on an unlighted pipe for the rest of the lunch. William Beebe, who had done a reverse-Piccard and dived the deepest any person had been, 3,025 ft (922 m) down in a "bathysphere" (from the Greek *bathos*, for depth) he had constructed himself, asked Piccard what he had seen "up there". Piccard replied: "No angels. What did you see?" "No mermaids," said the underwater man.

For Piccard's 49th birthday, a blimp – these commercial airships were the rage until the *Hindenburg* disaster in 1937 – was supposed to pick the professor up from his hotel and fly over Manhattan, but gusty weather scuppered the trip. Instead he celebrated with a party at his hotel. Robert Underwood Johnson, a celebrated American man of letters, read aloud a (pretty bad) poem he had written for the occasion (especially dedicated readers can find the complete text in the appendix to this book), and the hotel chef presented a cake topped with a sugar replica of the

F.N.R.S. Piccard measured the balloon's proportions with his slide rule and was quite satisfied.

Piccard left New York after a couple of days and travelled to Washington with his brother Jean, to give lectures. In one, sponsored by the National Geographic Society and delivered in the Washington Auditorium, he predicted that cosmic rays would eventually be useful for more or less everything: to fuel cars and planes, and to light cities. Piccard said, quite incorrectly, that the energy contained in a cosmic rays was a million times greater than that produced between molecules and atoms. "The raw materials cost nothing – water for example," he said. "The transformation of the atoms of three drops of water would produce enough cosmic rays and enough energy to light the whole city of Washington for a night."

"Across the successive stages of civilisation," he said, "one age, while exhausting natural deposits, has looked ahead towards a substitute for succeeding generations. When wood became relatively scarce, coal was discovered, and now that coal deposits are drawing toward their inevitable ultimate exhaustion, we look toward the liberated energy from cosmic rays for the energy of the future.

"When this source of power is made available, producing limitless energy almost free, coal will suddenly become valueless." Piccard advised those in the audience with shares in coal mines to sell them. He also said that cosmic rays might be able to power rocket planes to other planets. It is hard to see what Piccard based these optimistic predictions on: not much was known about cosmic rays, and none of his own research could have led to these conclusions; perhaps his natural optimism and faith in scientific progress carried him away. But although the specifics may have been misplaced, his vision of radical, green energy was ahead of its time and cast down a challenge that his

grandson Bertrand would resume. Piccard was more accurate about air travel by plane: New York to Paris would take
six to eight hours, he predicted; he envisaged businessmen
in New York being asked to drop in for lunch by friends in
Paris. He imagined an entire flight, from door to door, in
which the principles of stratospheric travel were expounded
by a cast of extremely knowledgeable flight attendants,
ticket inspectors and porters. Piccard also predicted that a
closed-capsule system like his own would one day carry a
human being to the moon. The afternoon after this lecture,
he called on President Hoover, accompanied by his brother.

Jean was much more at ease in the US than Auguste.
He had been there more than a decade and had married
Jeannette Ridlion. Like Jean, Jeannette was a twin,
although her twin sister had died at the age of three. She
had been born in Chicago on January 5, 1895, and was
one of nine children. When her mother asked her, aged 11,
what she wanted to be when she grew up, she replied "a
priest" and her mother ran from the room in tears. "That
was the only time I saw my Victorian mother run," she
later said. At 21, she still was set on the idea, writing an
essay: "Should Women Be Admitted to the Priesthood of
the Anglican Church?" Her undergraduate degree had been
in philosophy and psychology, at Bryn Mawr College near
Philadelphia, before she took up science at Chicago and
studied under Jean. She received her Masters in inorganic
chemistry in 1919 and they married the same year. Jeannette
was "very bright, had her own doctor's degree, and was
at least half of the brains of that family, technical as well
as otherwise," according to Robert Gilruth, a student of
Jeannette's who would later become director of the Nasa
Manned Space Center, which oversaw the Apollo missions.
"She was always in the room when he [Jean] was lecturing
or otherwise, almost always. She was something. She was

good." The couple taught at the University of Lausanne in Switzerland afterwards, before returning to the US in 1926. Jean taught inorganic chemistry at the Massachusetts Institute of Technology and became a naturalised US citizen in 1931; his colleagues described him as "simple, mild and brilliant". The Piccard house was always full of boys: "I don't know how many there were," said Gilruth later. "It seems like there was a dozen.... I remember the youngest one took the corn flake box and dumped it on his father's head. Of course, Piccard just brushed it off his head and said, 'No, no.' He was very gentle. He loved his boys, and he thought boys would be boys, I guess." The Piccards had three boys of their own – John, Paul and Donald – but also took foster children into their care.

When Auguste arrived in America, though, Jean was unemployed, having been fired from his job developing explosives at Hercules Powder Co; his academic studies of chemical reactions having briefly led to more practical and lucrative work. Although he was happy to see Auguste again, and to show him his new homeland, he resented his twin brother's success and subsequent celebrity; they had been equally feted as youngsters, and Jean had won a prestigious post at an American university before Auguste had even been awarded his doctorate. At their joint lectures, Auguste would each time tell anew his voyage to the stratosphere; Jean's role was to interject occasionally to help Auguste with his English pronunciation. As they completed the lecture circuit, it must have grated. Auguste had also said that he hoped to make his next ascension in North America, possibly at the edge of the Hudson Bay, to study cosmic rays further away from the equator. It would a "difficult and dangerous" ascent, he said: "The balloon might easily drift out over the polar ice cap or descend into the depths of the Canadian wilderness. The crew must be equipped and prepared to make its way back to civilisation." Canadian meteorologists were reported to be "apprehensive" about the planned trip. The organisers of the 1933 Century of Progress International Exposition, held in Chicago to celebrate the city's centenary, were also planning a balloon flight to the stratosphere and were hoping to lure Auguste; the brothers sat in the gondola together to inspect it. But Auguste had another project in mind, and he turned over all US ballooning plans to Jean, who was delighted.

The *Century of Progress* was a hydrogen balloon, the largest in the world, and it would give Jean a chance to match his brother. Dow Chemical had made the magnesium-alloy gondola; Goodyear-Zeppelin built the balloon out of rubberised fabric. It was 32 metres in diameter, with a volume of 17,000 cubic metres. Its envelope took 700 steel cylinders of hydrogen and miles of tubing to fill. Jean led the design and construction of the balloon, under the watch of the organisers of the Exposition.

He would not, however, fly it. For a start, he was not a licensed balloon pilot – someone would have to accompany him. Ward T. Van Orman was the initial choice – he had won the 1926 Gordon Bennett cup. But Van Orman did not like the idea of attempting such a dangerous flight with Jean Piccard. The two had met at the Goodyear plant, where Van Orman worked, and the latter was convinced that Piccard's eccentric nature and lack of aeronautical experience were dangerous. Instead, he recommended a friend in the Navy as Jean's pilot, Lieutenant Commander Thomas "Tex" Settle. Settle was an extremely able aviator – he would become the only human being in the history of flight licensed to fly a glider, an airplane, a free balloon, a blimp and a rigid airship – and he wanted a shot at the stratosphere too. He had listened to Auguste lecture in Washington, quizzing the professor on techniques and equipment afterwards.

Settle was delighted to be asked, but soon he also became worried that Jean would be a dangerous presence in the gondola; he asked to make the flight alone. Jean was becoming a problem on the project. His independent fundraising efforts at DuPont had proved unsuccessful, after he told representatives from the company that conditions for the balloon's take-off in Chicago could be dangerous. On another occasion, having been angered at a supposed slight, he complained not to the flight organisers, but to the President of the Exposition, a friend of Jeannette's father, who refused to see him. The Exposition Committee tried to remove Jean and persuade Auguste to return to the US to fly. Jean, who was supposed to fly as the science observer on the balloon, was grounded by the Committee two months before the flight. A threatened lawsuit did not materialise.

Jean's lack of legal retaliation was bought at a price. The organisers agreed to give Jean the balloon and gondola after the first flight, if Jean were to remain on earth as a "ground pilot". Jean did not go up in the balloon, but the Piccard name did, thanks to the popularity of Auguste's exploits: the flight was called "The Piccard-Compton Stratosphere Ascension from Soldier Field". Both sides spun the agreement well. Jean signed an agreement that he would not fly, writing "the reduction in weight thereby produced will most assuredly enable Commander Settle to reach a higher altitude." The Exposition's offices called Jean's decision "as sporting as it was astonishing". On August 4, 1933, while the balloon was being inflated, the general manager told 40,000 spectators: "The sportsmanship and unselfishness displayed by Dr Jean Piccard in surrendering his place in the balloon so that a greater altitude may be achieved through the lessened weight of himself and his equipment is a note of sacrifice that will not be forgotten." America would finally make it to the stratosphere.

The *Century of Progress* took off early on August 5, at 4.05 am. Just 15 minutes later, the gasbag lay wrecked less than two miles from the start point, in a Chicago railroad yard; the perennial problem of a gas-valve leak had brought it down, safely this time. As happened in France over a century earlier, a mob fell upon the gasbag with knives: this time, though, they were souvenir hunting. A squad of Marines drove the crowd away. The balloon was not damaged, and was commandeered by the US Navy. (Jean wrote to Auguste in December 1933 that "the Navy and the Army are very stupid...") In the meantime, on September 30, the *USSR-1* had risen to a reported altitude of 62,304 ft (18,990 metres) – beating Auguste Piccard's height by nearly 9,000 feet (the record was not official however, as the FAI did not recognise the USSR). The Russians celebrated with a huge rally in Moscow; a reporter said: "The psychological effect in Russia is comparable to the effect in the United States of Lindbergh's flight to Paris." The Soviet success convinced the US that the *Century of Progress* should be given another chance. On November 20, 1933, with a much smaller crowd watching this time, the *Century of Progress* took off from Akron, Ohio and reached 61,236 ft (18,665 m) – a new official record and the first successful flight from US soil to the stratosphere, but lower than the Soviets. It landed in a mucky New Jersey marsh only a few miles from where Jean Piccard lived.

After the record flight, Jean and Jeannette took control of the balloon. They decided to fly it to the stratosphere by themselves: Jean would conduct scientific experiments and Jeannette would pilot. "Energetic and forceful, she seemed to have a better chance of obtaining a pilot's license than Jean, who was preoccupied with restoring the gondola and balloon and convincing scientists to provide instruments to fly," wrote David DeVorkin, a curator of the Smithsonian

National Air and Space Museum and author of *The Race to the Stratosphere: Manned Scientific Ballooning in America*. Despite his lack of formal licence, Jean was an experienced balloonist and taught his wife how to fly. She also studied at Ford Airport: she would have to make three balloon flights with an instructor, one solo flight and one at night. Her official inaugural flight, with Edward Hill, a winner of the Gordon Bennett Cup and later flight director for the Piccards, was in May 1934. Jean took angel cake as a snack. Nine hours later, she landed roughly and the angel cake, which they had forgotten to eat, was crushed. On June 16, she flew her first solo flight and became the first female licensed balloon pilot in the US. Auguste wrote to his brother in June 1934, slyly winding up Jean even more: "Hopefully you will make your flight ahead of other competitors. It would be nice, if the name of Piccard through Jeannette, would once more be placed on the record list of the F.A.I."

Like Auguste, Jean had to fund the stratospheric flight by himself. The National Geographic Society said it was interested, until Jean told them that his pilot would be his wife, at which point it wanted nothing to do with the mission. This was less to do with outright sexism than fear of a public relations disaster. Jeannette later said that the "National Geographic Society would have nothing to do with sending a woman – a *mother* – in a balloon into danger." If Jean used another pilot, the society would of course provide funds and he could finally join his brother in the stratosphere. But he refused. Dow Chemical, who had backed the first Century of Progress flight, asked for their logo to be removed from the gondola and all references to Dowmetal, a trade name, to be removed from their publicity materials. Jean Piccard was "very, very hurt", according to Gilruth, but he found another sponsor: Henry Ford. He offered the use of a hangar, and brought Orville Wright to come and watch Jeannette's test flights. Eventually, Grigsby-Grunow Radio Company gave the Piccards several thousand dollars and other backers followed.

On October 22, 1934, the *Century of Progress* cast off, two hours behind schedule, the Piccards inside along with their pet turtle, called Fleur de Lys. Before take-off, a band had played "The Star-Spangled Banner" and the three Piccard children had presented their parents with a bouquet. Around 45,000 spectators watched, including Henry Ford, "who brought along 150 moppets [children] in buses to witness the spectacle". The balloon, though, was reluctant to lift off: instead of rising straight into the air, the gasbag drifted languidly along the landing strip a few feet above the ground. The ground crew pushed up the gondola and the balloon drifted towards trees fringing the field. Perched in the rigging, Jeannette frantically threw out lead ballast and the trees were cleared. She climbed back inside.

The balloon reached 57,979 ft (17,672 m) high. Jean had beaten his brother's record, but not Settle's. Jeannette became the first woman in the stratosphere: her female altitude record would stand for twenty-eight years until broken by Russian cosmonaut Valentina Terechkova on board the *Vostok 6*. She also proved to be an erratic pilot, making several impulsive and unplanned manoeuvres. The landing was not the smoothest, either. Eight hours after lift-off, the balloon came in low over the treetops and the Piccards put on the American football helmets they had taken up with them. The bag caught on tree branches and the gondola tore loose and dropped. Jean hurt his foot and fractured a rib. Jeannette checked that Fleur de Lys was unharmed and opened the hatch. "What a mess!" she cried. "I wanted to land on the White House lawn." The Piccards had set down on a farm near Cadiz, Ohio. Behind them, at the origin of the gondola's trail of destruction, the huge gasbag hung dismal and empty on a tall elm. Jean curled up in a blanket and dozed. Jeannette, asked by reporters whether she would repeat the flight, said: "Oh! Just give me a chance."

The Piccards were never given the chance, though. Jean worked for the thrill of revealing a hitherto unknown, of going where no one else had gone before, but he would not manage to return to the stratosphere. Anxious for the fame that Auguste had won, the American Piccards thought that their stratospheric flight would make them celebrities (they became minor ones, for a while) and lead to lucrative university positions; they prepared a press campaign, distributing brochures and releases – one was titled "Who Said We Couldn't Do It". But theirs had been the eighth stratospheric balloon flight and the novelty was wearing off; they had not even set an altitude record and the scientific results of their flight had been negligible; further flights were difficult to justify on a scientific basis: "The truth of the matter is that none of the experiments carried aloft by stratospheric flights in the 1930s required the presence of a human being," Craig Ryan writes in *The Pre-Astronauts: Manned Ballooning in the Threshold of Space*. "If science had really been the *raison d'être* of these flights, unmanned balloons would have made much more sense." Even Robert Millikan, who had supplied the scientific equipment for the *Century of Progress*, recanted, calling the scientific justification for manned balloon flights a "sham" and stratospheric ballooning itself "a fad".

Still, Jean and Jeannette wrote to dozens of colleges, trying to secure teaching posts in chemistry and even presidencies, but received only rejections. While they were lecturing, however, they met John Ackerman from the department of aeronautical engineering at the University of Minnesota. He secured Jean a non-tenured professor-ship at Minnesota in 1936, teaching and conducting aero-nautical studies: Jean would no longer be a chemist, but a full-time aeronaut.

His first invention, developed with Jeannette, was the plastic balloon. The phenomenon of multiples was once more at work: Max Cosyns in Belgium and Erich Regener in Germany independently created their own plastic balloons. The common motivation for plastic construction was its reduced weight, which should allow a balloon to reach higher altitudes. In 1936, Jean designed and flew a cellophane balloon built by his students. The balloon was unmanned; it had a diameter of only 7.6 metres and was made in ten-metre tapered panels which fitted together like an orange peel. Colleagues contributed equipment such as the radio and a telemeter that sent temperature and pres-sure data back down to earth. The balloon was tracked from the roof of the university, until radio contact was lost when its battery froze due to a lack of proper insulation. It reached 50,000 feet and over ten hours drifted for 600 miles, when it came down near Huntsville, Arkansas.

Jean's next innovation caught even Auguste's eye, who called it "of particular interest". Instead of using one giant gasbag, Jean, along with Ackerman, designed a cluster balloon, with hundreds of smaller balloons supporting a gondola. Two thousand balloons, he reckoned, would be enough for a record-breaking flight. The idea was that the craft would keep ascending until some of its balloons burst (because of the diminished air pressure), so there was little danger of going too high. In any case, he could descend at will by shooting individual balloons with a pistol. His first, test craft was the *Pleiades*, named for the seven daughters of Atlas who were taken to the sky to become a cluster of stars, and had only 80 balloonets. It was enough to carry him into the air in July 1937, from Rochester, Minnesota.

Six hours after the *Pleiades* lifted off, a farmer milking his cows in Lansing, Iowa was surprised to see a gangly, cheerful man with unconfined hair, wearing a damaged white suit, walk into his barn and say "Good morning!" Jean Piccard had reached 11,000 ft (3,353m) in the *Pleiades*, which "looked like two clusters of white grapes, floating along with the wind, with something resembling a bathtub, a coffin or a sweatbox dangling below," according to *TIME*. Piccard had decided to use three methods to shed balloons and control his descent: a hunting knife to cut the balloon cords, explosives on the cords and a .22 calibre pistol. But either the explosives or small arms fire set light to the balloons, which were inflated with hydrogen. Piccard barely managed to scramble down a tree before the gondola was consumed by flames. He was unhurt, though, and sent a classic Piccard telegram to his wife: "Landed safely, Lansing, Iowa. Balloon under perfect control. All equipment burned up."

Still, Jean was convinced of the method: "This flight was successful, in that it has proved to me beyond any doubt that multiple balloons are practical and feasible." But the Second World War halted further research into cluster balloons. Jean worked for the US Navy, researching the spontaneous generation of gaseous oxygen from its liquid form. After the war ended, Jean was part of a team sent to London to study German documents detailing their aerial progress during the war – especially the V1 and V2 rockets. In 1946, both Jean and Jeannette Piccard found work as consultants to General Mills, working under Otto Winzen, whom Jean had met at the University of Minnesota. In February 1946 Piccard and Winzen proposed a manned flight to the US Navy, using clustered balloons made of thin plastic; Jean described the plastic balloon as "a stepping stone to space flight". In June, the Office of Naval Research approved "Project Helios". General Mills and the University of Minnesota undertook to build a cluster of 100 poly-ethylene balloons for atmospheric research: *Helios* would reach 100,000 feet, near the very top edge of the strato-sphere, and stay there for ten hours while scientific experi-ments were conducted. Jean was named as project scientist responsible for gondola design and for testing the balloon film materials. But, just as during the preparations for the Century of Progress, Jean's acute sense of self-importance made his position in a large team impossible. Jean balked at having to file weekly status reports, complaining he was being treated like a lower-level employee, and he was annoyed, perhaps justifiably, that General Mills would own the patents to his ideas. But the final straw was again his devotion to Jeannette: he refused to continue work unless she flew with him. George Hoover, the Navy officer who had approved Helios, said, priggishly and incorrectly, that "Jean Piccard knew what he was talking about. But his wife...that's another story." Although Jeannette was an enthusiastic pilot, she lacked the technical invention of Jean and the greater flying experience of military pilots.

General Mills and the Navy fired them both in 1947; the Helios project eventually fell apart anyway. Piccard blamed Winzen in particular. Once more Jean had given up a shot at the stratosphere, deciding that without his wife there with him, it was a shot not worth taking at all. He never gave up the dream: one newspaper in 1952 said that "to Adventurer Piccard, no gondola probing the unexplored purple twilight of the stratosphere would be complete without him and his wife in it." The same year, the *Canberra Times* gave its front page to Jean, who claimed it would be possible to fly to Mars with cluster balloons within two years, if anyone would give him $250,000.

Jean died of a heart attack on his 79th birthday on January 28, 1963. His most important contribution to aviation was the use of explosives to release external ballast from inside a sealed cabin, an innovative and brave idea at the time (brave is perhaps an understatement: hydrogen and explosives don't play well together). Auguste was quite taken with this "graceful method" and described it in detail; each sack of sand "contains a detonator which electric conductors connect with a battery lodged in the cabin. A simple pressure on the switch suffices: the sack rips open and empties itself." The system was made for especially speedy unballasting and was used for the *Explorer 2* balloon: without Jean's invention, it would have not have cleared the trees on lift-off. Later, Robert Gilruth, as director of the NASA Manned Spacecraft Center, said that Piccard "used blasting caps on everything. It was great for me because it wasn't too long before I was using igniters on all kinds of spacecraft." Gilruth applied Piccard's system to the *Mercury* spacecraft – the US's first manned space flight – and to the Apollo vehicles. Piccard was a great inspiration on Gilruth: he said that Jean had "ways of looking at problems ... of simplifying things." Jean had never lost the love of the great heights. In his sixties, he said: "Going with open eyes into new territory is always an interesting and useful thing to do".

Jeannette would survive Jean by 18 years. After Jean's death, Gilruth asked Jeannette to work as a consultant to Nasa. She acted as a public relations liaison during the creation of Project Apollo; a photograph shows her wearing a mink stole and elbow-length gloves standing next to a mock-up of the Apollo Command Module, beaming and waving to the crowds. After *Apollo 11* landed on the moon, her interests shifted away from space and back towards her childhood fascination, religion. In 1971, she was ordained a deacon in the Episcopal Church. Three years later, along with ten other women, she was ordained a priest – the first in the US. All 11 had risked suspension from the Church; the bishops who ordained them risked being deposed. Five priests objected when a bishop asked if there was any impediment – one called them a "perversion", another "unlawful and schismatical". It was only in 1977 that the Episcopal Church finally recognised her ordination. She died of cancer on May 17, 1981. Don Piccard, her and Jean's son, born in 1926, would pioneer hot-air ballooning as a competitive sport in the US. In 1947, he made his maiden balloon flight, in a captured Fu-Go – one of the thousands of "fire balloons" launched by the Japanese to drift across the Pacific and into the US (around 250 made landfall). He was the first to cross the English Channel in a hot-air balloon, in 1963, and is still alive today.

*

The Piccards were, for a long time, synonymous with high-altitude ballooning. But during his visit to the US in 1933, Auguste revealed a new project. He would create a balloon that went down instead of up.

At that lunch in New York with Lindbergh, Auguste told the aviator that he wanted to go to the bottom of the ocean – in a balloon. Lindbergh was perplexed and asked for an explanation. Piccard said he had been planning such an expedition since before the war. "My gondola," said the Swiss, "would have been very much like the one I used for exploring the stratosphere, but the balloon would have been inflated with oil instead of hydrogen, helium, or other gases. This, being lighter than water, would have served to lift us and we would have carried ballast just as we do in ordinary balloons.

"If I subsequently decided to go up rather than down in a balloon, it was because observations of cosmic rays were to be made best in the upper regions, where they are assumed to be more numerous. I really have quite as much in common with submarine navigations as with aeronautical navigation."

In fact, Piccard had first had the idea when he was a first-year student at Zurich. He had read a book by the German zoologist Carl Chun which recounted the oceanographic expedition of the *Valdiva*. This ship had let nets down to a thousand fathoms and brought back fish "endowed with veritable headlights", as Piccard put it, to the surface. "But very quickly these lights grew pale and went out. The fish could no more endure the low pressure and the high temperature of the surface water than we could have endured the enormous weight of the masses of water beneath which they live." Piccard had not forgotten Jules Verne. He wanted to go down to the deepest parts of the ocean to observe these fish in their natural setting, in much the same way as he would go up to the stratosphere to observe cosmic rays in theirs, to "transport his laboratory into the environment to be studied". "Far from having come to the idea of a submarine device by transforming the idea of the stratospheric balloon, as everyone thinks, it was, on the contrary, my original conception of a bathyscaphe which gave me the method of exploring the high altitudes. In short, it was a submarine which led me to the stratosphere." Auguste had promised his wife he would make no more balloon ascents. He had said nothing about balloon descents.

The underwater plan would have remained a pipe dream, though. "The student became an engineer, then also a physicist," Piccard wrote whimsically of himself. "The idea of submarine exploration never left him, although for a long time he was not able to think seriously about the possibility of realising his youthful dream." But in 1937, the university in Brussels held a reception for King Leopold III. He asked Piccard what he was working on. Piccard was about to tell him of his latest research into cosmic rays, but somehow this didn't seem interesting. "Your majesty," the physicist replied, "I am planning to build a deep-sea research submarine, a 'bathyscaphe', for diving to the very bottom of the sea." King Leopold was extremely interested and pressed for precise information – when, where and how? When Piccard returned to his laboratory the next day, he told his assistants, who had no idea they were working on a scientific submarine, "Gentlemen, I told the King yesterday that we are going to build a bathyscaphe. We have no choice now but to do it."

The "bathyscaphe" took its name from the Greek, *bathos*, deep, and *skaphos*, ship. Piccard had been to the top of the sky. Now he was set on the bottom of the sea – from the heavens to the deeps.

Down

Auguste Piccard knew much less about submarines than he did about balloons. Submersibles had a longer history, though. Auguste himself was familiar with what he called the "most eloquent" Middle Age engravings that depicted Alexander the Great in perhaps the first-ever submarine: the Macedonian warlord supposedly shut himself into a crystal barrel and was let down into the water by a long rope from a boat. "Obviously, here we have merely a legend, which arose no doubt quite late in the Middle Ages," a sceptical Piccard noted. "Yet it is interesting." In 1578, William Bourne, an English mathematician, designed a prototype submarine which would be rowed underwater. Cornelius Drebbel realised Bourne's design in the early 1600s. A Dutchman, Drebbel designed and built telescopes and microscopes; Galileo was a fan. He also invented a chicken incubator, the mercury thermostat that kept it at the correct temperature, air conditioning, and owned a pub. In 1620, he was working for the Royal Navy and manufactured a steerable submarine with leather-covered wooden oars. He constructed and tested two more submarines before the final model. This had six oars and could carry sixteen passengers. According to some reports, he demonstrated it to King James I personally. Drebbel's submarine stayed submerged under the Thames for three hours, cruising from Westminster to Greenwich and back at a depth of about 12 ft (3.7 m). The king himself went on one test dive, so becoming the first monarch to travel underwater. Drebbel's science was on the right track; Robert

Boyle, who became interested in Drebbel's work, asked an "Ingenious Physician that marry'd [Drebbel's] daughter" how "he conceived it feasible to make men accustom'd to continue so long under water, without suffocation". Apparently, Drebbel believed that it was not the whole part of air, "but a certain Quintessence (as Chymists speak) or spirituous part of it, that makes it fit for respiration"; once this quintessence was used up, the remaining, nefarious part of the air could not support life. So Drebbel built a "chymical liquor, which he accounted the chiefe Secret of his submarine". Whatever this secret source was (the air supply remains a mystery), the successful demonstration of the craft greatly impressed Bishop John Wilkins of Chester, who wrote in his *Mathematicall Magick*, in 1648, of its advantages:

1. Tis private: a man may thus go to any coast in the world invisibly, without discovery or prevented in his journey.

2. Tis safe, from the uncertainty of Tides, and the violence of Tempests, which do never move the sea above five or six paces deep. From Pirates and Robbers which do so infest other voyages; from ice and great frost, which do so much endanger the passages towards the Poles.

3. It may be of great advantages against a Navy of enemies, who by this may be undermined in the water and blown up.

4. It may be of special use for the relief of any place besieged by water, to convey unto them invisible supplies; and so likewise for the surprisal of any place that is accessible by water.

5. It may be of unspeakable benefit for submarine experiments.

The Royal Navy, though, did not agree and Drebbel's sub never entered service. But the Dutchman inspired countless others. By 1727, 14 types of submarine had been patented in England alone. In 1776, during the American revolutionary war, submarines entered military service, with the single-seater *Turtle*, invented and commanded by David Bushnell This vessel tried and failed to sink the HMS *Eagle* in New York harbour (the British warship did not even notice it was being attacked – there is no record in the ship's logs); the submarine's low attack speed – its propellers were hand-operated – thwarted Bushnell's belligerence. In 1831, a Spanish diver called Cervo constructed a wooden sphere, went down into the water and was never seen again. In 1889, Balsamello, an Italian, constructed a 4.5-tonne submersible comprising two hemispheres, and dived to 541 ft (165 metres) down – a quite remarkable depth for the age.

The First World War was the first true theatre of submarine operations. During the war, the Germans built 360 submarines, the British 93. These submarines could go underwater, just not very deep. The most advanced U-boats of the time would collapse under the pressure at 200 metres (656 ft) below sea level. Modern US Navy *Seawolf*-class nuclear submarines have a collapse depth of about 730 metres. Pressure underwater increases roughly one atmosphere for each ten metres in depth: at 200 metres down it is twenty times the pressure at sea level and 300 metres will kill most humans, if they make it down that far. At the bottom of the ocean, deep-sea pressure could be up to 1,000 atmospheres; just over one million kilograms per square metre (211,621 pounds per square foot). Piccard might have said he was simply building a type of "free balloon", since, balloon or bathyscaphe, the principle was the same: an airtight cabin capable of resisting differences in pressure and suspended underneath a float. But the enormous stress on the cabin presented a different magnitude of engineering challenge. The thin aluminium walls of the *F.N.R.S.* would be entirely unsuitable. Fortunately for Piccard, unlike with his stratospheric expeditions, someone had already pointed the way. And Piccard had already had met that someone – at the young adventurer scientist lunch he attended in New York, in 1933: Beebe, the underwater man.

Charles William Beebe was born in Brooklyn on July 19, 1877, the son of a prosperous paper merchant. As a boy he avidly read Jules Verne, along with Rudyard Kipling, H. G. Wells and John Buchan. At 16, he wrote in his diary that "to be a naturalist is better than to be a king." Like Piccard, he was very tall, with "a bald head, and thin, eager features", according to an excellent recent biography by Carol Grant Gould. After graduating from Columbia University in 1898, Beebe became the first curator of birds at the Bronx Zoo, which had just opened. Soon he made his first expedition, with his first wife Mary Blair, into the heart of Mexico. He went on to produce a famous series of monographs on pheasants. This sounds more mundane than the reality: to research the work he lay for hours in the thick grass of the Borneo jungle, was tortured by peasants and narrowly avoided Dyak headhunters. It earned him a reputation as one of the most dashing explorers, which he made the most of back in the US: he was friends with Noel Coward and kept a lively house in New York which a young Katharine Hepburn visited – "he never lacked for female companionship," according to Gould. In the First World War, despite being too old to serve, he won special dispensation from Teddy Roosevelt to fly aerial reconnaissance missions over France. In 1923 he went to the Galapagos, where he studied marine iguanas. The iguana could move from land to sea quite naturally, and it prompted Beebe to do the same, quite unnaturally.

The most advanced conventional submarine of the time had not descended past 383 feet (116.7 m). An armour-suited diver had made it to 525 feet, but could barely see or move, resembling nothing more than a medieval knight being dangled on a cable. In 1928, Beebe announced plans for a cylindrical underwater exploration device. The cylinder was a terrible idea: no flat surface could resist the immense pressure of the deeps – at half a mile, more than half a ton on every square inch – without being unfeasibly thick. Beebe's "own ideas, the offspring of a mind versed in almost every sort of knowledge except mechanics, were totally impractical," Gould writes. Fortunately, a young, wealthy engineer called Otis Barton had a better idea: a sphere. The ball was the ideal shape for distributing pressure (as Piccard had found, though his was to resist internal, not external pressure). Each part of the surface, squashed by the water, would push against adjoining parts, which would themselves push back against their neighbours. This would strengthen instead of weaken the entire structure. This "bathysphere" would be lowered into the deeps by a cable some 3,500 feet (1,067 m) long.

Barton spent his inheritance building the bathysphere – "We were still in the plush twenties," he later wrote, and this is what he "wanted to do more than anything else in the world". After a few preliminary tests, Beebe and Barton sent the empty bathysphere down on its first deep dive. When it returned, the rubber hose that contained the electrical and telephone connections had twisted wildly around the cable; when they uncoiled it, they found it had wrapped around forty-five times. But everything still worked, and on June

6, 1930, the pair entered the bathysphere. "Finally," Beebe later wrote, "we were all ready and I looked around at the sea and sky, the boats and my friends, and not being able to think of any pithy saying which might echo down the ages, I said nothing, crawled painfully over the steel bolts, fell inside and curled up on the cold hard bottom of the sphere." They hid their fear, but both knew they were risking their lives: "If there was a leak, they'd be dead – shot through by arrows of pressurised water – before they drowned," Gould writes. At 787 ft (240 m) deep, Beebe made an entry in his logbook: "Since the beginning of humanity, thousands of humans have reached the depth where we now hang, to go on to even deeper levels. But all these men were dead, drowned, victims of war, of storms or other acts of god. We are the first living men to contemplate this strange illumination of the depths." After many successful dives, the bathysphere spent 1933 in Chicago, underneath Piccard's *F.N.R.S.* gondola, which was hanging in the Hall of Science at the Century of Progress exhibition. The next year, on August 15, 1934, Beebe and Barton rolled out the whole cable and reached a depth of 3,028 ft (923 m). "Only dead men have sunk below this," he once more gloomily observed. It would be 15 years before anyone went any deeper.

As with Piccard's stratospheric flights, Beebe and Barton's dives were not without serious complication. The bathysphere leaked – around the door, the telephone cable and the windows. In two tests, the sphere came up flooded, once when the door leaked and once when a quartz window gave way. On the second manned dive, 4 metres of telephone cable pierced the sphere, the coils writhing around Barton, prompting Beebe jollily to compare the scene to Laocoön, who died strangled by serpents ("there isn't much choice between a rubberised serpent and a real one when you're being squeezed to death," Barton later wrote). Barton seems to have acted as Beebe's unhappy comic foil; on one descent, Gloria Hollister, Beebe's chief technical assistant on the surface and also his lover, heard Beebe complain on the telephone of the once-more seasick Barton: "Oh God, Otis ö not now!" It became a catchphrase on deck.).

The danger could not always be laughed off. On another occasion, Beebe saw water trickling through the door seal. He phoned the surface to tell them to drop the craft quickly, hoping that the greater pressure would seal the door. It did. The bathysphere was also prone to being violently shaken, as the cable whip-cracked on the way down. After one empty test dive, the bathysphere came up heavy, filled with pressurised water. As Beebe unlatched the manhole, the bolt was torn from his hands and the metal hatch shot across the deck of the support vessel; Beebe was lucky not to be decapitated. But these misadventures did not deter him. Piccard said that "immense credit" was due to Beebe. "It is no exaggeration to say that it is he who opened the doors of the abyss to man." Jacques Piccard, Auguste's son, was at pains to point out that the bathysphere had little in common with the planned Piccard submarine – it was lowered by a cable and "designed for depths of little more than one-half mile. This is still the top of the ocean but the fact remains that these two courageous pathfinders saw things no man had seen before."

Despite his success, "Beebe was labeled an amateur by some hard headed scientists, and a romantic and fantasist by many others," Gould writes. Auguste too, although impressed with Beebe's device, had his reservations: "like all human works, it has some drawbacks." The most serious was the use of a cable. If this broke, sending the bathysphere down and down, "far beneath the surface, the observers would be condemned to a slow and terrible death." He compared the bathysphere with a tethered balloon, from the point of view of an imagined pilot:: "If only this rope would break, what a fine trip we would have," his pilot thought. "Very much to the contrary, the oceanographer, shut up in his tight cabin, is haunted by the terrifying idea that the cable may break." The bathysphere was consequently "a very dangerous device". It also prevented exploration of the greatest depths. The longer the cable, the greater its weight. Nylon could perhaps be used, but Piccard wondered "are we certain that no spoilsport would take it into his head to sharpen his teeth on it?"

Piccard's craft would be truly independent. The converse of the balloon, it would head down rather than up, with, crucially, a natural tendency to rise up: "it would be able to rise again as desired just as the balloon can descend whenever desired," Piccard wrote. It would not be a bathysphere, but a bathyscaphe – a ship of the great depths capable of independent navigation.

There were doubters. John Sheehan, who had carried out research with Beebe in Bermuda, thought that Piccard spoke "rather glibly" when he announced his plans in 1937; he incorrectly doubted Piccard's ability to release ballast, saying "no trigger mechanism seems feasible to be operated within the shell" and that the bathyscaphe "would certainly be no stable place from which to make observations."

Piccard once more knocked at the door of the Fonds National. He knew he would not get far with an official application for such an ambitious plan. So he casually spoke with members from the scientific board, asking them that if there were such a thing as a bathyscaphe, would it be scientifically useful? Of course, they replied. He approached the engineers and asked, if the money were available, would it be feasible to build his design? Perfectly feasible. Finally, he tapped up the financial committee, with the question that if the bathyscaphe could actually be built and prove useful to scientists, would they fund it? These three answers obtained independently, he went in front of the board members of the Fonds to tell them that they already thought a bathyscaphe was fundable, constructible and helpful to science. Nudged by King Leopold III, who had inherited his father Albert's admiration for Piccard, the fund obliged, equipping Auguste with a laboratory specialised for high-pressure studies, at the University of Brussels. Auguste again returned the favour, christening the new craft *F.N.R.S. 2*. The Fonds was concerned about the strength of any would-be submarine and ordered Piccard to make numerous preliminary trials. It would have been no problem to calculate the thickness of the walls of the sphere necessary to resist the great pressures, had it not been for the portholes and hatch: these variations necessitated the scale-model testing. Piccard constructed a tank to simulate the pressure of 1,600 atmospheres – the weight of a column of water at 10 miles (1,600 m) down. By using a pump, the pressure was increased progressively "until a violent explosion announced that the little sphere had been crushed. The pressure at which this took place was that at which the full-size cabin would also probably be crushed." Today at the Musée du Léman in Nyon, Switzerland, it is possible to see the results. Some of the small, hollow steel balls are intact. More have been torn and wrenched into pieces, the steel made to look as flimsy as paper. They must have been an extremely tangible incentive for Piccard to get his calculations right, each small, crushed sphere a *memento mori*.

Piccard was typically methodical. He listed four requirements for his bathyscaphe: it should be able to resist the enormous pressure "with all desirable safety"; it should be perfectly watertight; it should have portholes to allow the occupants to observe the external world and it should be spacious enough for two crew members. His stratospheric balloon had had a diameter of 2.1 metres and was made out of aluminium sheets 3.5 mm thick – a "luxury". Piccard had to keep down the weight of this new cabin as much as possible, which would result in a smaller interior. Beebe's bathysphere cabin had an internal diameter of only 1.3 metres (4 ft), for two men. Beebe and Barton spent hours here, but not comfortably, nor did they have to pilot their craft. Piccard himself went inside Beebe's diving bell, in the lab if not the sea, and found the situation "rather painful". (Piccard later offered Beebe a place in his bathyscaphe, and Beebe offered Piccard a seat in his bathysphere. Both declined: neither completely trusted the other's design.) He made some trials with mock-ups and settled for an internal diameter of two metres. Increasing the diameter of the cabin by only ten centimetres, to bring it into line with the *F.N.R.S.,* would have increased the weight by 1,600 kg, which would have required a much bigger float. Based on his pressure tests, Piccard went for a safety factor of four – the factor between the pressure at which the bathyscaphe would operate, and the pressure at which the bathyscaphe would be crushed. As for material, Piccard tried a magnesium alloy, which Jean had used to build his stratospheric gondolas. It did not prove strong enough for deep dives, so Piccard chose steel. This would be nine centimetres thick in most parts, 15 centimetres near openings such as portholes and hatches. "Thus conceived, the cabin would probably be crushed at a pressure of 10 miles of water," Piccard wrote. He was not planning on going nearly that deep. "At 2½ miles [4,023 m] deep we should then have what we want, a safety factor of 4."

Windows were a trickier problem, and a new one. Scientific theory was "completely lacking", so Piccard proceeded by trial and error with his scale models. "The concern with which we watched these experiments can only be imagined and likewise the joy we felt as the ideal solution appeared little by little: it was only after having found it that I was able to decide to go on to the construction of my submarine." Beebe and Barton had used fused quartz, but even small differences in pressure in the medium depths to which they ventured had resulted in leaks. In his laboratory experiments, Piccard used tiny peepholes of cones made from diamond (the King was, after all, ultimately footing the bill). But at the highest pressures, even these diamonds cracked regularly, albeit at pressures a hundred times greater than the actual windows would endure in the sea. Sheets of glass would not do either: any hole sufficient to withstand the pressure would offer a tiny field of view. Piccard tried conical blocks, which would enlarge the visual field. This time he consulted an expert, Professor Michels in Amsterdam, who predicted that the glass would crack as the bathyscaphe rose to the surface and the pressure diminished. Piccard tried other methods, inserting softer substances between the glass and steel, but these two resulted in cracks, if barely perceptible. In May 1939, though, Professor Guillisen, the father of Piccard's young assistant Jean, suggested Plexiglas – a relatively recent innovation patented by a German chemist in 1933. This proved successful. Plexiglas is slightly plastic: if part of the cone were pushed beyond the limit of its elasticity, it would go out of shape only slightly and pass the excess loads to adjacent load, spreading the burden uniformly though the entire piece, whereas glass, lacking this plasticity, could only yield to an overload by cracking. Piccard was delighted and called the windows "perhaps the finest feature of the bathyscaphe", with good reason. On the interior side of the glass, inside the cabin with its crew peering out, there would be a normal atmospheric pressure on the windows. On the other side the ocean would weigh on the Plexiglas with a force of roughly 450 tonnes. As Piccard pointed out, "the production of such items is not in the normal programme of industrial manufacture."

The cabin was complete. Now all Piccard needed was a means of travelling from the surface to the deep. Piccard started with the general concept, comparing the bathyscaphe once more to the balloon. "In spite of the difference of surroundings in which they move and of the quite opposed ends in view, the principle in question is the same: that of Archimedes." If the weight of an immersed body is lighter than that of the ambient fluid of an equal volume, the body rises. If the body is heavier than the fluid it disperses, it descends. A balloon rises because its envelope, inflated by a gas lighter than the ambient air, has enough volume to support the weight of the cabin beneath it. In the same way, the bathyscaphe was in principle lighter than the surrounding water: Piccard wanted the bathyscaphe not to sink of its own accord, but to rise. Ballast – water pumped into air tanks – would take it to the great depths; with this jettisoned, the bathyscaphe would return to the surface by its very design (compare this with Beebe's bathysphere, which, without its saving cable, would rapidly sink to the bottom of the ocean).

As with the first *F.N.R.S.*, Piccard required a sort of gasbag for his underwater craft. This float would have to be filled with a substance less dense than water, so that it would float at the surface. Gases would not be suitable, as they were too compressible. Just as the hydrogen in the *F.N.R.S.* expanded as it ascended, providing more lifting power, so too would any gas in the bathyscaphe shrink in volume as the craft descended, offering less lifting power. Maybe compression could be avoided, but this would require rigid walls able to resist high pressure. Conventional submarines operate on this very principle; their hull is filled with air.

But this is what restricts their depth: their walls would have to be extremely thick, and so extremely heavy, to resist the greater outside pressure. The bathyscaphe would have to go down much further and such a shell would have to be unfeasibly thick and heavy. Piccard abandoned gases and looked for a less compressible substance. A solid lighter than water was one option. It would have the added advantage of not flowing away if the float were damaged. Nor were solids nearly as compressible, so its lifting power would not decrease so much. There were two candidates: lithium or paraffin wax. Lithium "would certainly be ideal": its gravity was only 0.55 – in fresh water, one cubic metre of the metal would carry a weight of 450 kg. But lithium production was limited. Piccard made some enquiries and the most any manufacturer would offer him was 19 grams. Paraffin wax was not quite so buoyant: its gravity is 0.9. In fresh water, one cubic metre of paraffin would lift only 100 kgs. "The bathyscaphe would require a very voluminous float: its cost and the difficulties of transport would be considerable."

Solids rejected, liquid it would have to be – specifically, petrol. Lighter petrol would mean a smaller float. But too light and it would be too compressible, liable to explode. Piccard selected a mixture that would boil at between 60 and 80 degrees celsius; at freezing, its gravity was between 0.68 and 0.695, meaning a cubic metre of the liquid could bear a load of nearly 350 kilograms. The volume of any liquid, though to a lesser extent than gases, is a function of temperature and pressure. Piccard factored this into his design. At the bottom of the float, he constructed a passage that would allow seawater to enter and exit. In this way, the pressure would be the same inside and outside the float (the petrol would only be slightly more compressible than the surrounding water), allowing it to be built from relatively thin metal shielding. To determine how the volume of petrol varied under the effects of pressure and cooling, Piccard of course did calculations on paper, but he also perfected a new scientific apparatus which used mercury. Piccard determined that he would need 14.8 cubic metres of petrol to carry the cabin and its contents. The float's volume would be 30 cubic metres, with the petrol stored in six upright cylindrical tanks. Between the cylinders were tanks containing the petrol for driving and the ballast tanks, all encased in iron sheeting one millimetre thick. The float also contained the air tanks: flooded with water, they would take the bathyscaphe to the bottom.

Ballast was vital, much more so than on the F.N.R.S. If a balloon pilot runs out of ballast, he or she cannot rise any further. Any landing may be quicker and rougher than hoped for, but it would be a return to earth nonetheless. If the bathyscaphe, though, could not find a way to jettison ballast, it would never return to the surface: there was no way of pumping seawater out of the air tanks when full. "A method must be found thus," Piccard wrote, "which in any circumstances will allow the pilot to unballast, and which will never be in danger of a breakdown. The ballast is outside the cabin: the pilot must then in some manner work through the wall of the cabin. How is it possible?" Piccard toyed with a mechanical system, using a shaft and a stuffing box – the device used to keep propeller shafts watertight, while still allowing them to turn. This would be a "very delicate and dangerous organ", Piccard decided: he was not going to leave his life hanging on one piece of experimental equipment. He could see no other solution than to use electricity. In water especially, this conjured up the "double spectre of short-circuit and bad connection" but Piccard ingeniously turned these vices into virtues. The electric current, while it flowed, would hold the ballast in place. When the current failed or was switched off, the ballast would fall. All Piccard needed to fulfil these conditions was an electromagnet. This was the perfect fail-safe: in case of any electrical fault, the craft would automatically dump its ballast and return to the surface. There were three types of this emergency ballast: tubs filled with scrap iron, held in place by electro magnets and capable of being jettisoned one by one; gravel stored in four big tanks closed at the bottom by flap-valves, also held by electromagnets; and the two heavy storage batteries were suspended beneath the float, controlled by more electromagnets. All of these were "to be sacrificed in case of necessity". Necessity could manifest itself variously: if the float lost its petrol, if they became stuck in the bottom mud or in seaweed, or if the cabin became flooded with water, which would add a weight of 4,290 kilograms. Piccard wrote that "these last considerations cannot be calculated in advance", but he added a total of 4,290 kilograms of emergency ballast in case. It wasn't entirely enough: what if everything that could go wrong, did go wrong? For this is the nature of true disaster – a series of independent catastrophes which experienced individually might be survivable; together, they prove truly disastrous. "To provide for this," Piccard admitted, "it would be necessary to double or treble the quantity of emergency ballast available. But let us not forget that each of these occurrences is itself very improbable... it is less than the danger that each of us runs when we walk in a large city any day. Since we are not afraid to go about town, why should we fear to go down in a bathyscaphe?"

The emergency ballast was a fail-safe, but a bathyscaphe pilot would also need to unballast in small amounts for more delicate manoeuvres, or to slow the rate of descent. So Piccard used the small shot lead "sand" that he had taken into the stratosphere, storing it in two big tanks built into the float. The lower part of the storage tank was funnel-shaped, its aperture encircled with an electric coil. While current was running through it, the small shot was magnetised, forming a compact mass which plugged the orifice. Cut the current and the shot would flow like sand from an hourglass.

The bathyscaphe was now nearly done: it could go up and down, and keep its occupants safe. In this, the bathy-scaphe entirely resembled the free balloon, submerged. Piccard pushed the analogy further. Balloons are equipped with a trail rope, up to 50 metres long and weighing about 80 kg. As the pilot prepares to land, he or she brings the balloon down quickly and throws the trail rope overboard. This slows the descent, transferring the weight of the rope to the ground and so lightening the balloon; the friction of the rope's contact with the ground also slows the balloon's horizontal speed. The trail rope thus helps the balloon stay low, without unballasting sand or venting gas, until the pilot finds a suitable place to land – just as Piccard had dragged his trail rope over the crevasses of Gurgl. If the balloon rises again, the trail rope's weight is once again taken up by the balloon. The bathyscaphe too would have a trail rope, to slow the vehicle down as it approached the sea floor, and made of metal so that it would sink (unlike the hemp trail ropes of a balloon). There was one thing left to be designed: the propellers. These were not very powerful and would push the bathyscaphe along at a speed of about 10 centimetres per second.

The most important trials had been made and the construction of the bathyscaphe had begun, when the Second World War broke out. Jean Guillissen, Piccard's assistant who would have dived to the bottom of the ocean with him, was killed by the Gestapo. By 1938, Piccard himself had realised that war was inevitable. He built a house in Chexbres, on Lake Geneva, and moved there in 1940 with his family. During this time, he continued

research in aluminium construction for the Swiss government and for private industry. He also proposed the
construction of prefabricated houses for the victims made
homeless by disaster. Piccard kept up his subaquatic
interest too, creating a depth map of Lac de Géronde,
and in 1940 he published a paper in the journal *Actes de
la Société helvétique des sciences naturelles*, outlining a
complete design for the bathyscaphe and titled "Le projet
d'une exploration sous-marine belge". In this article, wrote
Théodore Monod, an oceanographic authority who would
accompany Piccard on his first nautical expedition, "everything was described, foreseen and calculated."

Six long years later, at the end of the war, the Piccard
family returned to Brussels. The funds given to him
before the war were still available, but the Belgian Franc
had massively depreciated: no more diamond windows.
The budgets were tight and many features of the prototype would have to be abandoned – "every nut and bolt
was expected to do the work of two," Jacques later wrote.
Auguste Piccard was now past 60 years old. If he was going
to the bottom of the ocean, he would have to do it soon.

Jacques

On October 26, 1948, Auguste Piccard once more returned to the world of men, this time after 12 hours spent underwater. As the *F.N.R.S. 2* rose off the coast of Dakar, Senegal, the porthole emerged from the water. "I could see the *Scaldis*, with the whole crew at the rails: I recognised my son, who is a head taller than the others: he would very much have liked to come with me. If one could have told him that five years later, he would go down too, but to 1,680 fathoms [10,080 ft, 3,072m], in a perfected bathyscaphe, the building of which he would have directed!" If one could have told Auguste that Jacques Piccard would not stop at 10,000 ft, but carry on down to 36,000 ft (11,000 m) – seven miles down and the deepest point on earth...

Ten hours earlier, Jacques had rowed out in a "little cockleshell of a boat" and tended to the ballasting for the descent. He was twenty-six years old. "I was excited and rather tense as the sinking bathyscaphe slipped from under me," Jacques later wrote. "Everyone aboard the cargo vessel was tense too. There were men who didn't have my father's confidence in this strange depth vehicle.

"Thus the story of the bathyscaphe began that afternoon off Dakar. I did not know then that I was to be part of the future story. Nor was I aware, that day as I watched the *F.N.R.S. 2* sink from sight from my little tender, that this would be the last time I would witness a descent from the vantage of the sunlit world. Ever after, for the next 12 years, I would be the one sealed inside the sphere looking out upon a watery world."

*

Like many boys growing up during the 1930s, Jacques idolised Auguste Piccard, the difference being that Auguste was Jacques's father. "It never occurred to me that my early life was anything but normal," he later recalled. "I was aware that not everyone had a father and an uncle who disappeared into the sky in balloons. This is something the Piccards did, though. Some people were wine merchants, some shopkeepers and others local officials. The Piccards made experiments." Auguste's way of playing with his young son was "to pose simple physical experiments. I was encouraged to work out the proper solution. My father was always patient with me. 'Never be satisfied with *a* solution,' he admonished. 'A true scientist must be patient and forever seek *the* solution.'"

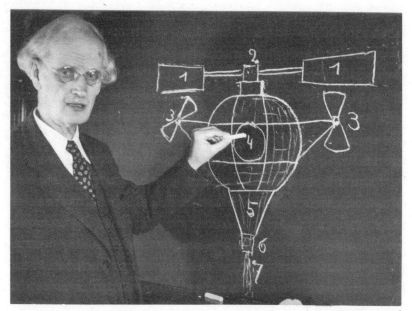

Auguste Piccard

Jacques's first memories were to do not with the sky or the stratosphere, but the sea. When he was three, the Piccard family holidayed at Arcachon Bay, on the Atlantic coast in southwest France. One Sunday, Auguste and Marianne took the children for a boat trip. The sky was grey and the wind picked up. "The captain shouted at us to take cover, to go down into the hold. I don't think I will ever forget that evening there. The sound of the water slapping against the hull, the frightened tourists, the smell of this boat," Jacques later said. "And above all the impression of feeling beneath the water level, of being in the sea... As far back as I can remember, I find myself there, in that hold, being rocked in caring arms, in a world already underwater."

Jacques was ten when his father went to the stratosphere. "It seemed not at all extraordinary to me – except that I was aroused at 1am. I was rarely awakened before dawn." But the excitement of the occasion rubbed off on him. Some photographs taken in 1932 show Jacques, wearing white shorts, helping with the balloon or trying on his father's wicker basket helmet, with Auguste standing behind him, a wide grin on his face. He would politely doff his hat to the dignitaries Auguste presented him to. Auguste took his family around the site of the flight, pacing the grass and observing each detail like a bird of prey. Jacques helped one of the seamstresses doing minor needlework on the balloon; he was fascinated with the aircraft. At school, his science teacher asked him to come up to the front to explain how the F.R.N.S. worked. Jacques knew only a few of the principles, but he explained the airtight capsule and the gas envelope to his admiring friends. The only boy among Auguste's children, he was determined to help his father and to follow him.

After secondary school, Jacques went to read economics and social sciences at the University of Geneva. But he also took a course in physics at the science faculty – "a way for him of maintaining the connection with Auguste at the same time as trying to find his own calling," according to Jean-François Rubin, who became friends with Jacques later in his life and was left a submarine by him in his will.

Jacques was tall and skinny, but more rugged and athletic than his father. He was the engineer who realised and lived the principles dreamt up by the abstract physicist. His aunt Jeannette told a local paper in the US, the *Sarasota Journal*: "he's a typical Piccard, logical and sharp. He's the sort of person who can lie awake all night thinking of things that could go wrong and then get up the next morning and do something about them." Jacques had intense dark eyes and spoke softly, but firmly. Those who worked with him say that there was never a lot of laughing and joking with Jacques, a combination of his natural reticence and his hesitance in speaking English. But he was charming – "everybody liked him and he was fun to be around," says Don Kazimir, who would later dive with him. "I know he was Swiss, but he had that French charm." When Jacques talked about his father's creations, especially the submarines, he explained the details using his large, expressive hands. During pauses, the tips of his long slender fingers pressed together with palms apart. Like his father, he abhorred drinking and smoking. He was, according to Robert Dietz, who worked with him later, an "anachronism – a one-man organisation, sans secretaries and sans assistants". He detested bureaucracy, small-minded thinking and especially the press – he would never forget the premature obituaries they printed for his father – but he was extremely enthusiastic about those projects he thought worthwhile. Jacques also wore two watches, on the basis that "there is an unwritten law that Good Swiss must wear two watches. Besides, I have two watches, why not wear them?" Dietz called him "a

Captain Nemo right out of the pages of Jules Verne". Indeed, Jacques made a similar sort of first impression as Nemo did on the narrator of *20,000 Leagues Under the Sea*, Professor Pierre Aronnax: "I made out his prevailing qualities directly: self-confidence – because his head was well set on his shoulders, and his black eyes looked around with cold assurance; calmness – for his skin, rather pale, showed his coolness of blood; energy – evinced by the rapid contraction of his lofty brows; and courage – because his deep breathing denoted great power of lungs... He was tall, had a large forehead, straight nose, a clearly cut mouth, beautiful teeth, with fine tapered hands, indicative of a highly nervous temperament." Auguste's fact had inspired Hergé's fiction. In Jacques, Verne's fiction became fact.

Jacques Piccard

When the Piccard family moved back to Switzerland at the start of the Second World War, Jacques was upset to find himself in a neutral country; born in Belgium, he now saw that country overrun and a king, whom he had met, exiled and imprisoned by the Nazis. The French-Swiss Piccards were on the side of the allies; Auguste sent a great number of the discoveries he made during the war to the British Ambassador in Switzerland, with the aim that they should help those fighting the Axis, but having lived through one world war, he was keen to protect himself and his family by staying in Chexbres. Jacques's mother Marianne, originally French, was more partisan: she had lost one of her brothers to a German bombardment in the First World War. So when Jacques, less pragmatic and more idealistic than his father, announced he would join the French Resistance, she understood better than Auguste. Neither parent approved though, and Jacques and Auguste had a bitter argument – the only time they are said to have rowed. Over time, the professor relented, with a great deal of reluctance.

Early in 1944, the twenty-two-year-old Jacques crossed the Franco-Swiss border into the Jura. He travelled north to Doubs and attempted to join the army of General Jean de Lattre de Tassigny, a hero of the French Resistance. The officer who interviewed him declared that a Swiss could not serve in the French army. Jacques replied that he was also a citizen of Dunkirk. With Dunkirk still in German hands, there was no way of checking, and Jacques was enlisted. He was sent to officer training, which was cut short when, lacking troops, the general staff sent all the young soldiers to the front. Jacques left as a sergeant and was incorporated into the Mountain Infantry, in command of four mortars and a squad of 15 men. There was not much war left, though. "We crossed the Rhine on a bridge of boats at Strasbourg. We headed along the Rhine on the other side and we crossed the Black Forest. Then we reached Lake Constance and we were in Austria... In all, it lasted a bit less than a year." Jacques's lieutenant was Edmond Kaiser, who would later found a number of charities, including Terre des Hommes, and work directly with Jacques's son Bertrand. "We performed acts of war, but I never saw a German," remembered Jacques. "We heard the cries of the SS, in a wood where there were three small valleys. We never saw them but we chased them. They left shouting loudly, 'We will return'. They never came back."

When the war ended, Jacques resumed his studies in Geneva and started taking part in his father's missions. He had never stopped idolising Auguste. He joined the bathyscaphe project out of "an incredible loyalty to his father", according to his own son Bertrand. Jacques dedicated his 1961 book *Seven Miles Down* to Auguste: "This book is dedicated to my father who invented, constructed and deployed the bathyscaphe..." Auguste had a high opinion of his son and returned the compliment, dedicating *In Balloon and Bathyscaphe*, published in 1954, "to my son, Jacques Piccard, in recognition of his invaluable help which made possible the construction of the *Trieste* and its deep sea diving". In the same book, he wrote that his son "more than ever held the reins in his hands. The study of economics had developed his feelings for synthesis... First in the yards and last to leave, always there when we wanted, Jacques knew how to maintain contact with the workman as with the engineer. Not a detail escaped him. Not an instrument but had passed through his hands; nothing that had not been subject to his personal control. He knows the apparatus better than I do. It was he who inspired all the enthusiasm which is indispensable in the carrying out of such an undertaking. What a privilege for me to have this time such an assistant and to be able to place my whole confidence in his intelligence as well as his overflowing energy." Auguste was never severe as a parent, but rarely overly emotional either: such praise was the expression not only of his estimation of Jacques as a project manager, but of his love for him as a son. In the dedication to the book, Auguste had also quoted *Genesis* i:28: "...replenish the earth, and subdue it: and have dominion over the fish of the sea, and over the fowl of the air, and over every living thing that moveth upon the earth." He omitted the first half of the verse: be fruitful and increase. Writing before Jacques went to the absolute bottom of the oceans, and before Bertrand was even born, Auguste seemed already to know the fruits of his seed would indeed dominate sea, then sky.

*

When he returned to the bathyscaphe after the Second World War, Auguste needed his son's help. He had reapplied to the Fonds National, who had given him the credit necessary to take up the work again. But they had stipulated that Max Cosyns, as the token Belgian, should share the supervision of the project, "with complete equality of rights and responsibility". Piccard had himself selected his stratospheric assistant as his underwater one too, but was unhappy with the new arrangement. "Such a division of command was no doubt necessary from the political point of view, but the formula hardly proved fortunate in practice. An achievement of this importance demands someone in absolute command: as this chief cannot physically perform the whole task himself, he must be surrounded by assistants over whom he has authority." No questions over who that chief should have been in Piccard's mind: that was simply how he worked. And indeed the Fond's division of command would ultimately thwart the *F.N.R.S. 2.*

There were no major holdups in the construction of the submarine, though. Piccard realised his pre-war design, with a few money-saving modifications. The finished cabin, made from steel described by the manufacturer as "indefatigable", was constructed by the Henricot Steel Mills of Court-Saint-Etienne, Belgium. Piccard wasn't going to take their word for it though: when metal is cast, bubbles and flaws can form in its middle, unapparent on the surface. Piccard borrowed a gram of radium from the Union of Mines of Upper Katanga, in what is now the Democratic Republic of the Congo. He placed this in the centre of the sphere and laid eighteen square yards of photographic film around the outside of the cabin. Piccard left these exposed for twenty-four hours. The developed film showed that although the steel was supposed be homogeneous throughout, there were lacunae in the material. The staff then took a sample of the defective part using a boring chisel and replaced this removed material with a pin in the shape of a truncated cone, made from more of the "indefatigable steel". The samples contained bubbles with diameters up to 5 mm. The steel experts said this should not have too much of an effect on the cabin; Piccard agreed, but resolved to extend the depth of the practice dives to be absolutely sure.

Another change in plan was for the petrol reservoirs in the main float. After they had worked out the dimensions for these, Cosyns, scouring the second-hand metals market, found aluminium tanks of exactly the right size. They had originally been intended to contain the fuel for V2 rockets, but the allies had seized them before they could be used. Piccard's team were "at the last moment" outbid, sadly. "It would have been a curious trick of fate if these vessels, instead of helping to propel engines of death and destruction through the stratosphere, had been used for the scientific exploration of the submarine deeps." It would have been another curious trick if Piccard had ended up using the work of his former pupil, Wernher von Braun, who years before had attended the professor's lectures and who had gone on to design the V1 and V2 rockets. (He would continue to be associated with the Piccards after he began working on the Apollo programme; his and Jacques's children became playmates.) Instead, Piccard used tanks supplied by the *Établissements Georges L'Hoir* in Liège – the same works as had supplied the two aluminium cabins for the *F.N.R.S.*

Piccard was also preparing another marine craft, the *Scaldis,* a 3,175-tonne cargo ship. "To say that this ship was conceived under a lucky star and that good luck always accompanied her would be an exaggeration," Piccard wrote. During her maiden voyage from Antwerp to Dakar, the motor powering the rudder broke down. As a result the *Scaldis* could not steer and struck a reef. Later, while Piccard and his staff were on board, the ship broke down in the middle of the Channel. There were numerous "fresh alarms" and when they finally got to Dakar, the single-screw propeller was found to have only two blades, instead of three, and so was hauled back into the dry dock. "After returning from our expedition she was sold to Bulgaria."

The *Scaldis* had a crew of 50, and Piccard and Cosyns took ten of their own retinue. Once the cabin and instruments arrived safely, the bathyscaphe was set up in the shipyard of Antwerp. A crane hoisted the submarine up and lowered it into the large hold of the *Scaldis*; the hold also doubled as a workshop. On September 15, 1948, the *Scaldis* weighed anchor and set sail for Dakar. There were a number of reasons for choosing this site for diving: they needed somewhere close to Europe, to save on transportation costs; somewhere sheltered from storms that could damage the bathyscaphe, and water at least 3.5 miles (5.6 km) deep.

The North Sea and the Channel were too shallow, and too busy. The Bay of Biscay and the North Atlantic were too often racked by storms. Cape Verde and the Gulf of Guinea both fitted. Piccard was leaning towards the latter – he liked the idea of going to the point where geographical coordinates are the simplest in the world – longitude and latitude zero degrees. But time was limited, so Dakar would have to do for now.

The *Scaldis* proceeded through the Channel, pausing only to break down because of a damaged engine and to say hello to a passing submarine, which greeted the *Scaldis* in Morse Code; unfortunately, none of those on board the cargo ship were proficient enough to decode the message. Onwards to Dakar, when a French Navy sloop came to meet the expedition. On board was Captain Jacques-Yves Cousteau. His ship, the *Élie-Monnier*, was a military vessel fitted out for oceanographic research. Cousteau came aboard. Piccard showed him the bathyscaphe. The Frenchman allowed himself to be impressed and said: "Professor, your invention is the most wonderful of the century."

At Dakar itself, the authorities gave the party a triumphant reception, as if the expedition were already a success. Piccard was less jubilant. "It seemed premature to me, and I thought about counting unhatched chickens. Several details of the bathyscaphe had yet to be verified and adjusted. I was realising the drawbacks of the expedition's being under a divided command, and I was regretting that I was not in sole charge." Cosyns also fell ill, delaying the first dives. Still, it gave the crew an opportunity to practise launching the bathyscaphe for the first time, which Piccard described as "spectacular". He wrote up the whole operation:

The submarine lay in the hold of the *Scaldis*: two hooks were raised above its float. On the cable of the crane hung a big hook with a beam attached to it. At its extremities hung two other hooks which were attached to the first hooks. The steam engine of the winch begins to work. Slowly the *F.N.R.S. 2* is lifted out of the hold. Its cabin is above decks: the crane turns. The *Scaldis* lists. The winch turns in the opposite direction, unrolls the cable and for the first time the *F.N.R.S. 2* makes contact with its element. The cabin enters the water: the float in turn is immersed to a third of its height. At this moment the cable slackens: the *F.N.R.S. 2* is afloat. It is light, for it has not yet been filled with petrol. As a precaution the float has been filled with carbon dioxide to avoid all danger of explosion at the moment of pumping in the petrol. Two hoses connect the *Scaldis* with the bathyscaphe. By one hose a pump sends the petrol from the reservoirs into the cylinders of the float. The other is used to evacuate the gas: driven out by the petrol, the gas flows back towards the reservoirs of the *Scaldis*, where it occupies the space which has become free. Slowly the bathyscaphe sinks, until the moment when the 7,040 gallons [26,649 litres] have been pumped in. Our calculations are shown to be correct...

On October 19, 1948, the *Scaldis* at last left Dakar for the island of Bao-Vista, accompanied by Cousteau and the *Élie-Monnier*, and two French naval frigates with a sea plane each, donated by Admiral Sol, commanding officer of the Dakar naval base. The *Élie-Monnier* took echo soundings along the way and marked out a zone where the bottom descended to a gentle regular slope. They dropped anchor there on October 21. Five days later, the first manned dive was made. Piccard was "rejoicing to be able to carry out at last" the first proper tests. Cosyns didn't feel the same way, and stayed on board the *Scaldis*, to Piccard's dismay. Professor Théodore Monod, another of the party, would go down with Piccard instead.

"For me, it was the great moment," Piccard said. The dive would be to only 25 metres down, but it was a vital proof of concept of the bathyscaphe: whether at 25 metres or four kilometres (2.5 miles), the bathyscaphe had to function in the same way, the only variable being the increased pressure. At 2.45 pm, Piccard climbed down the iron ladder into the hold of the *Scaldis* and squeezed through the 43-cm-wide manhole of the bathyscaphe. He reached back out to be handed some sandwiches and a flask of coffee. Monod followed him in, wearing shorts. The heavy door was brought up, put in place and bolted. Shut in, the professors could see nothing, nor could they communicate with the outside world. Looking out of the portholes, "we felt nothing at first, but all at once we noticed that the bottom of the hold was moving away from us: the winch had taken us in charge: here we were now above the deck of the *Scaldis*. Are we starting out for the stratosphere?" The crane stopped raising the submarine, turned and lowered it into the sea. "The deck of the ship seemed to slip beneath us, then the rails and the blue sea: then the hull of the ship appeared to rise. We went slowly down towards the water, till at last the portholes were immersed. The blue light penetrated the cabin. The sight was most beautiful."

Unfortunately, the F.N.R.S 2, once submerged, bobbed right back up ("prisoners, we could do nothing," Piccard knowingly wrote, referencing his stratospheric flight with an appropriate sense of the bathetic). Piccard was frustrated and betrayed his attitude towards any form of delegation: "If only I could have been two men; without losing my place in the cabin, have been present on the deck of the *Scaldis*!"

Down, slowly. Piccard made sure the same Dräger

apparatus that had kept him alive in the stratosphere was in good order and the two watched the sea. "In front of our portholes a swimmer passed." Piccard wondered whether it was Nicolas, the friend of Captain Nemo. "A picture illustrating *20,000 Leagues Under the Sea* has remained engraved on my memory: half a century has not effaced it. Aronnax, Professor in the Museum at Paris, and Captain Nemo in the semi-darkness of the saloon of the *Nautilus*: outside, in full light, the diver. Today it is I who am in the submarine. At my side there is indeed a professor of a Museum in Paris, but it is not Aronnax, it is Dr Monod. We are not in the *Nautilus* but in the *F.N.R.S. 2*. And we are in 1948." The swimmer was a diver from the *Élie-Monnier*, who moved away. When he returned a while later and looked through the porthole, he found the two scientists playing chess. "Why not? We had nothing else to do, unfortunately." The diver indicated the submarine was on its way down. Soon after, Monod said "We're at the bottom." "Without a jolt, without a jar, the *F.N.R.S. 2* had grounded at 14 fathoms [84 ft, 25.6 m]."

Monod and Piccard abandoned their chess and did some work. Piccard, perhaps inevitably, measured the cosmic rays ("the meter crackled loudly") and found that there was less radiation underwater. "At the end of quarter of an hour, having nothing to do," Piccard jettisoned the ballast – all twelve tubs of scrap iron – by pressing the switch – "in short, it's as simple as a modern lift." At 10 pm, they returned to the surface and were caught in the flat glare of the French Navy searchlights scanning the black water. The crane raised the *F.N.R.S. 2* to the surface, and Auguste caught sight of his son on deck. The winching took a long time; it was 3 am before the submersible was back in the hold.

It was an odd little trip, lacking the ambition or drama of the first flight of the *F.N.R.S.*, but it was the beginning of something incredible. For now, Piccard noted that the *F.N.R.S. 2* "behaved very well. There was no reason then for not going on with our programme." He told the press that "the bathyscaphe is not yet in perfect shape. The apparatus will have to undergo a major overhaul and it will need certain simplifications before it is absolutely right."

The *Scaldis* moved on towards the island of Fogo, another of the Cape Verde group, where Piccard made tests with an unmanned *F.N.R.S. 2*. One test was abandoned after the robot sub deployed all its ballast before it entered the water, the rough seas setting off the delicate device prematurely. On November 3, they tried again. The depth limit was set for 770 fathoms (4,620 ft, 1,400 m). Whatever depth reached, a timer would go off at 4.40 pm, which they thought an ample of margin of time, and the bathyscaphe would automatically return to the surface. But preparation was slow and it was 1 pm before the *F.N.R.S. 2* was in the water. Meanwhile, the *Élie-Monnier* took new soundings and found that there were now only 495 fathoms beneath them. As the *Scaldis* moved to a new spot, one of the towing lines snapped and the *F.N.R.S. 2* was adrift. Finally, they started again. At 4 pm, the bathyscaphe went down, giving only 40 minutes to reach the prescribed depth before the timer sounded. The bathyscaphe had a radar antenna attached so that the French frigates could find it in the fog. As this antenna dipped below the surface, Captain Laforce, the dour skipper of the *Scaldis*, told Piccard: "During the war I saw several ships go down just like that. Not one came to the surface again."

Piccard replied: "The *F.N.R.S. 2* is not like any other ship, Captain. This one will return." Inwardly, Piccard admitted "it was not encouraging" – even if he had entire confidence in the automatic pilot, he thought it unlikely it would make the desired depth.

At 4.29 pm, Piccard caught sight once more of the orange *F.N.R.S. 2*, now without an antenna. The *Élie-Monnier* examined the cabin and radioed to say they could see drops of water inside, showing that a joint was not tight. They brought the submarine alongside and night came on. Operations were difficult in the rough, heavy sea and a shark was circling the bathyscaphe, so the order was given to tow it back. But the *Scaldis* could only proceed slowly in this way. Worse, the *F.N.R.S. 2* appeared to be sinking: there was a leak in one of the reservoirs. "We therefore had to take a quick decision: the petrol had to be replaced not by water but by carbon dioxide." The petrol had to be sacrificed and run out to sea. "That would put an end to our diving and to the whole expedition, but we reckoned it better to sacrifice the petrol than to risk the loss of the bathyscaphe itself." Piccard gave the order that no one should smoke, which in other circumstances might have pleased him for its own sake, and jettisoned the petrol. The float emptied and the *F.N.R.S. 2* rose higher in the water; the *Scaldis* continued on its course for the bay of Santa Clara. "Meanwhile the bathyscaphe battled separately with the waves. Its plates groaned all night long." By midnight, the *Scaldis* had gone nowhere: it was only just holding its own against the current. The situation improved through the night and by dawn they were in the bay.

They brought the *F.N.R.S. 2* aboard. The ooze on its underside showed those watching that the bathyscaphe had indeed touched bottom, but how deep? Piccard opened it up and slid into the sphere. "To my great joy I could announce a depth of 759 fathoms [4,554 ft, 1,388 m]" – much deeper than the 3,048 ft record set by Beebe in 1934. In twenty-nine minutes, the bathyscaphe had made a round trip of 1.3 miles (2.1 km) down and up: its quick ascent had broken the antenna off. The water was the result of a minor leak that could have been fixed by a human pilot. This was no record though, as the dive had been unmanned. "Nevertheless, we had not set out to hunt records, and the fact that a habitable cabin had indeed come back from 759 fathoms had exactly the same value, from the technical point of view, as if a man or a guinea-pig had been shut up in it. Perhaps even a little more, since the construction of the robot constituted quite a presentable technical achievement." Jacques wrote that "a new era of deep-sea exploration had been opened."

That's the line the Piccards tried to spin, anyway, but with little success. The expedition was over. "A dream of forty years fizzled and died today," wrote the *New York Times*. The project had been a failure: a record certainly, but one made without anyone inside and one that had left them with a busted bathyscaphe. Piccard knew it himself, even if he protested otherwise. He had set out to reach the bottom of the ocean, but did not get anywhere close; nor had he been able to study the underwater environment at all. "My father was disappointed, but far from discouraged," said Jacques. "In his own heart, he still had confidence." Few others did.

A Race to the Bottom

After the tropical sun, the Piccards journeyed back in November 1948 to a Belgium that was grey and overcast. The weather reflected their reception. Jacques, always more sensitive than Auguste to criticism – or at least more prepared to respond to it – said that "the very people who barraged us with enthusiastic questions upon our departure now reproached us for having attracted world-wide attention to a project they said was obviously doomed beforehand to failure. It mattered not at all that we had laid the first stone for penetration of man into the sea, even if it was not brilliant granite in the sun."

"There were, without doubt, plenty of disappointments," Auguste wrote, "but, and I should like to emphasise this, the expedition was far from being a failure.

"It is not the first time that a scientific experiment has to be done over and over again until it can take place in perfect conditions." Piccard made the comparison with airplanes, when people were struck with admiration "every time we saw a few inches between the tyres and the ground." Maybe, but the *F.N.R.S. 2* had been badly handled. Monod, although convinced of the genius of the invention, said: "The fundamental error... was the failure on land to recognise marine realities. No, one cannot extrapolate from the lab to Nature. No, there is not a common measure between the test tube and the Ocean. They are two different worlds, each one with its own laws and technicians. Otherwise put, to make a viable bathyscaphe, you need physicists and skilled calculators, but you also need... sailors." Auguste was no sailor, nor was Jacques.

The Times of London wrote a kind summary, concluding: "There will be general sympathy for him in his disappointment"; the press closer to home was less understanding, slating the bathyscaphe and declaring Piccard's underwater adventures over. One report had said that "all its gear was unserviceable", another that "there was nothing left of the float."

"The first bathyscaphe did not realise all the hope that had been founded on it," wrote Piccard. "That is agreed upon." Piccard was by this stage used to public criticism, but this time it would have a direct effect on his research: the Fonds National decided "at once", according to Jacques, to have nothing more to do with the bathyscaphe. The fund itself had come under criticism for financing the mad Nautilean pretensions of a foreign professor and would not back any further expeditions. "They were reproached for having funds in an undertaking doomed from the first," wrote Auguste. "They had to pay more attention to these opinions because I was of Swiss nationality and I was not a sailor." In 1949, the Fonds National proposed that the French National Centre of Scientific Research and the French Navy take over the bathyscaphe and rebuild it at their own expense. But nothing happened for a year – what Jacques called a "paralysis of indecision". Jacques intervened, suggesting that he himself would raise funds for the reconstruction in Switzerland, then take it to Toulon for sea trials with the French Navy. "My father's full direction of the project would guarantee that its reconstruction would be in the hands of the physicist who invented the bathyscaphe... We would avoid the duality of leadership imposed in Belgium where Max Cosyns shared the authority with Professor Piccard because the latter was Swiss."

The proposal was accepted, in principle, but Jacques was

told to wait for a decision from the French Navy. It was a frustrating time. "We had to join battle with the inertia and inaction which destroys, or tries to destroy, so many new ideas in the embryo." In March 1950, he signed contracts with Sécheron, a Geneva firm, to build a new float. Petrol was sourced. In Paris, the Navy assured him that it would agree to any reasonable solution, so long as it did not cost them a sou; these things just took time. Jacques thought the Ministry of the Navy "an obscure world. It seemed an anthill of officials, full of goodwill, mulling about and without doubt submerged under unimaginable red tape. They appeared entangled in a spider web of rules which would leave even the best jurists desperately bewildered." As Jacques was preparing to ship the cabin of the *F.N.R.S. 2* to Geneva, everything changed. The Fonds National announced it would give the French Navy the *F.N.R.S. 2*, along with ample funds, so long as the Navy would agree to take it over completely: they wanted rid of Piccard's submarine, whatever it took. Another three months, but the French formally received the *F.N.R.S. 2* and nine million Swiss francs on October 9, 1950. Article 2 of the contract stipulated that the *F.N.R.S. 2* would be renamed the *F.N.R.S. 3*. Article 8 stipulated that Professor Auguste Piccard would be "invited to lend his collaboration as a scientific consultant" at the base in Toulon.

If Piccard had resented sharing command with Cosyns on the *F.N.R.S. 2*, he liked being stripped of all authority much less. "I may say that I began this work with enthusiasm. But the conditions under which I collaborated with them gradually became too painful for me: the work showed no progress: I had no rank: my situation was not easy." In 1952, he left the project. The *Times* of London observed that "like many inventors he loved freedom and could not afford it nor bear to hand over the children of his mind until he had tested them."

Jacques had been busy in the meantime. During the winter of 1951–2, dismayed with the French Navy's treatment of his father (according to Jacques, the collaboration "remained solely one-sided", they treated Piccard's notes as "mystic alchemy", Piccard was "cast in the role of a dreamer, more ingenious than practical. He had no rank, no authority."), Jacques had returned to economics, preparing a thesis on the economic possibilities of the Free Territory of Trieste. This city state had been created in 1947 by the United Nations Security Council, as a buffer between allied-controlled Italy and Tito's Yugoslavia. Researching the report, he met Diego de Henriquez, an eccentric professor who had collected a vast number of items from the Second World War for his War and History Museum. De Henriquez also had a dream, to make Trieste a centre of international science and culture. This included an ultramodern base which he hoped would launch the first rocket to the moon. He also proposed, on the spur of the moment, that Trieste be chosen as the site for the construction of a new bathyscaphe. Local industrialists, at de Henriquez's urging, contributed funds. Compared with the lethargy of the French Navy and the Fonds National, everything came together quickly. The Cantieri Riuniti dell' Adriatico would build the float; the Industrial and Electrical Company at Terni would forge, not cast, a new cabin; the Italian Navy would provide tugs and escort for dives in the Tyrrhenian Sea; Esso, later renamed Exxon, would supply the petrol for the float. And the new bathyscaphe would be called the *Trieste*.

Jacques was no physicist, not even, at that stage, an ocean-ographer or engineer. His unique skill related to finance, and he used that ability to create a monument of money to his father: "with Professor Piccard the complete master and solely responsible... finally to realise the bathyscaphe of which he had dreamed so long." It was a remarkable act of loyalty and devotion from Jacques. Auguste jumped at the chance to be "physicist-engineer in chief... It would be like before the war, when the *Fonds National* had granted funds to me alone."

Auguste saw no conflict of interest with the *F.N.R.S 3*: "if, instead of one bathyscaphe, two were constructed at the same time, the explorations of the great depths could only profit." Piccard had his way out and he would take it: "I had not much more to do at Toulon. They could henceforth get along with my help. Without delay I let the French naval authorities know about the proposal that had been made to me."

Piccard was criticised yet again, this time for "secretly" having done a deal to make a rival bathyscaphe and undermine the French effort. Some newspapers suggested that the bathyscaphe was now a French invention and that Piccard had taken knowledge of its plans with him to Terni. Indeed he had: there were only so many ways to design a bathyscaphe, and Piccard had considered them all. The similarities between the two craft: "in no way prove that one of the two machines was copied from the other. A biologist could say here that a cat's eye was not copied from a dog's eye, although the two animals descended from the same ancestor."

For the first time since he arrived from the stratosphere in Desenzano in August 1932, Auguste Piccard returned to Italy. He was delighted with what he found. The budget was sufficient, no more, but the professor was in complete control, the Italians were keen to collaborate and his son Jacques was by his side. According to his grandson Bertrand Piccard, "it was like a second youth: he thought when the float of the *F.N.R.S. 2* was damaged that it was the end of his career. He went to Italy and worked with Jacques, and this was a very important moment in their relation-ship, because they were working closely together." Auguste asked his son: "Could we wish for anything more?"

The new bathyscaphe was finished in barely 15 months. Unlike the *F.N.R.S. 2*, it was fully towable – a conclusion that Piccard had come to in 1938 and abandoned only because of expense. The calamity of the Dakar dives, when the too fragile *F.N.R.S. 2* had suffered in the high seas, would be avoided this time. The float, built at Monfalcone, a pretty little industrial town in north-eastern Italy, was a cylindrical steel envelope, partitioned into twelve parts and towable up to 8 knots. It had dark lines painted on its bright hull to show where each of these partitions was: in case of damage, the crew would be able to tell immediately which compartment had been damaged. Piccard was thinking like a sailor instead of a physicist, now: the float could resist waves up to 30 ft high.

The French *F.N.R.S. 3* reused the cabin from the *F.N.R.S. 2*, but Piccard's Italian bathyscaphe had a brand-new cabin in the same dimensions, forged rather than cast, making it stronger and more malleable than the original cabin. The forging shop at Terni was immense and Piccard was impressed enough to describe it. "It is so dazzling at first that nothing can be seen inside... A giant tool, suspended from a travelling crane, transports this radiant mass across the hall and places it upright on the bed of the press. Now imagine this press exerting 12,000 tons [10,886 tonnes], probably the most powerful in Europe, if not in the world, while its ram, actuated by three hydraulic cylinders, is lowered slowly: under its pressure the block is compressed and broadens out." The forge repeated this operation several times; newsreel footage shows the lofty Piccard, goggles on, paying close attention to every step: he was no longer the dreamer chalking on a blackboard with both hands, but surrounded by what looked like the molten bowels of the earth; not Captain Nemo, but Jules Verne's Professor Von Hardwigg journeying through volcanic tubes. "The whole surface is crushed bit by bit... Of a blinding white, the block gives out an intense heat and the men have to have masks for their faces."

Because the crew would enter the bathyscaphe while at sea, it was necessary to construct a long tube traversing the entire float, from top to bottom; the submariners would climb down a ladder, seal themselves in the cabin, then flood this tube. A telephone was installed, so that Piccard could be in constant contact with the surface. This required an opening in the cabin (and for other cables, such as the copper wires to carry the current to control ballast). These had to be completely secure: otherwise, at two and half miles down, 100 litres of water would break into the cabin every second, travelling at 60 miles an hour. "The crew, even if not stunned by the spouting water, would succumb to the pressure in less than seventy seconds." Piccard returned to the laboratory and tested each design iteration with small-scale models. At the same time as the bathyscaphe was being constructed, new scientific instruments, sourced from Switzerland, Germany and northern Italy, were assembled at Castellammare di Stabia, in the civilian ship yards of the Navalmeccanica.

Construction was not a complete breeze. Piccard once again had trouble with his familiar tormentor, the control valve: "the manipulation of the valve, very simple in the conventional free balloon, here became a difficult problem." And Jacques was not used to Mediterranean working practices: "My first sight was a small donkey cart blocking the way of a giant modern mobile crane. The donkey refused to budge. The crane driver refused to draw back. Flailing arms, shouting and cursing filled the air, but to no avail.

Amid these expletives both the donkey and the crane stood firm...

"'*Non si preoccupi* (Do not worry; it makes no difference).' This is the whole 'don't give a damn' philosophy, tinted with fatalism, which permeates southern Italy. Don't worry; it makes no difference. How many times I have had to fight against this sentence and against this mentality which refuses to accept responsibility! 'Have you checked the oil?' The answer comes, '*Non si preoccupi*'." Soon after he arrived, Jacques had to institute the firm rule that no one should, under any circumstances, use this phrase in front of him. He made sure to check every detail, nuts and bolts, of the craft that was being created to take his father and him 10,000 feet down. But there was affection on both sides: when a strike paralysed the whole shipyard, the technicians continued to work on the bathyscaphe, with the approval of the strikers.

By 1953, the new bathyscaphe was complete. When it was unveiled, it immediately prompted more controversy. One journalist, writing for *Science et Avenir*, wrote that "its builder didn't even have the shame to modify, even a little bit, its exterior appearance to distinguish it from the French plans [for the *F.N.R.S. 3*]." The chief engineer of the *F.N.R.S. 3* said that it was entirely a French Navy development and that Piccard had stolen ideas during his unhappy sojourn at Toulon. Piccard came back strongly. On December 12, 1953, he wrote in *Libre Belgique* that "it is with indignation that I have learned of these statements, which are completely false... It is false to pretend that during my studies with the French officer, I was travelling to Italy: there was no impropriety at all, on one side or the other. The opposite: a close collaboration between soldiers and civilians was shown to be impossible, and each party has taken control over that part to which they were entitled, each having their own views on the progress of oceanographic research."

There were now two bathyscaphes in the world, with the same goal of reaching the extreme depths. Piccard had, up to this point, been the trailblazing and peerless pioneer. Now he found himself in a race to the bottom.

The Trieste

On August 1, 1953 – Swiss National Day, as it happened – the colours were hoisted on the *Trieste*: the tricolour of the Italian Navy and the white cross on red of Switzerland. Tradition goes that ships are baptised with champagne; "Never having understood the relation existing between bits of broken glass, I left out this part of the ceremony," said Piccard. Instead, he let an Italian priest sprinkle holy water on the tubby bathyscaphe and officially christen it the *Trieste*. The giant crane of the Navalmeccanica yards lifted the zebra-striped craft deftly from her cradle, swung it out and laid it gently on the water. Hanging motionless in mid-air, the blimpish *Trieste* looked like it had been created to fly rather than dive. But making contact with the water, and settling deeper and more comfortably in its element, the *Trieste* was on its way to the great depths.

Eleven days later, Jacques and Auguste climbed inside, closed the hatch and went underwater, reaching a depth of 30 ft (9 m). The *Trieste*'s flagpole remained above the water. The next day, ten miles southwest of Cape Cepet near Toulon, Captain Nicolas-Maurice Houot and Pierre-Henri Willm, an engineer, took the rival *F.N.R.S. 3* down to 5,088 feet (1,550 m), breaking William Beebe's depth by 582 ft and setting a new depth record. On August 14, the *F.N.R.S. 3* recorded 6,888 ft.

Piccard, only just pulling up to the starting line, was already well behind in the race with the French bathyscaphe. But talk of records annoyed him: when one reporter, from *La Meuse*, asked one too many questions about the duel with the *F.N.R.S. 3*, Piccard pushed his glasses up to the crown of his head, the better to show off his angry expression.

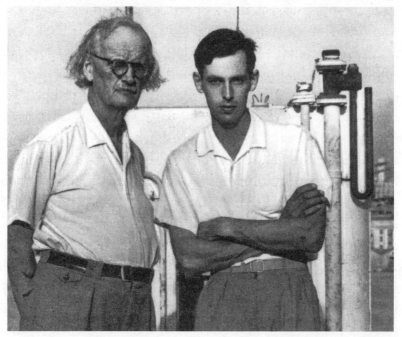

Auguste and Jacques Piccard topside on the Trieste

"Records...Records... I am a physicist, not a record-hunter." Later he told another newspaper: "As I've said several times, it isn't a boxing match or the Tour de France. If, in a few days, the *F.N.R.S. 3* reaches 4,000 metres [13,123 ft], certain papers will not forget to say that the *F.N.R.S. 3* has beaten the *Trieste* or even that the French Navy has beaten Piccard. It would be better to say that we actually have two marvellous research devices." In a dig at his doubters, he also said: "For my part, I should be happy that France has contributed to proving that I made no mistake in creating the submarine equivalent of a stratospheric balloon."

After two weeks of test dives in the harbour of Castellammare, the *Trieste* set out for Capri. The island sloped down underwater to a submarine hollow, 3,600 ft

(1,100 m) deep. At 6 pm on August 15, the tugboat *Tenace* slowly and tediously towed the *Trieste* out and the *Fenice*, a fast corvette from the Italian navy, accompanied the flotilla, carrying fifty journalists. At gloomy first light, the Piccards made their preparations. A speedboat, carrying an unidentified but "celebrated movie star", according to Jacques, came close to observe the dive. "Soft words proving vain, the *Fenice*'s hoses went into action, thoroughly dousing the craft. It moved off."

As Auguste and Jacques unrolled the guide rope, the electro magnet holding its catch failed and the 350 kg cable sank to the bottom of the Mediterranean. They decided to dive without a rope. The Piccards entered and started their descent. A few minutes later, they returned to the surface, after accidentally jettisoning three tonnes of ballast thanks to a short circuit from a broken electrical cable. As happened off Dakar, Piccard had to make a decision: continue the operations or go back to port. But the latter "would have taken a week at least, and we could not spare the time, as the season was already advanced." Piccard could not afford any further delays if he was to catch up with the French, and Jacques had a solution: refill the faulty ballast chute, and block it mechanically. They would dive using only the aft ballast tub. The morning was lost, but by afternoon they were ready. "At last the telephone was disconnected from its socket and the bathyscaphe went down; slowly the light grew less."

Father and son were calm. "Neither my son nor I could believe in the possibility of any fatal accident," Auguste later wrote. "However, it must be admitted, seeing the light decrease while the gauge indicated increasing pressures has something impressive in it...until now, those who have come back from the kingdom of shadows can be counted on the finger of one hand. And yet we had confidence in the laws of nature." Piccard senior was afraid of only one thing: to return to the surface too soon. They settled slowly into the abyss, the weak blue light coming through the 20 cm portholes and dimly lighting the cabin. The shadows grew darker as the light fled. "All became grey, then dark grey, then black."

At 1,500 feet (457 m), with a pressure forty-five times that at sea level, the Piccards turned on the lights. Auguste saw a luminous spot cross the porthole – "A living thing!" he wrote in the logbook. The deeper the *Trieste* went, the more the two submariners saw: "Each depth possesses its particular fauna," Auguste wrote. But this was not a zoological dive; they made straight for the bottom. Under the spotlight outside, Jacques, by the porthole, saw a circular surface appear under the cone of light and called out "Steady on!", like an aeronaut. But they were already on the bottom. "So soft was the ooze that we felt no shock," wrote Jacques. Nor could they see anything: mud, disturbed for the first time in aeons, covered the porthole; the *Trieste* was four and a half feet deep in the slime.

"During the descent we had been rejoiced to think of the discoveries we should make, once on the bottom. And we saw nothing." The *Trieste* had gone down too fast and so too deep into the mud. The main aim of the dive had been to prove the strength of the bathyscaphe, but the sight on the bottom was disappointing and troubled Auguste. What good was a laboratory at the bottom of the ocean if the scientist couldn't see out of it?

After 15 minutes spent on the bottom making some technical observations, Auguste and Jacques decided it was useless to remain any longer. They would jettison the ballast and return to the sunlight. Jacques turned the switch to empty the iron scrap. Nothing happened. "The silence was total, a real silence of the tomb," Auguste wrote. Several minutes later, the *Trieste* suddenly lurched upward. Auguste rushed to the porthole, in hope of seeing the sea floor. The churned-up sediment obscured it; by the time it cleared, the bathyscaphe was long gone.

"As we approached the surface, darkness first gave way to grey light then growing into a limpid blue," wrote Jacques. "A gentle bump followed by a slight rocking indicated our return to the surface some forty-five minutes after leaving the bottom."

Despite the mess at the bottom, the dive was a success. Capri was no longer deep enough. On September 25, the *Fenice, Tenace* and *Trieste* – refitted in Castellammare – sailed for the island of Ponza. A vast, sandy submarine plateau stretched out around the island, nearly 2 miles (3 km) deep – deep enough to beat the *F.N.R.S. 3*'s recent record. The first dive was aborted, after a rough tow during the night, so the scientific flotilla made land. The commandant of the port met the *Tenace* in a launch. On land, the mayor welcomed the Piccards. Auguste was fascinated by the crayfish that constituted Ponza's main trade. Jacques made a shallow test dive alone on September 29, to inspect the bathyscaphe for damage. The next morning they headed for the dive site and an attempt to go deeper than anyone before.

Once again, the sea picked up. It was "only" a "medium" swell: no problem for a battleship, but not for a bathyscaphe. Auguste, thinking of the botched Dakar dives, doubted whether the operation would be possible. But "all the dockyard workers who were with us – electricians, mechanics, fitters, engineers – metamorphosed themselves suddenly into wonderful sailors. All together we were a united crew; we had only one thought, to succeed."

Jacques gave the signal to start. Auguste put on his lifejacket and boarded the launch. He struggled to haul himself onto the deck of the bathyscaphe; Jacques was there already and held out his hand to haul his father on board. At 8 am, the 160 kg door of the cabin swung shut. Eight minutes later, the tube connecting cabin and surface was flooded and at 8.19 the dive started. The *Trieste* gurgled as its snorkels filled with water, then settled slowly. At 8.36, the *Trieste* was 1,000 feet (305 m) down and the water outside was nearly dark. The weather forecast predicted deteriorating conditions, so the dive had to be fast. The red bulb of the newly installed tachometer blinked on and off, faster and faster as the *Trieste* picked up speed, matched by the ever-increasing gradient on the pressure gauge. Auguste and Jacques took turns piloting and observing. "Time passed quickly," wrote Jacques. The barograph traced its curved line: 6,900 ft (2,103 m), the depth from which the *F.N.R.S. 3* returned without seeing the bottom. There was still 3,280 ft (1 km) of water beneath the *Trieste*: any deeper and the Piccards would have gone lower than anyone else. Auguste was reminded of Alberto Santos-Dumont, who devised some of the first airships: *por mares nunca d'antes navegados*. "We too were entering a virgin sea," Auguste wrote. "My feelings were like those that I felt on May 27, 1931 when, with Kipfer, I entered the stratosphere. But the analogy stops there: here there was neither sun nor moon nor stars, nothing but opaque shades."

The *Trieste* continued diving, fast. The Piccards let some ballast out to slow the descent at 8,248 (2,514 m). Divetime 63 minutes, there was a slight rocking jar. The *Trieste* was once more on the mud. But this time the porthole was clear: Auguste and Jacques could look upon something no one had seen, the sea at 10,392 ft – nearly two miles down. It wasn't much of a sight. "The sea floor was a featureless and lifeless coloured plain fading in the distance to blackness," Jacques wrote. But at least they could see it. The Piccards shook hands then got on with their observations.

They released the ballast and for a few minutes, the *Trieste* did not budge, although the Piccards could see, through the aft porthole, the pellets pouring out from the tank. Oceanographers had warned that suction might keep them on the bottom, but soon water started swirling in front of the porthole and the *Trieste* was on its way up, quickly. Phosphorescent animals appeared and the darkness receded. "The first rays of light pierced the liquid layer: daylight became apparent, clearer and clearer," Auguste wrote. "Suddenly we were being tossed on the waves."

At 10.35 am, Auguste Piccard returned to the surface for good. As planned, he had made his last dive. For the next six years, Jacques would pilot the *Trieste*. But for now, two miles down was a new world record. Auguste was happy, but not with the record: "that was not what I was after: the fact that the bathyscaphe had at last shown what it could do was enough for me."

There wasn't any deeper to go, at least not in the Mediterranean. Auguste thought of Uqba ibn Nafi, a Muslim general who conquered much of North Africa. According to Edward Gibbon, when he reached the Pillars of Hercules and saw the ocean, which seemed to stretch out for ever, he spurred his horse into the sea, raised his eyes and sword to the heavens and cried: "Great God! If my course were not stopped by this sea, I would still go on, to the unknown kingdoms of the West, preaching the unity of the holy name, and putting to the sword the rebellious nations who worship other gods than Allah." Piccard had a self-effacing idea of how he might wield his own scimitar. "I could, in my turn, have pulled out my slide rule and cried: 'Neptune is my witness that the ground alone stops from opening up the deepest oceans to scientific exploration!'" Piccard knew that the *Trieste* "could without danger reach the greatest depths". Jacques would put that belief to the test.

Tossed on the Mediterranean, the *Trieste* waited for the *Tenace*. The Piccards blew the water from the entrance shaft, sending up a geyser of seawater. They went up the shaft and opened the hatch. Standing upright on the tower of the *Trieste*, waves sweeping the deck, father and son waited for the longboat to fetch them; the 68-year-old Auguste found crossing into the wave-rolled launch more difficult than the dive to 10,392 ft. They came aboard the *Tenace* to tell what they had done. Auguste leaned on his son and whispered in French: "You speak, Jacques. The credit is all yours." Jacques smiled, but demurred. "For a moment, father and son clung to each other, as if too moved to speak," a journalist from *TIME* reported. Auguste resumed: "It was very important, very lovely. And I must say that the chief merit of this undertaking goes to my son Jacques. It was he who guided the *Trieste*." The achievement, according to Auguste, was what he had "foreseen. It is possible for man to descend into the sea depths using means created by him. The problem is to overcome physical obstacles by using physical principles." There was no risk. "Everyone," he remarked, "is in the habit of trusting a railway bridge. We trust the eternal laws of physics."

The *Tenace* arrived at Ponza a few hours later. The Piccards, entering the gangway, saw the crew drawn up on deck, and were saluted by six sharp whistles. When an officer objected that these were the honours given to an admiral, Admiral Girosi replied: "Admirals of the abyss, they deserve it." Not bad for two Swiss landlubbers. The inhabitants of Ponza came out into the street or threw flowers from the window; the Mayor of Ponza made the Piccards honorary freemen of the island and a fisherman presented them with the sword of a swordfish as a souvenir, taken from the Red Sea. They also threw a feast of crayfish.

The professor spent the next day violently sick, thanks either to seasickness or the crayfish.

The *Tenace* left Ponza the next day. Jacques made a dive south of Ischia with the engineer and a photographer to 2,142 ft (653 m), "so as not to lose the habit" and to test some underwater videocameras. Auguste watched the *Trieste* descend without him as part of the crew for the first time. The aerial, then the two flags flying from the masthead, sank below the waves.

After a long wait, the *Trieste* emerged from the sea. Its flagstaff was bent and its deck rose much higher than usual. Auguste was concerned. The *Trieste* had reached the bottom, evident enough from the mud smeared on the portholes. But while there, a suffocating gas had invaded the cabin, after a short circuit from the videocamera had burned the insulation. In the restricted space of the cabin, a little thing like this was enough to poison the air. If seawater breached one of the cases containing the accumulators, chlorine would be released; this gas had killed several submarine crews. Jacques, panting, acted quickly, cutting the current to the topside magnets and dumping all the ballast tanks. They fell away into the abyss and the bathyscaphe rocketed toward the surface, far quicker than its critical speed of ascent, zigzagging wildly like a tennis ball released from the bottom of a pool. The oscillations had turned the craft as much as 45 degrees and bent the flagstaff, but saved the crew's life. Jacques said that the ride was "not unpleasant". They were keen to suppress any suggestion that bathyscaphe diving was dangerous. Afterwards, Auguste wrote breezily: "All's well that ends well!"

The *Tenace* towed the *Trieste* back to Castellammare on a calm sea, making a speed of six knots. It was night when they reached the harbour as fireworks lit the sky. "The little town was en fête: the bathyscaphe, in whose construction the population took so large a part, had come back to its home port." The Piccards were again made freemen of a town and given a procession.

After, they travelled back to their home village of Chexbres, on the verge of the Vaudois vineyards. The syndic, pastor and the council of the commune, with a gendarme and a horticulturist, assembled before the Piccards' villa and, aware of his love of nature, presented Auguste with a beautiful blue cedar. They planted it and put up a plaque commemorating September 30, 1953.

That late-summer, Jacques married Marie-Claude Maillard. The two had grown up together; her father was the priest in Chexbres. He died while she was still young, leaving her and her mother to take care of her disabled sister Antoinette and younger brother Olivier; her mother was forced to open her house to lodgers as a source of income. Marie-Claude was a brilliant musician and aspired to be a concert pianist; her mother supported her in the ambition to study with the great piano teachers of Paris. This required passing an examination at the Conservatory in Lausanne: in the middle of her rendition of the fifth of Chopin's Études, which employs only the black keys of the piano, she froze. She never played seriously again. Instead, she and Jacques became engaged, marrying two years later. She devoted herself to her marriage and, later, to her children.

The *Trieste* slept the winter in the yards of Castellammare. She did not lack the will to travel, but the funds. In 1954, the *Trieste* made some observational dives, sponsored by Fiat, to a maximum depth of 492 ft (150 m); on one dive, Jacques took Marie-Claude as his observer (she said she was delighted to see "how the *Trieste* looks from the inside" – and she still holds the record for the deepest descent by a woman). In 1955, the *Trieste* spent the whole year in port; once more, there was no money: each dive cost just over $8,000 in today's money, not counting the cost of an escort ship or tug; each exotic zinc battery pack would today cost $100,000.

It had taken Auguste Piccard 20 years and an unimaginable effort to realise the bathyscaphe; it existed, and could undoubtedly dive deeper, but instead it was gathering dust on land. In the meantime, the French Navy had taken the *F.N.R.S. 3* down to 13,260 ft (4,042 m), on February 15, 1954, much deeper than the *Trieste* had gone. Jacques called the smashing of his and his father's record a "fine accomplishment". Although he too was not interested in a record for its own sake, Jacques did want to show what his father's submarine was capable of: "This was a dive we could not match in the Tyrrhenian Sea off Italy. No such depth existed... When it now became evident that no record-shattering descents could take place off Italy in the course of our routine diving, part of the Italian public interest flagged." Jacques was constantly searching for funds, even offering the *Trieste* wholesale to the US National Science Foundation, arguing that "for great depths, the bathy-scaphe is the only existing means of permitting man to make direct observations," in a three-page, typewritten letter. He received no reply. Auguste took to dreaming of new underwater ships: a passenger submarine called the *Dolphin* that would cross the Atlantic at 70 mph; the meso-scaphe, a "submarine helicopter" for exploration of the medium depths. "If circumstances, financial and other-wise, do not permit me to construct this new apparatus myself," the 70-year-old Auguste wrote, "I hope that some day someone will be found to take my project in hand and bring it to a happy conclusion."

Auguste was back to dreaming, and Jacques had all but given up on ever taking the *Trieste* down deep again, when he made a trip to London in spring 1955, to lecture at the

Royal Society of Arts. There he met Robert Dietz, an ocean-ographer attached to the US Navy. Piccard mistook him for a journalist, after he read the title "attaché" on his card, and ignored him, but later that day the two got talking at Brown's, a hotel in Mayfair. Jacques had been trying to entice officers from the US Navy's Sixth Fleet, headquartered at Naples, to inspect the *Trieste* (and contribute some funding), but to no avail. Now he had an audience, and he was captive: Dietz later wrote of the "conviction in his intense dark eyes" which "transmitted his dedication to ultra-deep diving even more than his words. The *Trieste* to him was an animate being of flesh and blood." Jacques invited Dietz to visit the *Trieste* at Castellammare. Several weeks later, the American met Piccard at the Hotel Quisisana, in Sorrento. Jacques took him to the shipyard where the *Trieste* was dry-docked and showed him a pair of three-metre-long, ski-like pontoons made out of aluminium, with foot straps – a spin-off project from the bathyscaphe (Jacques had tired of being rowed out in a skiff each time to the *Trieste*). He guided Dietz down the entrance tube, through the vault-like door into the tiny cabin. "I felt myself to be inside the works of a giant Swiss watch," Dietz wrote. "As he explained the *Trieste*'s workings, I realised how personal this strange creation was to him. Nothing was labelled. Only Jacques Piccard knew what actuated what, and why."

Dietz thought Piccard a one-man organisation, a "backyard Edison" – one who was outdoing the well-financed laboratories of government agencies and militaries. "Over the past decade, the two most powerful nations on earth have spent billions of dollars for rocketry, hoping eventually to send a man to the moon for direct observation. In contrast, two citizens of landlocked Switzerland with only private assistance succeeded to take man to the deepest hole in the ocean." Dietz was sold, and started to sell the idea to his own Navy. "Clearly, the operational capabilities of the *Trieste* per se, as a man-o'-war, were nil. But the oceanographic potential was boundless and the best navy in the world must have the best oceanography." The *Trieste* would dive again, but Jacques was right: the Mediterranean was not deep enough. Only the largest, and deepest, ocean would do. "For years, lack of funds had frustrated my desire to take the *Trieste* even into the world ocean beyond the Strait of Gibraltar," Jacques wrote. "Perhaps now, the Pacific was in her not-too-distant future."

The Piccards had gone beyond the sky. Now they would go beneath the sea.

Project Nekton

On July 10, 1959, Captain John Phelps, the Commanding Officer and Director of the US Navy Electronics Laboratory in San Diego, sent an official report to Admiral Arleigh Burke, Chief of Naval Operations in Washington, and to the Chief of Naval Research and the Chief of the Bureau of Ships. Its subject was brief – "Project NEKTON Assist Project; request for" – and its language was to the point, if acronym-heavy:

1. It is requested that the Office of the Chief of Naval Operations authorize assistance and logistic support for bathyscaphe (*Trieste*) operations (Project NEKTON) in the Marianas Trench, between November 1959 and February 1960.

2. The *Trieste* purchased by ONR from the Piccards (Auguste and Jacques) is being modified for dives in the deepest known submarine trench in the world (Marianas Trench). A new and stronger sphere has been procured by ONR and the buoyancy hull is now being enlarged to provide the greater lift required. The modified craft with new sphere is being prepared for shakedown dives late July through most of August 1959 off San Diego.

3. A period of favorable weather conditions in the Marianas normally exists during November, December and January. Operations at this period this

year will be possible only through early consideration and approval of our request by CNO.

4. We have every reason to expect a successful operation if CNO authorizes the necessary assistance. The bathyscaphe in 56 successful dives has proven itself a reliable diving vehicle. The new high strength sphere gives a further factor of safety. Jacques Piccard, operator-pilot on the 56 dives will be with Project NEKTON, under contract with ONR. NEL will have two operator-pilots (one naval officer and one civilian) trained and authorized prior to completion of the July-August check-out operations near San Diego. Only proven techniques and equipment will be used.

5. It is urged that rapid handling must be accorded this request in order that all action desks may see it within the very limited time remaining for action.

A huge document, detailing the assistance and support the *Trieste* would require – "from thumbtacks to tugboats," according to Jacques Piccard – accompanied the five bullet points. Admiral Burke "reluctantly", according to one account, approved the request and with that, the last great geographic conquest of Earth was under way. Project Nekton was now official. Its mission: "The study of the ocean's physical, biological, geological and chemical characteristics".

"Project Nekton was never supposed to be a deep dark military secret," Jacques wrote. "It was a technical and scientific effort, not a military operation. The code name was mostly a matter of having a convenient short title." But also to avoid attention: "We could talk about the idea without stirring up idle curiosity... We did hope to keep the plan reasonably quiet." There were reports that the *Trieste*'s real mission was to help with nuclear submarine warfare; that the US Navy was anxious to construct a submarine capable of operating as deep as 12,000 feet (3,658 m), to avoid sonar and depth charges. "*Trieste* research on how to kill an enemy sub far down is likely to change depth charges considerably," *TIME* magazine reported. Jacques Piccard didn't think that the *Trieste* was a deep, dark military secret, but those in charge may have hoped it would indeed prove one. Piccard said he did not know "the official thoughts of the US Navy for supporting Project Nekton. As a foreign international, it was not my place to inquire. I was never cleared to know any of the Navy's inner workings."

Competition was an undeniable and fully apparent motivation, though: Piccard knew that for the last few years, the French Navy had been working on a so-called super bathyscaphe, capable of descending to 6 miles (10 km). Its design extended that of the *F.N.R.S. 3*, with a stouter sphere and longer float, and it could carry three crew members. Auguste Piccard had also in 1956 received a clipping from a Bulgarian newspaper: it described a deep-sea vehicle the Soviets were supposedly building, called a "hydrostat".

Robert Dietz had come up with the project's codename the year before. Nekton is the catch-all term for the free-swimming animals of the sea, as opposed to the plankton that are directed by tides and currents. "Fish, squid, sharks and whales are nekton – and so is the *Trieste*," Dietz told Piccard, who thought the name apt. But Project Nekton had been in the planning a lot longer, since 1956, when Jacques had taken Dietz to the bottom of the Mediterranean in the *Trieste*. Afterwards, Piccard had gone to the US for 100 days "that shook my world". He visited several oceanographic institutes and there found scientists "receptive to new ideas, new methods. There was a creative ferment in the atmosphere." They were, he wrote, "kindred spirits". Jacques, a financier turned diver and engineer, was growing into a scientist, too. In 1954, he had dived with Professor A. Pollini, a geologist at the University of Milan; in January 1957, Piccard travelled to Gothenburg, Sweden, as an observer at an international meeting of oceanographers, where he met Soviet scientists for the first time, and Japanese researchers ("For piloting bathyscaphes, the Japanese are a logical choice," he wrote, thanks to their small stature – in the diving bell *Kuroshio*, "three scientists in addition to the pilot were crammed in. And a small boy was added in the final moments to fill a small vacant space.")

Oceanography was a newer science in America, one made necessary by the Cold War. The sea was another front: "to the Navy, it was an absolute necessity, the very key to survival." The US Navy had set up the Office of Naval Research at the end of the Second World War, finding that sponsoring professors was an effective way of achieving its research – and military – aims. At a symposium in Washington at the National Academy of Sciences, Dietz and Piccard presented papers on the *Trieste* and a "bathyscaphe resolution" was adopted, urging the US government to take up the technology: "The scientific implications of this capability are far reaching", it read.

Although his father had condescended to the skyscrapers of New York, Jacques fell in love with America. It was quite the swoon: "The contrast to small mountain-girt Switzerland was overpowering at first," he wrote. "I like the American informality and overt friendliness... I sensed a disregard for tradition, and a greater willingness to accept new things."

In February 1957, the ONR offered Jacques a contract, but not in the US. Instead, they would back fifteen summer dives off Naples, to evaluate the *Trieste*. If Jacques was disappointed not to be in his new favourite country, he was delighted to have its representatives in old Europe, among them his uncle Jean. The twins, now aged 73, resumed their childhood pastime of being mistaken for one another.

"The entire summer was bright with scientific excitement and achievement," Jacques wrote. The science team stayed in a hotel still maintaining the dilapidated Bourbon grandeur of old Naples and spent their days climbing all over the *Trieste*, inspecting the bathyscaphe inside and out. They dived with Jacques at the helm, as often as three times a day. The *Trieste* was fitted out with an underwater telephone from the US Navy. Although electromagnetic transmission is difficult underwater, forbidding radio communication between surface and deep, water's acoustic properties are easily exploited (whales sing for a reason). These telephone calls were initiated by a pitch near high C; the sound was then changed to a higher frequency to make it easier to aim and to sound better. The other benefit was that the bathyscaphe's occupants could listen to the sounds of the sea in clarity: the whistling of porpoises and the "crackling brushfire sound" of snapping shrimp. Jacques logged 26 dives, spending seventy hours below the surface.

Throughout that summer another motivation had lurked beneath the surface of bright scientific success. Over coffee one evening, Dietz made it explicit: "An important reason for working with the US Navy this summer is that it could open the door for an eventual assault on the deepest spot in the world." "You mean the Challenger Deep?" Jacques asked. Dietz nodded, "Exactly. Who else but the Navy could easily support such an operation? They have the facilities, ships and a base near at hand. It's true that we can expect a few oceanographers to argue that it is a diversion from more pressing scientific dives. But I'm sure most of us will agree: if the capability exists, it *must* be done."

Piccard did agree. "Until man placed himself on the

bottom of the deepest depression on earth he would not be satisfied," he wrote. "There is a driving force in all of us which cannot stop, if there is yet one step beyond."

*

The Challenger Deep lies along the Marianas Trench, about 200 miles from Guam. According to one modern hypothesis, it is a tear in the tectonic plate that bears the ocean and earth of the whole Pacific. From 1872–1876, a British science ship, HMS *Challenger*, circumnavigated the globe, discovering 4,700 new species and taking 492 deep- sea soundings – using a total of 144 miles of rope. Two of these, taken on March 23, 1875, reported a depth of 26,850 ft (8,184 metres) below, the deepest of the expedition and the first discovery of the Marianas Trench. In 1951, another British ship, also named HMS *Challenger*, returned to the spot to take new measurements. It used more precise echo soundings and found a maximum depth of 35,760 ft (10,872 m). They called the hollow the Challenger Deep, a name that may as well have been designed to goad explorers (Jacques said it "has a fine ring to it!"). It is the deepest point on Earth: "Now that we know of the Challenger Deep, it can no longer be ignored," Jacques wrote. "The bathyscaphe was designed to take that step beyond. Once she touched down in the Challenger Deep, there would be no place on earth, from the highest mountains to the frigid poles, that still thwarted man's entry. It would be the last great geographic conquest."

The summer's scientific success led to further negotiations with the ONR. Jacques was "anxious not to sell the *Trieste*; I had a deep personal interest in her." He offered a lease, but the ONR preferred to buy it outright. Jacques and Auguste eventually agreed, hoping to use the sale price to build Auguste's mooted mesoscaphe. "A price was set based on the assumption that the *Trieste* was a somewhat used ship." On January 8, 1958, the *Trieste* sold for $200,000 – about $1.6 million today. As part of the contract, Jacques agreed to stay on as a consultant, and train two new bathyscaphe pilots. A clause in the contract provided that Jacques Piccard kept the option to pilot the bathyscaphe during "dives presenting special problems". As the *Trieste* once more became a going concern, Jacques was otherwise distracted: on March 1 that year, in Lausanne, Marie-Claude Piccard gave birth to the couple's first child, a boy they named Bertrand.

The contracts were formalised and the *Trieste* loaded aboard the USS *Antares*, a transport ship. After a long trip, the bathyscaphe arrived at her new base, the Navy Electronics Laboratory (NEL) at San Diego, on August 23, 1958. "The tiny *Trieste* seemed minuscule in the company of aircraft carriers, transports, submarines and destroyers," Piccard wrote. The press was nonplussed, one local paper describing the *Trieste* as a "weird-looking water-balloon"; when Don Walsh, a lieutenant assigned to Submarine Flotilla One, first saw the disassembled craft on board the submarine tender *Nereus*, he thought it "all looked like an explosion in a boiler factory". Still, everyone was impatient to see the *Trieste* in action; the *San Diego Union* carried pictures on its front page each time the bathyscaphe was lifted out to sea for harbour tests. Piccard would take his own time. "It was difficult to explain that one doesn't jump aboard a bathyscaphe and go diving," Jacques wrote. He constructed facilities for the mooring, docking and dry-docking of the *Trieste*, and trained up the army of specialists who saw to the submarine. This time, money was not a problem. Piccard's support in Italy had been "quite limited", according to Charles Bishop, a Navy captain. Here in San Diego, Jacques had the best-equipped Navy in the world behind him. And the military bureaucracy that had hindered Auguste in France, leading to him abandoning the other bathyscaphe, did not apply to Jacques in San Diego: "The protocol of 'going through channels' was specifically suspended for me. My requests received immediate attention, quick action followed." He no doubt found it gratifying.

In December, the *Trieste* was finally ready to dive. The first observer inside the sphere was not a scientist, but a journalist, there to take pictures and prepare an eye witness account for television. Piccard was peeved: "it was not appreciated how precious such a plunge would be at this stage... I had no choice but to comply reluctantly." The photographs came out badly, and the TV show was cancelled before it was even made. But the journalist nevertheless returned to San Diego with authorisation for a second dive. Piccard dry-docked the *Trieste* and flew to Europe, to escape the ordeal and to oversee the forging of the new bathyscaphe sphere in Germany: this would be bigger and heavier, and require a larger float. When he returned, in April, Lieutenant Don Walsh had been assigned as a submarine officer, along with other scientists and technicians: "the bathyscaphe project was finally shaping up."

The *Trieste* started making serious dives to the sea floor immediately off southern California. "Diving in these plankton-rich waters was a new and exhilarating experience," Jacques wrote. "The limpid blue of the Mediterranean is the colour of pure water with little life, the 'desert' colour of the sea. Teeming with microscopic plankton, this water acquired a greenish-yellow cast cutting down its transparency; at 600 feet it was already almost black." Amid the pressure of leading an undertaking as sprawling and ambitious as Project Nekton, the dives renewed Jacques's joy in the deeps: "When descending through the dancing light of

The Trieste *is lowered into the water*

the sunlit zone, on through the bathyal twilight zone and into abyssal darkness, I realise that we need not go to Mars or even to the Moon to find a strange new world. Alice, stepping through the looking glass, found no more of a wonderland than this."

The dives proved useful scientifically, too: "On every dive there was a biological wealth. The 700-fathoms bottom of the San Diego Trough was ploughed over and churned by animals, like a battlefield as seen in miniature." The observers found ophiuroids, also known as brittle-stars, "writhing and twisting like the snakes on Medusa's head", according to Jacques; the bottom-dwellers had previously been supposed to be quiet and lethargic. Piccard and his observers made friends with black cod: "One even tried to enter the sphere," Jacques wrote. "With his mouth pressed against the port, as though trying to fathom the nature of this transparent solid, he looked like a fish in a goldfish bowl. But it was I who was in the bowl. I was a captured specimen of *Homo sapiens* on display alive in their world."

The most scientifically productive dive was also the most dangerous, undertaken with a researcher from the NEL, who measured the velocity of sound underwater, according to certain variables. This called for a hovering dive – difficult because of the *Trieste*'s depth instability. "We had just finished hovering at 85 fathoms [510 ft, 155m] and were slowing, settling deeper, when we heard a sharp implosion followed by bubbling sounds. Then a little later, a second implosion startled us. An implosion is a simple collapse of some air-filled device or component. Under the high sea pressure, this kind of collapse can be as violent as an explosion. Such implosions are disquieting, needless to say. The force could be sufficient to rupture the skin of the float with dire consequences." Jacques continued the dive. Back in port, he found the camera fitted beneath the float had failed, causing the implosions: it was one of the few components Jacques had not designed himself. Less seriously, Dietz and Piccard put half a dozen eggs, wrapped in cotton, in a porous plastic box, strapped topside one dive. Egg shells are semiporous, allowing water to pass in and out of the egg, and thus equalise pressure inside and outside the shell; the bathyscaphists were eager to see whether the eggs would survive, as a "striking demonstration of the principle of the *Trieste*'s fragile float, which also permits water to enter". Every egg returned to the surface intact. Less resilient was the towboat of the *Trieste*: one afternoon, returning to harbour, the old, leaky vessel broke down. The bathyscaphe, 600 feet behind, caught up, rode over it and smashed it to splinters, causing it to sink. "The accident created quite a little excitement."

The dives were successful scientifically, but Project Nekton was merely treading water before the outrageous challenge that lay ahead: Challenger Deep. "That late summer of 1959, one could sense the increasing tension in the air. Although the fact never appeared in directive or memorandum, we all knew what we were shooting for...

"Logistics, procurement, tests and training all pointed to one objective. It was destination Guam, the Challenger Deep, the Big Dive." In August, at the request of Jacques, Auguste Piccard arrived at San Diego to help the team with its preparations and work through the final problems: reunited with his son and the submarine he had started work on decades ago.

Test dives were made with the new sphere on September 11 and September 15. The window of opportunity for diving in Guam, as outlined in the memo that made Project Nekton official, was narrow. On October 5, the *Trieste* was separated into two and loaded onto the USS *Santa Mariana* for transport to the Pacific. A short article appeared in the back pages of the *New York Times*, saying that the "reconditioned *Trieste* would search for ocean depths down to 20,000 feet [6,000 m]." For once, the press had made an understatement.

Lieutenant Don Walsh, who had volunteered for the programme as a pilot, established a temporary base at Guam, in the northern half of the 225-square-mile island, among the sprawling US Navy and Air Force commands there. Walsh commanded five navy men. Among the civilian party were Giuseppe Buono, Piccard's original chief mechanic from Castellammare, who had followed Jacques and the *Trieste* ever since, Dr Andreas Rechnitzer, the scientist in charge, Charles Hill, the battery man, photographer John Pflaum and the researchers Denvil Harris, Kenneth Jair and Ernest Virgil. Robert Dietz went as a consultant; two other scientists would join them later. The diving party assembled and Auguste returned to Europe.

*

Before the deepest dive, the *Trieste* made several merely extraordinarily deep dives in the Pacific from her Guam base. On the third dive, on November 15, Piccard piloted and Rechnitzer observed, tape-recording his description. The two, shivering with wet clothes in the cold cabin, heard "strange little cracklings, like frying bacon", the source of which they could not identify – certainly not the snapping of the shrimp they had observed in the Mediterranean. At 17,640 ft (5,377 m), Rechnitzer was still identifying living organisms: "One of the particles has remained out front of the window for some time," he spoke into the recorder. "It appears like a hawk fluttering when it's just about to take its prey. It looks like a beat-up ctenophore. The hawklike object was a pteropod!" Rechnitzer, an expert ichthyologist, was delighted with this sea slug, and the other animals he saw through the porthole: the pelageic annelid, mysid shrimps, isopods, more pteropods, medusae, unidentified crustaceans ("his palpitating friends"), an animal that looked "like an Egyptian's cap": the extreme depths were, contrary to prevailing scientific thinking, teeming with life.

The near-freezing water became cloudier, but Rechnitzer could soon see the salt-and-pepper ocean floor out of the porthole. "We are coming to the bottom, Jacques, WE ARE ON THE BOTTOM." The *Trieste* was 3.4 miles (5.5 km) down. Rechnitzer was excited because they had beaten the record the *F.N.R.S. 3* had set off Dakar in 1954, by a mile. Jacques thought this "of no great moment"; he still had the same distance deeper to go, another three and a half miles, to the very bottom of Challenger Deep. More important was that "the rebuilt *Trieste* had passed her high-pressure test."

Not quite.

Piccard began the ascent and the *Trieste* came up very rapidly. "Coming up, coming up, coming up, coming up," Rechnitzer said out loud. "50 metres and coming up, 40

metres, 35, 30, 25, 20, 15, TWO VIOLENT EXPLOSIONS!"
The tape recording ended, immediately. The explosions
sound like rifle volleys. Fortunately, the *Trieste* was already
on the surface. Piccard blew the water from the antechamber, threw open the porthole door and crawled out of
the bathyscaphe. Neither he nor Rechnitzer could see any
obvious fault, so they relaxed and warmed their bodies in
the tropical sun.

Back in Guam, Piccard reentered the cabin. The source
of the explosions was immediately clear. The central ring
of the sphere, which bound the two forged half-spheres,
had shifted slightly; the epoxy resin glue holding it had
failed. The sphere was thus very slightly ajar and water
was trickling in. The *Trieste* needed to be repaired before
it dived again. "We could not rebond the sphere short of
sending it back to Germany," Piccard wrote. "Was Project
Nekton finished?" According to Walsh, the Project Nekton
team "decided not to bother our masters at NEL with this
particular situation" – telling them would have meant the
end of the attempt on Challenger Deep. Instead, one of
the engineers at the Naval Repair Facility, John Michel,
improvised. He was not overly impressed with the Piccards'
sphere in any case and so planned to replace the windows
in the door and front portholes with aluminium ones he
had machined because, in his words, "although a world-
renowned physicist, Auguste Piccard was not an engineer."
What Auguste had thought the crowning feature of his
bathyscaphe – its occluded Plexiglas portholes – was a
design fault in the rough and ready environment of Guam,
as they were almost impossible to make on site. Michel did
not stand on ceremony. "Jacques, although a sharp individual and versed in several disciplines, is also not an engineer," he wrote. "He would have had a fit or a heart attack
if he could have seen what my alternative plan was." Michel

sent Jacques away, then, using a forklift that held a piece of timber as a battering ram, "bumped" the sphere sections together, three or four times, until they were out of alignment by less than a millimetre. He also built a series of metal bands that would hold together the sphere mechanically, fixing gasket compounds and rubber strips from a car along the joints' surfaces with the help of Giuseppe Buono. These improvised modifications complete, "We were confident that we had a good and safe fix," Walsh said.

The *Trieste* made some more dives, to test the new method of holding the sphere together, including to 5,700 ft deep off Guam on December 18. On January 6 the next year, with a wild sea running, the flotilla left Guam for the Nero Deep – a hollow in the Marianas trench discovered by the USS *Nero* in 1899 while it was looking for a cable route between America and the Far East. At the time they had thought the 31,614-foot-deep hole the deepest on the planet. For Piccard and Walsh, it would serve as a useful dress rehearsal.

The descent was normal – about three feet per second. Just over two hours and 19,500 ft (nearly 6,000 m) down into the dive, there were two sharp implosions, one quickly after the other. Jacques straight away hit the ballast switch, releasing about 900 kilograms over 90 seconds. The *Trieste* slowed, then hovered. Piccard said to Walsh: "No, nothing is wrong, let's continue down." Into the tape recorder, Walsh said: "no reason for apparent damage has been perceived."

At 3,600 feet further down, another implosion, but Piccard steered the *Trieste* deeper. At 23,000 feet (7,010 m) the bathyscaphe stopped: there was no more ballast, and the *Trieste* started to rise. Jacques tried to valve off gasoline, but the control was not working and so the craft could not shed some of its lighter-than-water buoyancy to become heavier. On the way back up, "those implosions were still on my mind", Jacques wrote. The bathyscaphe's ascent was more sluggish than usual; Jacques wrote in his log: "Maybe we are losing gasoline."

Back on the surface, Jacques saw the gasoline valve was badly damaged, and that the petrol had bled from its container. The implosions were because of faulty stanchions – a worker had failed to drill holes into these pipes so that they would flood with water on descent. The damage was only superficial, though, and the *Trieste* had shown it could go down to 24,000 ft. Now it was time for the real thing: Challenger Deep.

There were two objectives for the dive: reach the very bottom and look for signs of marine life. Governments around the world had been looking to discard their radioactive waste in the great depths, because it was assumed there was no life down there. A living fish would mean that there was oxygen at the bottom of the ocean. Oxygen is produced only in the upper layers of the sea, by phytoplankton, so this would mean that currents were circulating oxygen from the surface to the deepest depth. The *Trieste* was to establish whether this was the case; if not, the abyss could provide a limitless dumping ground for nuclear waste.

Three dives to the bottom there had been planned. But because of the delay in refitting the *Trieste*, only one dive would be possible; the waves around Guam, now big and rolling, would make the reballasting and other preparations necessary for a second dive impossible. The *Trieste* had just one shot at the ultimate deep, the Big Dive. And it would not include Jacques.

One morning, a few days before the scheduled departure for the Challenger Deep, Piccard was working topside on the *Trieste*, when he was pulled aside and told that Don Walsh and Andy Rechnitzer would make the ultimate dive. The decision had been made months earlier, when Walsh had stood in front of Admiral Arleigh Burke as Navy commander of the *Trieste* and asked him to approve Project Nekton. Burke had asked who would make the dive; Walsh replied that it would be Rechnitzer, the chief scientist, and himself, as the ranking US naval officer; Lieutenant Larry Shumaker would take command of topside activities. Burke agreed (and added: "I want you to tell Shumaker that if the *Trieste* does not come back, then you, Walsh, are the lucky one because I will have Shumaker's balls."). This was news to Jacques, who protested furiously, arguing what he called "his moral right". It suddenly meant little to him whether the bathyscaphe succeeded, if it were without a Piccard on board. He remembered his uncle Jean, forced out of so many planned assaults on the stratosphere. But Jacques, with his care for each detail, was not so easily jettisoned. He invoked the clause in his consulting contract: "My contract states that I reserve the right to make any dive that 'presents special problems'. Wouldn't you say that a dive to the bottom of the Challenger Deep presents a special problem?" Jacques of course had a copy of his contract in his cabin, with the stipulation outlined in typewritten black. Messages were sent back and forth between Guam and ONR in San Diego; the matter then went to Washington. The command there said that those who had signed the contract were no longer active with the US Navy. Jacques countered that those who had signed the US constitution were no longer active at all, but the document nevertheless carried some weight. After a further short delay, new orders came, along with an apology: Piccard and Walsh would dive. "I was deeply gratified by this forthright and honourable decision," Jacques later wrote. He would have preferred to dive with a scientist like Rechnitzer "in order to gather the maximum amount of scientific information". Just not if it cost him his own place in the submarine.

Still, Walsh was "an excellent choice" in Jacques's view. Walsh, 28 years old at the time, immediately offered to step aside for Rechnitzer – "I was just a new boy," Walsh remembers now. "I had only been on the project a year at that point." He pointed out that Rechnitzer was a commander in the Naval Reserve; if Rechnitzer were put on active duty, a Navy man would still reach the bottom. "That would have been the fair thing to do," Walsh says. "It wasn't magnanimous of me to offer. It was just." The Navy, though, disagreed: Walsh would go down.

Walsh had been born in Berkeley, California, and grew up watching ships and boats sail out of the bay there. His mother raised him alone during the Depression, working as a cashier for a large mail order company. Walsh wanted to fly planes in the Navy, but less than perfect eyesight meant he failed the physical examination. So he decided to fly underwater instead, and joined the submarine division. His commander, Commodore Styles, had promised Rechnitzer to assist in finding qualified submarine officers to join Project Nekton; Walsh send out the message to all the submarines on the West Coast, asking for volunteers, and included himself. "Three months into it I was ten times deeper than I'd ever been." Now he had deeper still to go.

There was another, less critical issue. During the first dives in San Diego, the American flag had flown from the *Trieste*. Jacques asked whether the Swiss standard could also be flown. The white cross had flown in the Mediterranean, after all – so where was it? He was informed by a junior officer that the Swiss flag had been lost. Happily, Jacques had a spare; he "agreed to correct this unfortunate loss" and the Swiss flag flew alongside the star-spangled banner. A few days later, though, it mysteriously disappeared once more. "I had another." The last dives in San Diego were made entirely flagless. "I suppose my seemingly inexhaustible supply of Swiss flags may have had something to do with it." At Guam, both Swiss and American flags were in good supply to start, but they were soon both gone. "A civilian had ordered them removed. It would seem that the Navy's 'five-foot-shelf' of regulations does not yet cover flag protocol for a bathyscaphe." For the deep dive, there were no flags flown on the *Trieste*. One British journalist tried to turn this into a minor diplomatic incident; Jacques told him that the Swiss, having no navy, "were not accustomed to getting their flag wet". In fact, there were several American flags inside the bathyscaphe. And hidden at the bottom of the pile underneath them, one Swiss flag, which would thus go deeper than any American.

On January 20, a US Navy tug, delightfully named the *Wandank,* and the destroyer escort *Lewis* left Apra harbour in Guam for the Challenger Deep, 300 miles (485 km) away. The already limited window of opportunity for the dive shortened, as the weather worsened. The *Wandank* towed the *Trieste* at a "stately" five knots; the window of opportunity for the dive was narrowing as the weather worsened. The towline broke on the way, costing a few more hours, and another day was lost while the *Wandank* made only one knot against huge head seas. "These delays stirred up anxieties," Piccard wrote.

On the evening of January 22, the *Wandank* and *Trieste* arrived on the dive site. That night, Auguste Piccard, now 75, telephoned his son. "Jacques, I have faith. You will manage it, the great dive."

"No," Jacques replied. "It's not me who will do it. It's you, through me."

The Deepest Dive

In the grey predawn of dive day, Saturday January 23, 1960, Jacques Piccard stepped out onto the deck of the USS *Wandank*. A mile away in the distance, he could just make out the lights of the destroyer escort, the USS *Lewis DE 635*, as the big waves carried her above the horizon and back down beneath it. Piccard felt the thumping shockwave of an explosion and saw a tower of white water shoot into the sky – the 800th attempt by the *Lewis* to find the Challenger Deep using depth charges. Throughout the foul-weathered night, Rechnitzer and a team of scientists had been trying to find the deepest spot, by dropping half-kilogram sticks of TNT off the side of the ship. They started their watches when the block exploded, then stopped them when the return echo was heard on the *Lewis*'s fathometer hydrophone. As the seas rolled harder, and the wind gathered, Jacques saw flares drop from the *Lewis*, then felt the *Wandank* churn towards them. "Directly below was the basement of the world. As the distance between the two ships closed, I could make out the dye markers." The *Lewis* had found a "target zone" a mile wide and seven long, with an echo delay of 14 seconds – a depth of around 35,700 ft (10,880 m), about seven miles down. "The big moment was coming up fast."

The dive was scheduled for 0800 that morning – still a few hours to go – but Jacques was quite awake. The *Wandank* rolled and pitched; in his bunk, he had listened "to the sound of the wind and pound of the surf". To help himself sleep, he did not count the customary sheep, but the bags of shot hauled aboard the *Trieste* and poured into the ballast tub – "soon to rain down into the darkness, bound for Challenger Deep". Anxiety, not the sea, kept him up. "I could tell myself that this was just another dive. It wasn't, of course, and I knew it." First, this would be his last journey with the *Trieste*, after more than 60 dives and 15 years. Second, it was to the deepest hole in the deepest ocean. And third, it would be the only shot at completing a Piccard dream more than half-a-century old.

But the seas were bad. The first attempt to launch the transport boat failed. Twenty-five-foot waves forced the crew to abandon the attempt. They used a rubber raft instead. "It was uncomfortable," Walsh says. "We got good and wet." Jacques would soon have to make a decision: dive, or stay on the surface and wait another day? "The sight that met my eyes when we boarded the wallowing bathyscaphe was discouraging, to say the least. Broaching seas smothered her. The deck was a mess. Everything was awash." The tow from Guam had taken its toll. The surface telephone had been carried away; the tachometer, which measured the rate of descent, was damaged and not working. The vertical current meter was dangling from just a few wires: "I was worried." Buono asked Piccard: "Do we dive?" and Piccard asked himself the same question. "Was it sheer madness to dive seven miles into the sea under such conditions?" Walsh was also disconcerted. Piccard went below to investigate. He turned on the electromagnets, which worked. The time was 0800. The *Trieste* had to carry out the 14-mile round trip to the ocean floor and back before darkness; to dive that day, Piccard couldn't wait much longer. 0900 was the cut-off point. "It is all very well for a man seeking adventure to take chances. I wasn't looking for an adventure. I wanted a successful and uneventful operation. I wanted to leave nothing to chance. Essentially things were in order. I made the decision. We would dive."

Walsh agreed. Buono climbed around the *Trieste* to disconnect the tow line. Piccard removed the pins that held the ballast mechanically. Below, Walsh checked a new electric thermometer.

Topside on the *Wandank*, the ship's radioman handed Rechnitzer, who was looking for a cup of coffee, a message. Rechnitzer read it, with no visible reaction, then handed it to John Michel.

FROM C.O. AND DIRECTOR U.S. NAVY ELECTRONICS LABORATORY to DIRECTOR US NAVY PROJECT NEKTON.

CANCEL DIVING. COME HOME.

The administration back in San Diego had grown concerned about the repeated pressure failures – the implosions – on the *Trieste*. If one were to occur on the bottom of the ocean and kill the divers, it could be a public relations disaster: Project Nekton was therefore suspended. Michel was furious; Rechnitzer nonplussed. "Let's find some more coffee," he told Michel and the two walked to the mess. Recaffeinated, Rechnitzer said he should go back to the radio room to check in. There he found the radioman. "Radioman, send a message."

FROM DIRECTOR PROJECT NEKTON to C.O AND DIRECTOR U.S NAVY ELECTRONICS LABORATORY.

"TRIESTE" NOW PASSING 20,000 FEET.

On board the *Trieste* – a quarter of a mile away from the *Wandank* and still very much on the water's surface – Piccard was unaware of Rechnitzer's intervention. The bathyscaphe was nearly ready. Buono clasped hands with Piccard then Walsh and wished them "Buona fortuna". "Grazie," Piccard replied. "Arrivederci." Then he swung shut the heavy steel door, and "turned up the bolt that would seal us securely in our vault". Inside the sphere, the buffeting of the sea was more exaggerated: Piccard wanted to dive as quickly as possible. It was 0815.

The two quickly went through a check list. Several important instruments were missing; Piccard would have to calculate the rate of descent and ascent using only the *Trieste*'s watch – the same Swiss chronometer Auguste Piccard had taken into the stratosphere – and the depth gauge. Jacques thought of his father now. "I see him close to me, just as if he was flesh and blood in this metal sphere. I see him smiling softly, like he used to smile at me when I was a child. He is beaming, but he scarcely lets it show. I start the descent. I am his hand, I am his eyes…

"Through the aft porthole I could see water flooding the antechamber. I opened the oxygen valves and checked the air purification system. We could expect to dive momentarily. Had our tachometer been operative, the very instant of descent would have been apparent. As it was, we simply had to wait to see the pressure gauge going.

"I wanted to log that instant. My eyes were on my watch. Suddenly, at 0823, the rocking ceased, the sphere became calm. I glanced at the depth gauge. The needle was quivering.

"We were on our way down." Walsh and Piccard looked at one another and both sighed in relief. After the fraught departure, each was calm and sure of the task in front of them. Neither was afraid. According to Walsh, "If you're scared, you don't belong there, You're on your game, you've done everything you can to reduce the unknowns, you've practised emergency procedures over and over. That's what we did." The two were focused and didn't say much. "There wasn't a lot of laughing and joking. Well, there never was much with Jacques anyway, but even less so on this thing."

The *Trieste* went down slowly, breaking stubbornly through the thermal barriers in the water. At 0900, she had descended only 800 feet (24,000 m) – an average descent of four inches per second. At that rate, it would take more than 30 hours to complete the descent. But the pilots were cautious: they did not know what lay beneath them. Piccard was "chilled" at the thought of slamming into the wall of the trench. "We were through the sea's twilight zone," Piccard wrote. "Beyond the port there was darkness, but not yet total blackness. Descending into the sea, the night comes slowly like a northern dusk."

At 1,000 feet, Piccard switched off the cabin light to look into the deeps. Only a faint sunlight reached the *Trieste*. Their descent picked up, to three feet per second – the *Trieste*'s "terminal velocity". In the meantime, Walsh made contact with the *Lewis* using the acoustic telephone. "The tenuous connection with the surface world is a pleasant diversion," Jacques said. "Why, I don't know. We were now far beyond the reach of assistance." The water temperature dropped and the sphere grew colder. Walsh and Piccard changed out of their wet clothes and ate some chocolate, the only food aboard. On the last dive, Piccard had brought Swiss Nestlé. This time, Walsh provided fifteen American Hershey chocolate bars.

At just before 0930, and 4,200 feet down, Piccard and Walsh noticed drops of water entering the sphere – through a cable lead-through, down the wall and into the bilge. The lead-through had always been perfectly water-tight before. Piccard spoke to Buono, up on the *Wandank*, on the telephone, to check that his topside preparations had gone off well. They had, but the weather on the surface was deteriorating, the Italian engineer said. "I signed off feeling completely detached from nature's vicissitudes in the world of the sun."

The *Trieste* went deeper, at 200 feet per minute. The leak stopped, but another started. "We continued to plunge. Black water rushed upward past us." The bathyscaphe kept on, down through all the records it had established in the preceding weeks, to 20,000 feet (6,096 m) – nearly four miles straight down. This was the maximum depth of the normal Pacific sea floor; the *Trieste* was about to drop into the Marianas Trench, "leaving the abyssal zone of the ocean and entering the hadal regions". The Hadal zone, beneath the Abyssal, takes its name from the ancient Greek god who ruled the underworld, abode of the dead, and constitutes only one per cent of the ocean bottom. Hades was also known as "the unseen", a title that suited these pitch-black waters. "This was a vast emptiness beyond all comprehension."

The bathyscaphe continued – 23,000 feet – the deepest the *Trieste* had ever gone. "For the first time, man was descending so deep." Weak, musical tones reverberated around the cabin. The *Trieste* was out of voice range, but still in acoustic contact with the ships on the surface. An even number of tones sent in reply mean all was well, an odd number the opposite. A Mayday signal was five tones. Walsh transmitted two tones: OK. At 1144, the *Trieste* was at 29,150 feet (8,885 m) – as deep under the sea as Mt Everest is high. And more to go. "There was, perhaps, a mile of water still beneath us..."

Midday, at 31,000 feet, Piccard turned on the echo sounder to try and find bottom in its 600-foot range. No echo bounced back. "Trying moments were ahead. We were venturing beyond the tested capabilities of the *Trieste*. On paper she could descend safely to ten miles and the sphere alone much more. I had confidence in those calculations. She was a complex of nuts and bolts, metal, plastic and wire. But a dead thing? No. To me she was a living creature with a will to resist the seizing pressure. Above me, in the float, icy water was streaming in as the gasoline contracted, making the craft ever heavier and heavier. It was as if this icy water were coursing through my own veins."

The tones of the acoustic telephone were quiet now. Only the hissing oxgyen and hum of electronic equipment broke the tomb's silence. Piccard peered out of the window looking for the bottom. "But there is only water and water." Perhaps the echo sounder was not working. Piccard did not know what the bottom would be like. Dietz had speculated that it would be similar in consistency to soup; Russian scientists on the *Vityaz* had tried to lower cameras into the trench to take photos, but had only come up with blank negatives; the second HMS *Challenger*, in 1951, however, sampled the oozy bottom, made up of old marine fossils. Scientists speculated that the same water could have lain there for more than a million years. "Could we sink and disappear into this material before being aware that we had contacted the bottom?" It was an "uneasy thought".

Piccard did not have much time to ponder. Six minutes later, they felt an implosion. It was strong but muffled – more a bang than a crack, different to the high-pitched pops that had scored earlier implosions. "The sphere shook as though in a small earthquake." Walsh looked at Piccard, anxious but calm. "Have we touched bottom?" "I do not believe so," Piccard said, and both waited for something to happen. Piccard tried the outside lights, but they did not turn on. Piccard and Walsh didn't say a word, but by a look agreed to continue down. "We knew that if we came back up that would be the end of the project," Walsh says. "Forever. So we went down."

The *Trieste* reached the bottom of the Challenger Deep, 36,000 feet (10,973 m) – or where the bottom was supposed to be. Perhaps, they thought, they had missed the bottom floor. Walsh kept his eyes on the echo sounder; Piccard divided his attention between the porthole and the fathometer. An echo came. "There it is Jacques! It looks like we have found it!" The bottom of the earth was only 250 ft (76 m) beneath them.

Walsh reeled off the soundings as the *Trieste* approached: "36 fathoms [216 ft], echo coming in weakly – 32 – 28 – 25 – 24 – now we are getting a nice trace. 22 fathoms – still going down – yes, this is it! 20 – 18 – 15 – ten – makes a nice trace now. Going right down. Six fathoms – we're slowing up, very slowly, we may come to a stop. You say you saw a small animal, possibly a red shrimp about one inch long? Wonderful, wonderful! Three fathoms – you can see the bottom through the port? Good – we've made it!"

After seven miles diving down through the deeps, the *Trieste* came to a rest, with no further to go. "The bottom appeared light and clear, a waste of snuff-coloured ooze. We were landing on a nice, flat bottom of firm diatomaceous ooze. Indifferent to the 180,000 tonnes of pressure clamped onto her metal sphere, the *Trieste* balanced herself delicately on the few pounds of guide rope that lay on the bottom, making token claim, in the name of science and humanity, to the ultimate depths in all our oceans – the Challenger Deep." The time was 1306 and the depth gauge showed 6,300 fathoms – 37,800 feet, just more than seven miles.

Walsh and Piccard shook hands, and took some quiet pride in contemplating their achievement. Jacques did not say anything, but Walsh could see that "he felt a great sense of personal triumph. This was a dream of theirs, he and his father, and now he was representing the clan Piccard in real-ising it. He was realising a family dream." Jacques looked out the porthole: "The sea floor fascinates me. I think that I can make out the figure of father dancing on it. I realise something. We are at the bottom of the deepest trench on the planet. Thanks to the genius of Auguste Piccard."

Walsh telephoned the surface: "On the bottom of Challenger Deep. Six Three Zero Zero fathoms. I say again, Six Three Zero Zero fathoms."

The depth was wrong – the gauge had been calibrated in Switzerland for fresh water. The actual depth was about 2,000 feet less, at 35,800 feet (10,911 m). But it was certainly the very bottom – 1.7 miles deeper than Everest is high. "Mission accomplished," Jacques later said. "An unbeat-able record, absolute. No one will ever go deeper, without digging into the earth." Piccard and Walsh sat there, silent.

Then Piccard saw something extraordinary. Beneath the bathyscaphe was a flatfish that looked like a sole – about 30 cm long and 15 cm across. "Even as I saw him, his two round eyes on top of his head spied us. Eyes? Why should he have eyes? Merely to see phosphorescence? The flood-light that bathed him was the first real light ever to enter this hadal realm. Here, in an instant, was the answer to the question that biologists had asked for decades. Could life exist in the greatest depths of the ocean? It could! And not only that, here apparently, was a true, bony teleost fish, not a primitive ray or elasmobranch. Yes, a highly evolved vertebrate, in time's arrow very close to man himself.

"Slowly, extremely slowly, this flatfish swam away. Moving along the bottom, partly in the ooze and partly in the water he disappeared into his night. Slowly too – perhaps everything is slow at the bottom of the sea – Walsh and I shook hands." The flatfish was indeed an extraordi-nary find. The enormous pressure from the water column above – 1,000 times greater than at sea level – would pose a challenge to even the smallest and most resilient living creature, let alone one with a backbone to be crushed. And to spot such a large animal, when the seven miles of water before had offered none, within the limited field of view of the porthole, directly under the spotlight... On top of that, Walsh says: "We couldn't see the bottom. We had stirred up the bottom sediment to the point where we really couldn't see. It was like looking at a bowl of milk." Before the dive, Andy Rechnitzer had told Piccard: "My friend, you have found a nice little hole. All that I ask is that you see a fish at the bottom. Apart from that, nothing else matters."

The improbable sighting was hugely significant. "One immediate conclusion: ocean trenches are not safe places for dumping radioactive wastes, since their water does not stay put," *TIME* concluded. Indeed, with the discovery of the fish, the US abandoned its plans to dump nuclear waste in the trenches – an achievement greater than the absolute record, in Jacques's estimation. He later told his son Bertrand, "OK, we have the record, just because no one went down there before. But the really important thing from that dive was the discovery of life at the deepest depths." Did he really see the fish, against all odds? Piccard was the only one to see it; Walsh did not, only hearing Piccard's description, which was later written up as part of the report. Piccard also said that he took pictures of the fish, and even filmed it on his 16 mm Bolex camera (both would have taken some time for what seems a fleeting moment), but that the Navy subsequently lost his materials. Jeffrey Drazen, a marine biologist at the University of Hawaii at Manoa, has suggested that no fish can exist deeper than 8,000 metres down. Other scientists have charitably suggested that Piccard saw a sea cucumber. At a reunion in Switzerland decades later, Walsh and Piccard met once more. A journalist asked them whether they had in fact seen the fish. The two did not answer, but exchanged a smile.

For 20 minutes, the pair made observations. "The ivory ooze was almost flat," Jacques wrote. "There were none of the small mounds and burrows such as those so common in the Mediterranean. Nor was there the usual churning of the sea floor by the bottom living animals. No animal tracks could be seen anywhere." The bottom of the earth was alien, but more pristine than any planet. Jacques exposed some film to check the levels of cosmic radiation: this was, after all, a Piccard expedition, and cosmic rays must be measured. He then switched on the aft searchlight. Walsh looked out and shouted: "I see now what caused the shock at 30,000 feet!" The plastic window that separated the antechamber from the sea was riven with horizontal open cracks. The window itself was still in place: no danger for now. "But I realised at once that it could mean some real trouble later on."

The antechamber was the only way to escape the sphere. If the plastic window gave way, the two "would be in a desperate predicament". Walsh and Piccard would not be able to leave the *Trieste* on the surface, unless they completely flooded the sphere and used aqualung equipment. The original plan was to stay thirty minutes on the sea floor: this would give an arrival of 1700 and thus only ninety minutes before nightfall to carry out whatever emergency measures might prove necessary. Instead, at 1326, Piccard cut the current on the electromagnets for 36 seconds, releasing 360 kilograms of ballast. The 136-tonne *Trieste* sluggishly lifted off the bottom. "The long seven-mile return trip to the world of man began."

As the *Trieste* climbed, the gasoline in the float expanded and the bathyscaphe ascended faster, peaking at five feet per second. On the way up, Walsh tried to make contact with the surface ships and warn them about the possible emergency because of the cracked window, but he had no success. At 13,000 feet (3,962 m), Walsh heard the pings of the *Lewis*'s sonar, and the *Wandank* desperately trying to hail the *Trieste*. But he could not establish a two-way contact.

The sphere continued up. "We were borne upward from night into grey predawn. Faster and faster we rushed towards the light of day."

*

Before the dive, it had been arranged that the *Wandank*, by means of radio and telephone, would tell Marie-Claude Piccard, in San Diego, when the *Trieste* was on its way back to the surface. She had been in constant contact with Jacques before the dive. Now she had not heard anything for more than eight hours. She knew the dive schedule to the minute and still no call. It was a "terrifying moment for her", according to her son Bertrand. "Everything was organized and planned and she had no news."

*

John Pflaum, a photographer on board the *Lewis*, was the first to spot the fluorescent strips of the *Trieste*'s tower, the moment it came up. "There she is! Right on her ETA!" The *Lewis* powered to the scene. Normally, the bathyscaphe crew appeared topside directly after surfacing. But fifteen minutes later, no one on board could see Walsh or Piccard. Nor had any contact been made since before they had begun the ascent. Had the sphere flooded? Would they find two dead men when they themselves opened the hatch?

Piccard very slowly pushed air into the antechamber, so that as little pressure as possible would push against the cracked window and cause it to give. "Walsh, slowly, very slowly, fed three bottles of compressed air into the antechamber. I watched, tensely, through the port controlling the bleeding of the air." The air forced out the abyssal water from the antechamber. The pair hauled open the door, and climbed up the ladder and finally topside, into the sun and heat. It had been eight hours and 33 minutes since they had closed the hatch. From an underworld of shades, Piccard and Walsh had come back alive if late, their clothes wet, their teeth chattering, their arms aloft.

*

"We were happy to be the first, but we didn't expect to be the last," Walsh told CNET, a technology website, in 2005.

Half a century after Piccard and Walsh first visited the world's deepest point, the Marianas Trench was once more in the news. Steve Fossett, a commodities trader and balloonist who would compete with Jacques's son Bertrand to be the first to travel around the world in a balloon, planned a solo journey to the bottom, but died in a plane crash in September 2007 before he could see it through. Richard Branson, the billionaire entrepreneur, bought Fossett's submarine, the *Deep Flight Challenger*, and prepared for his own assault. Branson's space company is called Virgin Galactic; his submersible sails under the Virgin Oceanic banner. Two other companies – DOER Marine, backed by Google executive chairman Eric Schmidt, and Triton Submarines – set their sights on the deepest dive. But they were all beaten to it.

On March 26, 2012, more than half a century after the *Trieste*'s historic dive, James Cameron made a solo descent to the Challenger Deep. The explorer-filmmaker – creator of *Titanic* and *Avatar*, among other movies – dived to

35,787 feet. While this is 13 feet short of Piccard's officially reported depth, that is less than the margin for error
of the two subs' depth gauges. Cameron spent more than
three hours exploring two miles across the ocean floor, "a
very soft, almost gelatinous flat plain" in his description,
until a thruster failure prevented him from going on, and
his submersible, the *Deepsea Challenger,* returned to the
surface. During those hours, he did not see any fish, only
shrimp-like bottom feeders. "There is a vast frontier down
there that's going to take us a while to understand," he told
the press. "The impression to me was it's very lunar, very
isolated. I felt as if, in the space of one day, I'd gone to
another planet and come back."

It may not be isolated for much longer: as well as records,
resources also lie on the ocean floor. Silver, gold, copper,
cobalt, zinc and rare earth metals – precious due to their
use in modern electronic devices – have all been discovered in deep-sea deposits. De Beers mines diamonds from
the sea bed; Japan, India and China have launched mining
operations along the tectonic plates; China is also planning a mobile, nuclear-powered deep-sea mining station,
manned by a crew of 33. This underwater gold rush could
tarnish the deep-sea environment before it has been properly studied, or understood.

But at least we too may get a glimpse of the deep.
Cameron captured his whole journey on camera, something
Piccard and Walsh could not have done. The footage will
eventually show on cinema screens, and a mass audience
will finally be able to see what just a handful have looked
upon. Cameron dived alone, but was watched over by a
large topside crew. Among them was Don Walsh, whom
Jacques's children had over the intervening years come to
call "Uncle Don". Before Cameron's descent, he emailed
Bertrand: "I wish your father could be here in person to

witness the completion of our unfathomable journey."

So far, twelve men have been to the moon. Only three have been to Challenger Deep. The Apollo astronauts "went with rockets and fire up their asses and walked around in funny suits planting flags," Walsh told the *Daily Telegraph*. "With diving, you just disappear quietly into the depths and hope you come back up."

Middle Waters

Only a few days after they returned to the surface, Piccard and Walsh were in the White House. From Guam, a Navy DC4e had flown them to Hawaii, then to San Diego, and finally Washington, where the two met President Eisenhower, on February 3, 1960. "It was a nice day, to say the least," Walsh remembers. The two bathyscaphe pilots received a plunder of medals and honours: the distinguished public service award, the highest distinction possible for a civilian, from the hands of the President; the Theodore Roosevelt Distinguished Service Award, Citizen of Honour of San Diego, life membership of the National Geographic Society, among other honours. Eisenhower afterwards wrote Piccard to say that meeting him was a "distinct pleasure" and that Jacques "had the gratitude of all of the people of the United States for helping to further open the doors of this important scientific field. All good wishes for your continued success." A year later, the *Los Angeles Times* published a list of the young men who had conquered frontiers, including Yuri Gagarin, Charles Lindbergh, Christopher Columbus, Wilbur Wright, Roald Amundsen, Edmund Hillary and Jacques Piccard.

Piccard left the *Trieste* and Project Nekton shortly after and returned to Switzerland, where the reception was less effusive. Walsh, Rechnitzer and Shumaker went back to Guam for Project Nekton II, planning to make more dives up to the beginning of the typhoon project. But the *Trieste* would not dive deeper than 20,000 feet again. The Navy felt that the implosion-prone craft had ridden its luck, and the *Trieste* went back to San Diego and the NEL. Walsh worked over several months to upgrade the *Trieste*, installing a manipulator, the first of its kind, and fittings for underwater cameras and lights. "It was cutting-edge," Walsh says. "We were right at the beginning of something that led to, in my estimation, over 200 manned submersibles being constructed in the 1960s, 1970s and early 1980s. We can see our fingerprints, our DNA, in all of them. It's fair to say, even the unmanned submersibles of today still have our fingerprints on them." The *Trieste* carried out 60 research dives in the summer of 1961; two years later, it was called into more pressing service. On April 10, 1963, the USS *Thresher SSN-593*, the newest US nuclear sub, diving 215 miles (350 km) east of Cape Cod, sent a garbled message on their underwater telephone: "...minor difficulties, have positive up-angle, attempting to blow." She was not heard from again and no trace could be found: the *Thresher* was declared lost, her 129-man crew presumed dead.

The *Trieste* was the only craft capable of scouring the depths where the *Thresher* presumably lay. The bathyscaphe was transported to Boston and made the first dive on June 24, 1963. Journalists asked Piccard if he was ready to pilot the *Trieste*: "Naturally, I'm ready," but in the end commander Donald Kaech and M. Kenneth Mackenzie took the submarine down. After months of unsuccessful dives, which turned up only assorted debris, the *Trieste* found a "tangled mass of twisted metal and debris of all kinds", according to the *Marine Technology Society Journal*, and a piece of pipe inscribed "593 Boat" on it, which identified the wreck as that of the *Thresher*. The *Trieste* was showing its age: it was worn and its battery compartment finally failed. The Navy retired it that year. A new bathyscaphe, the *Trieste II*, combined the original but refurbished Krupp sphere with a new, larger float. This submarine continued the *Thresher* search, confirming the site in September 1964, and dived until 1980, when she was finally retired. Auguste Piccard's vision and design had proved remarkably durable over the years. It is worth repeating: no submarine has ever gone deeper than the *Trieste*.

When Jacques returned to Switzerland, it was not as the conquering hero of the deep. He was made an honorary member of the Société Académique Vaudoise, the Swiss Institute of Naval Architects and the Helvetic Society of the Natural Sciences, and that was it. Auguste's stratospheric achievements had been won in view of his native mountains and countrymen; Jacques's supreme feat had happened on the other side of the world, in the service of another country's navy. Switzerland politely shrugged.

After conquering the Challenger Deep, Jacques now had to find something else to do. "He had to keep moving forward," Walsh says. "His sole financial support was doing that sort of thing." Within the year, Jacques wrote and published a book telling the story of the *Trieste*: like Auguste, he was diligent at mentioning those who sponsored his efforts. At the same time, Jacques and Marie-Claude had their second child, a girl called Nöelle.

At a loss, Jacques decided to build another submarine. Not a bathyscaphe this time, but a mesoscaphe – a submersible for the middle waters. Auguste had come up with the idea years before. One evening in October, 1953, he and Jacques had sat on board the *Tenace,* running at six knots in a calm sea. The *Trieste* was being towed behind; two days before, she had set a depth record. But, Auguste thought aloud, it wasn't necessary to make ultra-deep dives to study the ocean. With modern steel, a hull could be made that would be capable of descending to "respectable depths – intermediate depths". The craft, lighter than water, wouldn't need a float. It would be like an underwater helicopter, with a propeller on its vertical axis to make it descend. "What I would like is to call this new vehicle a 'mesoscaphe', signifying that it is a vessel for intermediate depths." Auguste could not find funding, even with Jacques's assistance, and the project was put on hold as dives with the *Trieste* continued. In February, 1961, Jacques went to America to seek $500,000 to build the mesoscaphe, but returned empty-handed. "On my return to Switzerland I immediately went to work on the future mesoscaphe," he wrote in *The Sun Beneath the Sea*. He turned a vacant apartment in Lausanne into a new laboratory and installed high-pressure testing equipment. Auguste and Jacques went to work, happily building and breaking experimental models. In October 1961, Jacques spoke with a director of the forthcoming Swiss National Exposition, to be held in 1964, and convinced him to commission a mesoscaphe to take tourists down into Lake Geneva. But a final decision was delayed.

*

On March 25, 1962, Auguste Piccard died of a heart attack at his home in Lausanne, at the age of 78. He had been in good health until right before his death, but as Marianne came to his aid, he said: "No point... It's the end!" A few months before, Jacques had taken a young Bertrand to visit his grandfather. "I don't remember his voice," Bertrand says. "But I remember a real grandfather who was extremely nice with his grandson, very affectionate. When I visited him in his house, I ran up the stairs, went into the living room and he was sitting in the armchair with his back to the door. So I ran and turned around and jumped onto his knees. He was very affectionate."

His father's death left Jacques "completely devastated",

according to Bertrand: "It was a disaster." The person he looked up to more than any, whose course he had followed, then taken over for himself, was gone. How much would his future achievements count if Auguste could not acknowledge them? Jacques "kept a veritable cult for his father", observed Jean-François Rubin, who knew him well. In every page of his writing, Jacques keeps saying that his father was the inventor, the genius, and that he was just the means. He was "completely loyal to his own father", Bertrand remembers.

A month after Auguste's death, Jacques's one-year-old daughter Nöelle died in hospital, from hydrocephalus. "It was absolutely terrible," Bertrand says. "He was very depressed." Nöelle's death more or less destroyed Jacques's marriage to Marie-Claude; Jacques, the rational scientist, refused to confront his loss; Marie-Claude, the musician, could do nothing but, and there was nowhere for them to meet. Within the family, their relationship became something *non-dit*. "It was not easy for them to cope with it, it introduced a lot of problems." Bertrand says. Even though Jacques and Marie-Claude had two more children – Marie-Laure, in 1963, and Thierry, in 1965, Nöelle's death remained "a big burden" – one the couple endured until Marie-Claude's death in 1987.

In public though, Jacques kept his customary detachment and blunted affect, not giving much away. In his book *The Sun Beneath the Sea*, the only clue to Auguste's death is the subtle shift in person from "we" to "I". The mesoscaphe that he had hoped, like the *Trieste*, to build with his father, would instead become a memorial to him. It was the natural way for Jacques to overcome his grief.

On December 10, 1962, the steering committee of the Exposition officially charged Jacques with the construction of the mesoscaphe. There could be only one name for the submarine: the *Auguste Piccard*. She would be the star attraction of Expo 64: Jacques wanted thousands of visitors (up to 108,000, he calculated) to see with his eyes and look upon life underwater. Just as Richard Branson is today pioneering space-tourism, opening up a remote realm to the public, so Jacques invented sub-aquatic tourism. The interior of the *Auguste Piccard* was modelled on the cabins of airplanes, with "an attractive appearance", "warm colours" and "an open space". "The wide, long cabin is well lighted, has many portholes and two rows of twenty armchairs apiece, upholstered in reddish orange and provided with seatbelts as in an aeroplane." There were television screens, too.

But Jacques was too used to the trailblazing spirit of the United States; he had forgotten the small thinking that could blight old Europe. His budget was abundant, true, and the mesoscaphe was completed on schedule at Monthey, some way from Lausanne and about 12 miles from Lake Geneva. A train took the submarine to Bouveret; here the shipping department gave Jacques a certificate of clearance for the departure of "1 mesoscaphe (one)". But this was the point "when the drama of the mesoscaphe – for there was one – started to unfold. Not too definitely disturbing yet; nevertheless there was menace in the air." (Perhaps only Jacques could turn the decisions of bureaucrats – as unwelcome as they were – into something that sounded quite so forbidding.)

In the meantime, they baptised the mesoscaphe. The sleek, long white submarine, with an orange line at the level of the bridge, stood by Lake Geneva. A Swiss flag waved above the conning tower. "The ceremony was half magnificent, half rustic; that is to say that it was a complete success." Jacques held the six-year-old Bertrand in his arms. A Protestant pastor and a Catholic chaplain both blessed the submarine. Then Auguste's widow Marianne officially named the submarine after her husband, "the name associated with the very origins of the exploration of the deep sea – Auguste Piccard", and this time they smashed a bottle of champagne on the side, with "some reluctance". The *Auguste Piccard* sloped into the water, a year after construction had begun.

But very soon a "committee of experts" from the Expo declared that the mesoscaphe was unfit to dive. They were terrified, Jacques thought, at the responsibility of so many civilian lives in such an experimental craft. The entire team of the mesoscaphe was dismissed and a new staff appointed by the Exposition, delaying the launch until two months after the show had begun. Jacques found it "impossible" to continue working with the Exposition because of their "outrageous" technical demands. He ended up watching the first dive of the mesoscaphe from a launch; he was furious – at what he called the "weakness", the "pettiness" of the rule-following – it was a "virus which had infected everyone". (Once again Jacques was a pioneer – complaining of health-and-safety-gone-mad years before it was fashionable to do so.) Eventually, the case went to court. "The door opened and the representatives of the Exposition entered, thoroughly confident that they would win and that justice was for sale to the highest bidder as it had been when the Borgias set about buying their tiara," Jacques wrote, comprehensively abandoning the understatement that he had used to describe his journey to the bottom of the earth. "But justice was no longer for sale, and the decision hit them like a club. They went out with their heads down, tails between their legs, and were seen no more." After detailing all this at quite some length in a book, Jacques graciously wrote that he was not angry with the organisers, as their defects were only human. He had always been just as sensitive to criticism as his father, if not more so, and he didn't let this one go either. In Jean-François Rubin's 2007 book, Jacques, writing only a year before his death, still railed against "la bêtise humaine!" (human stupidity) that the Piccard family had always bumped up against: the "misunderstanding, the jealousy, the pettiness" they had met.

As righteously indignant as Jacques was with Expo 64, he was eventually delighted with the *Auguste Piccard*. During the summers of 1964 and 1965, it dived nine times a day, six days a week, and carried 33,000 passengers to the bottom of Lake Geneva, 1,000 ft (310 m) down. "What a difference between a naval submarine, a blind brute which could do nothing but sow terror and death (and for which nevertheless submariners could have such a passion, for one can love a monster as well as an angel), and the mesoscaphe, delicate, elegant, gracious, supple, as easy to control as an aeroplane in fair weather and built for the sole purpose of taking innocent tourists for a ride."

After the Exposition, the directors sold the mesoscaphe for $100,000 (they had originally set the asking price at $2 million). And, once again, Jacques had nothing to do. "After the submarine for the Expo 64, my father had no work, had no money and told us: 'Soon I will have to sell the car because I cannot afford to keep it,'" Bertrand Piccard recalls. When Jacques did not have a project on, he "suffered completely", according to Bertrand. "He suffered a lot from the lack of supports for his projects." Thierry Piccard, his fourth child, says: "Our father was a brilliant guy, but probably not so much a business man. He was idealistic: as soon as he had invented something clever, something new, he thought someone would sign a contract." (This affected the family: when Thierry came to choose his university studies, he eschewed science in favour of finance: "I observed how hard it was to make a living out of his interest in science.")

One morning in 1965, though, Jacques took a call. It was from Marc Bailly-Cowell, from Grunman's Ocean Systems. "I wonder what you're doing at present. Would you like to work with us? Have you any free time?" Plenty. But Jacques replied: "I can find time if you have something interesting to do." To his family, he said: "This would save us completely."

Two weeks later, Bailly-Cowell arrived in Lausanne and Jacques showed him around his laboratory. He went to the US soon after and discussed a project designated PX-15 (Jacques called all his projects PX, for Piccard Experimental. The original *F.N.R.S* was PX-1, and so on), a mesoscaphe for the exploration of the Gulf Stream. They signed a contract in a day. "He came back with the contract and said: 'We're going to make a submarine, we're going to hire people, build a team' – and that was an absolutely great moment," Bertrand remembers.

The new mesoscaphe would be built in Monthey once more – Jacques already knew all the manufacturers, and also "why not admit it? – to re-establish a certain credit which the Swiss manufacturers had seen as slightly tarnished through the adventures of the late Exposition."

The Gulf Stream is a transatlantic, underwater river, that flows from Cuba and America, turns east at New York, then divides into two branches, one skirting the coast of Great Britain and France, the other heading south to Africa. Piccard was not the first to be excited by it: in 1492, Christopher Columbus noted the presence of a current in the region; in 1513, a Spanish explorer, Ponce de Leon, officially noted a current "more powerful than the wind" and Spanish ships sailing from the Caribbean to Spain began using it. The first scientist to make a study of it was Ben Franklin. Before the War of Independence, and before he journeyed to Paris to observe the first balloon flights, Franklin was Postmaster General of the American colonies. At that time, customs officials in Boston were complaining that it took official mail two weeks longer to cross the Atlantic than it did private fishermen. Franklin investigated the problem himself, seeking the advice of his cousin, Timothy Folger, a Nantucket whaling captain, who told Franklin that the merchant ships travelled on the Gulf Stream, speeding their voyage. Franklin worked with other captains to chart the Gulf Stream and volunteered the information to Anthony Todd, secretary of the Post Office in Britain, who ignored it. Today, cargo vessels factor the ocean current into their journeys as a matter of course.

Beyond shipping, though, the Gulf Stream has a huge effect on the weather and climate of the western hemisphere "and consequently on customs, habits, character – in short, on western civilisation as a whole," Jacques wrote. His basic idea was to drift underwater in the Gulf Stream for a month, "in a submarine big enough for an operating crew and a scientific team to live in". Drifting voyages had long been carried out on the surface; in 1947, Norwegian explorer Thor Heyerdahl had drifted nearly 5,000 miles (8,000 km) across the Pacific Ocean in a raft he built himself. But this would be the first drift done underwater. The rationale was classic Piccard: if you wanted to study something, whether the stratosphere or the great depths, you had to immerse yourself in it. Thus the oceanographers would spend a whole month underwater, studying their surroundings.

Most military submarines cannot float freely underwater, as they must always adjust their buoyancy to their depth: when they go deeper, the armour plates of their hull are compressed by the colder, denser water, meaning they lose buoyancy which they offset by unballasting. The new mesoscaphe, though, would float at a depth between 590 ft and 2,000 ft (180–600 m), with little effort required to keep it neutrally buoyant, thanks to its non-compressible hull: when the mesoscaphe dived, it sank through the warm, less dense water until it reached the colder layers. This denser water would support the submersible: in effect, it would be floating, underwater.

There was another reason for the project: "During long voyages, the crew must live and work together in a situation such as might be encountered during long stays in an earth-orbiting space station," wrote Nasa's Wernher Von Braun. As such, Nasa would have a man, Chester May, in the mesoscaphe, to observe and evaluate the crew at work, rest and play, "and to relate the experience to the development of future Nasa space stations". Three automatic cameras would take a photo of the interior every two minutes, creating an archive of 64,800 photographs that would be used to help design the living quarters of a planned space station, to launch in 1971.

During the winter of 1967–8, the PX-15 was fitted out and in 1968, Jacques took his young family – Bertrand was ten, Marie-Laure five and Thierry just two and a half – to Florida, just north of Palm Beach.

The mesoscaphe launched on July 15, 1968, and on August 21, they christened it with water from the seven seas. Several names had been considered: Argonaut, Atlantis, Sea Search, Sea Home, Sea Monster, Sea Queen, Exploranaut, Ulysses, Odyssey, Gulf Stream Conquest, Gulf Quest; but they had eventually settled on calling the sub the *Ben Franklin*.

Six men would spend a month on board the *Ben Franklin*, drifting along the Eastern Seaboard of the US. Jacques packed a bag with books, including *Au Fond des Mers en Bathyscaphe* by his father, along with *Moby-Dick* and *Doctor Zhivago*.

The *Ben Franklin* left port on July 14, 1969; after a seven-hour tow to the dive site, the nylon tow rope was thrown off and at 8.34 pm, "we closed the door of our prison: it was our own way of celebrating the fall of the Bastille."

The comfortable interior of the *Ben Franklin* could not have been more pleasant than the dank, cramped sphere of the *Trieste* – apart from one detail. "It lacked one aspect that in our first designs at Lausanne I had planned to give it: inner walls of mahogany and a general arrangement similar to the interior of a nice yacht," Jacques wrote. "I had thought that a good warm interior, perhaps even some tapestries – let us say the interior of a gilded cage – would ease a long sojourn aboard." Unfortunately, Grunman deemed any wood a fire risk. What about mahogany imitation instead? Jacques's answer was gloriously scornful: "In my turn I did not take to this compromise. No plastic imitation produces the effect of mahogany in European eyes, any more than stucco could replace marble under the chisel of the Greeks." Lack of mahogany, real or imitation, aside, the rest of the cabin was agreeable. A long corridor ran bow to stern, wide enough for two people to pass. At the bow a room served as meeting place, dining-room and living-room. There was a shower and a galley (although Jacques refused to eat any of the boil-in-bag rations, instead sustaining himself exclusively on several fruit cakes Marie-Claude had packed for him). The berths were long enough for Jacques too, by design, and his bunk had a porthole 30 centimetres from his pillow. He would "spend hours lying on that bunk, staring into the infinitude of the seas, ready to seize upon the tiniest speck of plankton, the smallest fish, the least trace of life". At the stern, was the pilot's station. Most visitors to the *Ben Franklin* "are surprised by the free space and roomy arrangements". Anyone viewing it today in the Vancouver Maritime Museum will agree that the interior was indeed ahead of its time, looking very 1970s.

The crew included Don Kazimir, a young submarine captain who had carried out intelligence-gathering patrols off the coast of Soviet Russia, near Murmansk – spending weeks underwater and following Russian nuclear submarines out of the port to record their sound signatures ("at the height of cold war, kind of exciting," Kazimir remembers). Kazimir, "called 'Ka' in the American fashion", was Captain and Grunman's representative on board. Erwin Abersold, another Swiss who had worked with Jacques on the construction of the *Ben Franklin*, was the pilot. Two oceanographers, Frank Busby and Ken Haigh, seconded from the British Royal Navy, also travelled. "Only one thing aboard displeases [Haigh]: the instant tea!" Jacques wrote. "I agree with him." Chet May was the Nasa engineer. And Piccard, whose job description was the "somewhat pompous title of leader", made six.

They all had a very pleasant time. Each day May took samples from the skin, washbasins, toilets, floor, the ceilings and the portholes, and grew them in cultures for later examination in the Nasa labs. Each day he also had crew members play a proto-videogame, to record the quickness of their reactions, called the Space Skills Test. May himself wore a hat at night with electrical sensors that monitored his brain signals while he slept. There was a dartboard and the crew was in constant contact with the surface via acoustic telephone; if they preferred, they could write letters, shoot them out the airlock, and float them to the surface and the support boat following above. Everyone brought cassettes for the player aboard, including *Yellow Submarine*: "on the fourth and fifth [day] it begins to be tiresome," Jacques wrote. Two weeks into the dive, he despised the tape machine: "Concentration would be possible only if the cassette player broke down. It is a good instrument however; at first the others were afraid its batteries would run down too soon, but Ken found a stock of reserve batteries that would serve the purpose. There is nothing to be hoped for in that quarter. So much the better for those who love modern jazz and western music." Kazimir was fond of playing "On the Road Again" by country singer Willy Nelson – "it pepped everyone up," he says – but not Jacques.

On July 16, the Apollo 11 mission launched; the crew of the *Ben Franklin* listened to the countdown on the underwater telephone. On July 24, they found out about the success of the moon landing and subsequent splashdown of the command module. Some days, the *Ben Franklin* would dive to deeper depths. Afterwards, people were kind of wired and tense, according to Don Kazmir. "So when Jacques went to bed – he didn't approve of this – I broke out little bottles of liquor – Scotch or Bourbon, just a small bottle, those little sample sizes," he says. "Everyone had theirs. And that was a time when alcohol had a great medicinal benefit, because it just relaxed everybody. You're not feeling any alcohol, but it's relaxing. We did that each night. We never told Jacques."

Halfway through the mission, the Gulf Stream ejected the *Ben Franklin*. The only solution was to return to the surface and be towed back into the place – without opening the hatches, so that the *Ben Franklin* would remain sealed for a month and not interrupt the NASA survival experiment. Jacques didn't want to go out in any case: he remembered Alain Bombard, who had crossed the Atlantic in a small lifeboat in 1952, living off what he could catch from the water. Midway through that voyage, he met a liner and was invited aboard. He accepted, thinking he could use the break, but was deeply depressed when he returned to his small skiff. Up they went, to the surface, then back down again, with no drama, and continued on their way.

On August 14, 1969, one month and 1,444 miles (2,324 km) after it first dived in Florida, the *Ben Franklin* surfaced just north of New York and this time opened its doors. The mission had been a complete success and, in all honesty, quite dull. The expedition was nowhere near as dangerous as the *Trieste*'s assault on the Challenger Deep. Piccard's account of the drift, *The Sun Beneath the Sea*, dawdles along uninterestingly (an entire chapter is given over to "The Visit of the Tunas"). But the month-long dive was as useful as anything Jacques Piccard had done to date. The mesoscaphe had made many biological and chemical observations in the Gulf Stream. Throughout, she had measured the temperature, the speed of the current, the speed of sound in the water, salinity, luminosity, and so on. They had thousands of photographs of the underwater environment, and 65,000 pictures of life aboard the submarine from the automatic cameras. "The most tangible result of the whole expedition is probably the perfecting of a new method of research and observation in the ocean... For the first time a group of observers was able to spend a month under water and carry on without interruption a great number of observations over a distance of 2,800 kilometres. We had the sensation while living so long in the sea of learning to know it as never before; observation of the flora and fauna was made easier by the drift of the mesoscaphe which gave it the same speed as that of the water."

After the *Ben Franklin*, the Piccards left America. Florida had been idyllic: "For me, it was a little bit of paradise on earth, made of sun, palm trees, beaches, discoveries," Thierry Piccard remembers. For a long time afterwards, the family would say: "Ah, if only we could return to Florida." Switzerland was depressing.

Jacques didn't lack ideas, but again struggled to find

work and funding during the 1970s. Aged 50, he launched an international ecology institute. At the same time, he built a new "pocket submarine", the *F.-A. Forel*, named after a Swiss scientist who pioneered the study of lakes, founding limnography as a science to stand alongside oceanography. Throughout the 1980s, this submarine made numerous dives in various European lakes, evaluating the quality of water and other measures. He was passionate about conservation, complaining about "the pollution of the ocean, the rivers, the air", the "pollution of the food" and "also pollution by noise". Not much was clean enough for Jacques, and in fact he predicted that humanity would not make it to the 21st century because of what he termed "widespread suicidal pollution".

In 1987, Marie-Claude died of intestinal cancer, quite quickly after a wrong diagnosis. Her and Jacques's relationship had never recovered from the death of Nöelle, but she spent her last hour conscious in the hospital, holding Jacques's hand and talking, alone together, without their children. Jacques was relieved, unknotting the problems which had hurt the marriage for more than 20 years, and deeply sad. "He missed her a lot," Bertrand says of his father. Jacques suddenly grew old: "My mother was always extremely supportive to my father, helping him a lot, in the most difficult moments." He still had new ideas for submarines. The ideal ship would be like the *Nautilus* dreamt up by Jules Verne: "Its realisation is technically feasible right now!" he wrote – the real life Nemo deprived of a ship. "Such a ship would be expensive perhaps, but not much less than a single jet bomber." Another submarine, designated the PX-44, was an elaborate tourist craft: six-seater subs, with huge portholes, would take visitors to the bottom of Lake Zurich. However, the company supposed to commercialise the craft went bust... In total, Jacques, following

Auguste's start, went all the way up to PX-50 in his experimental projects. "And there were only five which were built, and all the others were just drawings and designs in his drawer," Bertrand says. "He made the *Trieste*, *AP*, *Ben Franklin*, *Forel*, and the last one, the PX-44, which was a tourist submarine. So he made five out of 50. You see the number of disappointments he had.

"He was desperate to find some more support for his submarines, he was fully occupied with this. He was so sad not to be able to build a couple of last submarines that he was still active until two years before his death, he was still trying to contact people to get support, he still had some drawings that he wanted to realise. He was very absorbed by that part.

"He put his life into his submarines, more than into his own happiness." Jacques, without his father or a grand mission to guide him, kept trying to find new, elaborate ways to slip beneath the surface and disappear from view. In *20,000 Leagues Under the Sea*, Captain Nemo exclaims: "Ah, monsieur, to live in the bosom of the sea! ... There I recognize no master! There I am free!" Jacques Piccard would have recognised the sentiment. The *F.-A. Forel* was retired in 2005: Jacques would never dive again. But he would watch another Piccard take up the journey.

Bertrand

Just before eight o'clock on March 1, 1999, the *Breitling Orbiter 3* stood 55 metres tall, fully inflated and tugging at its moorings in Château-d'Oex, Switzerland. The hybrid helium and hot air balloon was Bertrand Piccard's third – and final – attempt at circumnavigating the Earth non-stop, after two abandoned flights. Five other balloon teams were racing to do the same.

Hundreds of spectators had gathered. His three daughters – nine, six and four years old – gave Bertrand a balloon-shaped biscuit to celebrate his 41st birthday. Then Bertrand embraced his 75-year-old father. Neither could hold back tears. Bertrand told Jacques: "Thank you for giving me the energy with which to prepare for our journey round the earth." Then he climbed inside the bright red gondola and pulled shut the hatch. Jacques Piccard kneeled down and made sure the bottom porthole was tight; an unsealed porthole had scuttled Bertrand's second attempt. Then Jacques took a handkerchief from his pocket and carefully cleaned the seal, as he had done before each of his bathyscaphe dives. Looking at his son through the glass, he could not hide the fear on his face.

The firemen from Château d'Oex let go of the ropes holding the *Orbiter 3* to the earth. The balloon, the same size and shape as Auguste Piccard's *F.N.R.S.* of 60 years before, but with a dazzling silver sheen to the envelope, lifted off. Inside the gondola, Bertrand wrote in his logbook: "bon moment avec Papa". On the ground, Jacques once more craned his neck to watch a Piccard rise into the clear sky.

*

"In all this flying I never felt I had to prove anything to my father or grandfather," Bertrand Piccard says, sitting on a low sofa in a living room that looks out over a steep hill down to Lake Geneva, in March 2012. There is a bronze bust of Auguste in one corner of his Lausanne house. The study is full of metal cast models of famous aircraft and of his father's submarines; there are propellers, old posters advertising glamorously presented airlines; books by Jules Verne, Charles Lindbergh, Auguste, Jacques and Bertrand himself. The bill of the swordfish presented by the Ponzan fisherman to Auguste is there too. On the desk is part of the hatch to the *F.N.R.S.*'s gondola which, some years after the flight, was found by a skier in the Tyrol mountains; the skier's great-nephew sent it to Bertrand after he read about his exploits in a paper.

Bertrand Piccard does not have the stature of his father or grandfather, standing around 5 ft 10 in tall. There is more than a passing resemblance to Patrick Stewart, the English actor who plays the captain of the Starship *Enterprise*, Jean-Luc Picard – a name inspired by the real Piccards. Bertrand's eyes are a striking, clear blue and he keeps the little hair that remains on his head cropped short. When he is not speaking, he looks intent; something like a bird of prey which has just spotted its quarry and is tracking it. But his smile is ready and quick, and creases and softens his face.

Bertrand was born on March 1, 1958, and grew up in Lausanne. He spent some of his very early days in his grandfather's laboratory, happily playing with models of the bathyscaphe: "For me, it was just one more toy," he wrote in his 1999 book, *A Trace in the Sky*, and he "wondered why so many people were telling me that they felt honoured to have met my grandfather, that they would never forget his tall slightly stooping figure, his charisma and his modesty; or that they had once caught sight of him while walking in the streets of Brussels, Paris or Lausanne, but had not dared approach him." Bertrand himself spotted the resemblance to Professor Calculus, "but he was my grandfather and I found it all very normal."

Just as "perfectly normal" were his father's journeys to the bottom of the oceans and seas. Bertrand didn't read Jules Verne as Jacques and Auguste had: "my daily life at home seemed to be taken straight out of his books. When I went to the cinema with my father to see *20,000 Leagues Under the Sea*, I sat next to Captain Nemo, the real one, mine. How could a kid like me see it otherwise? For me, there was nothing strange in seeing my father on television, or side by side with the most important people in the world, or receiving a medal from the President of the United States, that's what I'd been used to from early childhood." At two, Bertrand used to run behind the television when his father appeared to check where he was. He became more aware of his family history at the age of six, when Jacques started building the PX-8 – the mesoscaphe that would become the *Auguste Piccard*. "At the moment I really started to feel it was something special."

At the same time, the six-year-old Bertrand took his first step into the world of aeronautics. Herman Geiger, a Swiss aviation pioneer, flew Bertrand around the Matterhorn in a Piper plane – his first 13,000 feet, and his first experience of being airsick. "This was the real stuff, I was flying," he later wrote. At a function, King Baudouin of Belgium asked a ten-year-old Bertrand what he wanted to be: "A stuntman, your Majesty."

When Bertrand was ten, Jacques moved the family to Florida in preparation for the *Ben Franklin* mission.

Bertrand helped paint the hull of the mesoscaphe; when the *Ben Franklin* made for sea, Marie-Claude and the rest of the family ran along the dike as far as they could, following the tugboat out to sea. Bertrand had given Jacques a walkie-talkie; he listened as his father's voice grew weaker, until all he could hear was static. For the duration of the mission, the Piccard family marked out the *Ben Franklin*'s underwater voyage on a map, using red pins.

When he wasn't at sea, Jacques took his family to tour the submarines stationed nearby, and to Cape Kennedy, busy with the Apollo launches. While Jacques went down, Bertrand looked up – to the sky and to people like Bill Anders, of Apollo 8, the first mission to go around the moon, and Jim Lovell, who would later captain the nearly disastrous and heroic Apollo 13 mission. Charles Lindbergh, one of Auguste Piccard's original heroes and later a lunch companion, was also there. "My father was completely at ease with these astronauts," Bertrand told me. "It was really exciting for me, because I saw that all these people making extraordinary things that I could see on TV and in the newspapers, they were just human beings who were passionate about what they were doing." Bertrand watched six launches, from Apollo 7 to Apollo 12. Wernher von Braun took Bertrand to watch Apollo 11 take off, while Jacques was drifting underwater. Bertrand recorded the countdown on the tape recorder he carried around Cape Kennedy to interview astronauts and technicians. "When I saw these people there at the launch, Charles Lindbergh and the astronauts, I thought, OK, that's the type of life I would like to have."

Bertrand's brother Thierry, seven years younger, wasn't nearly as impressed. When his mother woke him to watch the Apollo moon landing, he protested that he would rather go back to sleep. It wasn't that the explorer gene skipped Thierry, who now works in finance and is close to Bertrand. "What was clear for me," Thierry says, "was that Bertrand has lived very special moments as a teenager that my sister and I did not have. He met the astronauts, he was completely impressed by the exploring and pioneering atmosphere. He was certainly strong influenced by that. He was completely pushed by that experience in Cape Canaveral: he would be doing the same thing now even if he was not a Piccard." The Piccard genes were perhaps less important to Bertrand than being brought up ringside at the space race, where moonshots were a matter of course. When the Piccards left Florida, Wernher von Braun wrote Bertrand an autograph: "To Bertrand Piccard, who, I hope, will continue the Piccard family tradition of exploring both inner and outer space."

The return to Lausanne at the age of 12, after the *Ben Franklin* had completed its mission, was a shock. "It was not easy to get back to Switzerland after two years that were so exciting and extraordinary," Bertrand told me. "I have to say I was little bit depressed. I had the impression that the most beautiful time of my life was behind me, when I was 12 years old."

Bertrand thought that everything worth doing had been done. "We had walked on the Moon and, from now on, astronauts would be scientists, not pioneers... I felt intensely nostalgic about an extraordinary epic which I would not live again... In my eyes, aviation had reached its limits and yet I still wanted to live intensely."

In 1974, Bertrand found an outlet for this craving, in the new sport of hang gliding. For Bertrand, it was "love at first sight. I had thought that aviation made it possible to explore everything, including the Moon, that there was no more room for inventions, and suddenly I realised that back in the Apollo days the simplest flying machine didn't exist.

And its simplicity is precisely what makes it interesting, because it doesn't rely on technique, but on sensitivity and intuition."

Bertrand needed permission from his parents to fly, though. "My father had two faces," Bertrand says. "One face was the face of the explorer who went to the Marianas trench and had absolutely no fear of that, because he had calculated and built the submarine with his father and trusted it completely. But of course, for his family, he was much more careful and he was much more protective. He was a very protective father." But in the end, Bertrand convinced Jacques to let him fly a hang glider. He made his first flight in front of his entire family, promptly crashing onto the roof of a chalet, straight into a chimney. Jacques "really thought I had been killed. I'm very thankful that my father gave me the right to do crazy things like that at 16."

The accident did not deter Bertrand: flying offered him the sensation that there existed "another potential state for human beings, a state where you are much more conscious, much more aware, than in normal life. It's the first time that I understood that in normal life, most people, even me, we are living on autopilot, we are doing the things automatically, because we are trained to do it, we are thinking the same as usual. Suddenly, you are out of the state of lethargy; suddenly, you are facing some risk, facing a situation that is out of your routine, so you are suddenly aware and much more concentrated, much more efficient. And suddenly you *feel* you are much more alive... That changed my life completely, my way of understanding human beings." At the age of 16, Bertrand wanted "to go beyond human and technical limits, to know fear and audacity, to increase my freedom".

He was soon made aware of those limits, though, when a friend was killed flying. Bertrand had helped him with his hang-glider equipment minutes before he struck a rock

face. Bertrand became more introspective, trying to understand what had happened: he read books on astrology and
the *I Ching*, the Chinese divination text. While the rest of
his friends were out dancing, Bertrand was pondering the
purpose of life. He could not discuss these topics with his
father: "He trusted science and calculation completely. He
was more rational than intuitive. Or let's say – he didn't
trust his intuition. Probably he was very sensitive, but he
didn't trust it." Bertrand instead confided in his mother
Marie-Claude, talking for hours over long walks in the
countryside. "I could feel the presence of a sweet light of
harmony inside me," he wrote. "If I didn't have this type
of mother, I would not be what I am. Because my father
transmitted this taste for exploration of the outer world,
with the higher goals, but through my mother I got all the
interest for spirituality, philosophy, psychology – this is a
really important part of myself. That part was missing for
my father. If he had had a little more access to that part,
he might have had a less difficult life at the end. Because he
was really putting the reason of his life into his submarines,
more than into his personal development." According to
Thierry, Jacques "believed only in what was scientifically
proven. My mother believed in everything that was not
scientifically unproven."

Bertrand kicked back against his father's authority,
achievements and approach: "I rebelled against my father for
all the psychological things. For my father, something had to
be proven to be possible. For me it's the opposite: for me you
have to prove it's impossible before I stop believing it.

"Sometimes we were really arguing quite a lot when I
was a teenager. I was speaking of oriental, eastern medicine, he would say there's no proof it works, and I would
say I don't care, I see the result, it works because you see the
result – you don't understand why but you see the result.

"My father had to prove it was possible to believe in it. So he was always looking for proofs. And everything – new submarines were possible because he could prove that he could design and calculate them and it was possible to build them. But if you speak of intuition, spirituality, psychology, there is a lot that cannot be proven. And he didn't like the things that could not be proven." Jacques was "a bit cold" according to Thierry Piccard. "It was difficult for him to express emotions." And Bertrand was a teenager "who really challenged everything," Thierry says. "For someone who prides himself on knowing everything, that was difficult. They fought about anything." Bertrand was likewise frustrated: "Bertrand had always admired our father. But he was expecting that he would keep doing things as great as he had done in the earlier years." Bertrand expected Jacques to keep living up to himself, to renew himself as a Piccard with each exploit.

Disillusioned, Bertrand reconsidered the "inner space" Wernher von Braun had encouraged him to explore: "I now wished to go deeper into that theme from the psychological point of view, so, why not study medicine and psychiatry?" He would not follow his grandfather's trace in the sky.

"Before I started studying at university, people would often ask me whether I was going to be 'like dad' or 'like granddad', inferring the difficulty involved in bearing that name and in feeling obliged to continue with a tradition of scientific research and invention." While he was young, Bertrand had seen following their path as a given: a Greek minister at a reception in Athens called the teenager "the Swiss hope". "It was easy to represent the 'third generation' when you had a whole life ahead of you, rubbing shoulders with extraordinary people who were so indulgent with a teenager who hadn't proved anything yet... I still thought I could do it all." But soon Bertrand had to decide, between the "glory of perpetuating the family tradition and the desire to draw nearer to the meaning of Life". At 17, Bertrand and Jacques had a conversation in their mountain chalet. He wanted to become a psychiatrist, Bertrand said, but he had his doubts: "Maybe it's not too bad to build submarines like you did." Jacques replied: "No, you shouldn't do the same thing that I did. Because what I did was pioneering. If you do the same, it won't be pioneering. You can also really have your own life, your own goals, and don't be obliged to build submarines."

Bertrand started studying psychiatry at the University of Lausanne. He married Michèle Rathle; the two had had an on-off relationship since she was 16, Bertrand 19. "It was a little bit too serious for our age at the beginning," Michèle says. "We met a little bit too early," Bertrand replies. "But it's better to meet too early than too late." On dates, Bertrand had taken Michèle flying.

Bertrand did not completely leave aviation behind: he would skip lectures to fly and get "a weight off my shoulders". He took three years off university to set up a micro-light company, Piccard Aviation, which ultimately failed, and he set various hang-gliding records at the same time. At 20, he pitched his hang-glider out of a multi-coloured hot-air balloon, 10,000 feet above Château-d'Oex, as part of a daring aerobatics display. During a loop-the-loop, he nosed the hang glider up and fell 1,300 feet. He recovered the flight, but he had completed the loop. Bertrand gave another aerobatics display. After an easy first loop, his glider started vibrating. The craft porpoised and his speed picked up. Bertrand, "much to [his] disgust", realised that he would have to use the emergency parachute. As he made to pull on the release handle, the glider shuddered violently and began to disintegrate into a "tangle of tubes and cables".

He started falling. "It was like being a contorted puppet

falling with remains of a hang glider, spinning and swirling towards the ground." The sky "spewed" him out at 90 miles per hour. "There was nothing I could do to stop the violence." Bertrand wheeled as he fell, fast. Thinking of his wife and his six-month-old daughter, he felt guilty. He reached for the handle of the emergency parachute among the centrifuging, plummeting debris. It wouldn't open: the bag escaped his hands, unrolling its strap. But now he was no longer rotating so violently. The parachute was open. Bertrand was upside down, his head pointing toward the coming ground, his feet to the sky. The trees and electric lines were coming fast and there was no way he could control his fall. He hauled himself upright, as he came in hard and crashed. "I collapsed among the remains of my hang-glider."

"Life then carried on." But Bertrand had been bloodied, and he changed. He realised hang gliding was not the real freedom he had always understood it to be, merely "fascination". He had thought his "craving" for exploration was part of the family tradition. "Neither of them accepted that a man should content himself with living on the firm ground, and they explored the sky and the sea," after all. His father and grandfather had certainly taken risks and rejected limits, but never for their own sake. Bertrand was just chasing thrills. "One of my life cycles had come to an end."

Bertrand took another blow, when his mother Marie-Claude died in 1987, four months after being diagnosed with cancer – "It was the wrong diagnosis, the wrong treatment," Bertrand says. "And in four months, she was gone." While Jacques redoubled his efforts with experimental submarines, Bertrand abandoned flying and dedicated himself to psychiatry instead. "Once you experience that there is this other level of consciousness, you have two possible ways. One is to search it out like a drug, in order to get out of normal life, to have these flashes of adrenaline. And this will quite often lead to accidents, because people will try to go further than their limits. The other way is to bring this state into your daily life." Eventually, he began talking to Michèle about his consultations with patients with the same passion he had felt for microlights. He wrote a psychiatric thesis with the title: 'Ordeal: A Learning Experience'. The clinical cases Piccard was most interested in were to do with trauma, from accidents or childhood abuse. He would use hypnosis. "You have a patient under hypnosis, disassociated into an adult part and a child part," Piccard explains. "You teach the adult to speak to the child and explain what happened in the past. And say that your parents couldn't take care of you because they were working all the time, or depressed, but today I am here to take care of you. When the session is over, you can feel the patient healing. This is so fabulous. Of course you cannot change the facts of the past, but you can change the emotion that is related to the past."

With physical accidents, Piccard used a different technique. He would ask a patient, again under hypnosis, to visualise the accident on an imagined screen, as if it were a scene in a film. The patient also has a virtual remote control in hand. By fast-forwarding and rewinding the scene, stopping and starting, the patient can revisit and re-understand the accident, "so that he can break the automatic link between the memory and the emotion".

Piccard used the same technique on himself, but not on an imagined screen. A spectator had recorded the hang-gliding accident that had nearly killed Piccard, filming as Piccard tumbled out of the sky. He gave him the tape. "Physically, I was going forwards and backwards, still, slow motion – exactly like in the hypnosis session. But it was true. It was on the television, I had a remote in my hand. So

I could heal myself like this."

Bertrand dedicated himself to his medical practice and, so in his mind, ended the glorious generations of the Piccards. Put simply: "I broke the family tradition."

Bertrand had forgotten something though. No Piccard had ever chosen exploration as a career: exploration had found them as they pursued other activities, whether that was studying cosmic rays or economics. One evening in January1992, Bertrand took his seat, the only one still free, at a dinner held for the Château-d'Oex balloon festival. He sat next to Wim Verstraeten, the Belgian whose balloon Bertrand had hang-glided out of a couple of times. Verstraeten was preparing for a balloon race across the Atlantic and he needed a teammate. At that time, 16 attempts had been made to cross that ocean in a balloon; only five had been successful, the first in 1976 in a helium-filled balloon. In 1987, Richard Branson had made the first journey in a hot-air balloon. Five people had died attempting the crossing. Chrysler, the carmaker, and Cameron Balloons, the largest hot-air balloon maker in the world, were organising the first-ever such race. Verstraeten liked the idea of taking a psychiatrist with him and asked Bertrand if he would fly with him (undoubtedly, he also had an eye on the publicity that would come from Auguste Piccard's grandson making a balloon flight). Bertrand had no licence, nor could he fly a balloon. He had always flown against the wind, with it blowing in his face, more or less in control. Flying in a balloon meant being at the whim of the wind instead – "like losing control and being led towards the unknown". Bertrand accepted. He was worried that the decision was a hasty one, but soon received myste-rious reassurance. During a trip to Shanghai to study tradi-tional Chinese medicine, he came across an antique shop, full of medals. He took a coin at random and asked the shop owner what the four characters on one of its sides meant. "When the wind blows in the same direction as your path..." –Bertrand bought the coin almost before the salesman could finish – "...it brings you great happiness." Bertrand understood the coin as a clear sign, "an imperative answer".

He convinced Breitling, the Swiss watch manufacturer, to cover his salary for the two months he would spend away from his psychiatric practice, in return for any publicity he could bring. Like his grandfather and father, Bertrand wore two watches, one on each hand – but to make sure that whichever angle he was photographed from, a Breitling would be visible.

Five two-man crews would race 3,000 miles (4,800 km) across the Atlantic, each in a technologically advanced prototype balloon, the Cameron-Rozier 77. A Cameron balloon dealer would be pilot, taking a co-pilot "chosen essentially on media coverage criteria", according to Bertrand. In the British balloon, Don Cameron, the Scottish founder of the hot-air balloon company, would fly with Rob Bayly, a producer from the BBC and later director of *The Antiques Roadshow*. Troy Bradley and Richard Abruzzo helmed the American balloon – Abruzzo's father Ben had been the first to cross the Atlantic in *Double Eagle II*. The German crew was Erich Kraft and Jochen Mass, a former Formula One racing car driver, and Evert Louwman and Gerhard Hoogeslag made up a Dutch crew. *Chrysler 1* – Verstraeten and Piccard's balloon – would be a Belgian Swiss combination, just like the *F.N.R.S.* Piccard also had to learn how to fly a balloon. He had time for only five hours of lessons before the race began.

In the early morning of Wednesday, September 16, 1992, the five balloons stood nine storeys high in Bangor Raceway, in Maine. Thousands lined the racetrack fence. In the four hours before, ground crews had filled the balloons, underneath the track's spotlights. Before the pilots climbed into the balloon, Piccard sought out Richard Abruzzo. Abruzzo had seen his own father take off in *Double Eagle II* and Bertrand could "feel this race was made for the two of us. He was going to be reunited with his father over the Atlantic, and I would be reunited with my grandfather. We each had a family episode to live out," Bertrand later wrote. Abruzzo was slightly taken aback at Piccard's direct and personal approach – both his parents had died in a plane crash only a few years before – but shook Bertrand's hand. Before he climbed into his gondola, Bertrand told the *Bangor Daily News*: "I hope I won't wake up in my bed in six hours' time and find this was all a dream."

At 3.04 am, Verstraeten cut the ground strap and *Chrysler 1* lifted off, followed at five-minute intervals by Germany, Great Britain, the Netherlands and the United States. The race was on.

At daylight, Piccard and Verstraeten flew over the east coast. They descended to just above sea level. "The wind was pushing us towards the open sea in absolute silence and we felt drawn to the horizon," Piccard wrote. They left US airspace, on a heading to South Africa, which was hardly desirable, so they rose to find a different wind. As they did, they heard a "long ghastly creaking noise, followed by several other shorter ones". The seams of the envelope were straining and the helium couldn't overflow. Other sounds, "dreadful creaks that sounded just like when you tear a rag apart. I was paralysed with fear, my throat felt tight." The pressure would either burst the balloon, or it would unblock the overflow and return to normal. Piccard and Verstraeten donned their life jackets. They took the balloon down to sea level and proceeded on at 11 miles per hour, so low that the antenna of their high-frequency radio was trailing in the Atlantic. Bertrand, already exhausted and hungry, started hallucinating and saw a plane coming right at the balloon. It turned out to be a fishing boat and was safely avoided. Piccard now wished he could wake up in Bangor and find the flight had been only a nightmare.

Piccard went to the gondola's single berth to sleep. He tried self-hypnosis, a technique he had first used as a teenager during his revision for school exams, listening to Leonard Cohen records for hours. He tensed each muscle in his body as hard as he could, then released it, and focused on the regularity of his breathing. He felt his body go to sleep while his mind remained active, "a state of conscious sleep that was new to me: my body was profoundly resting while my mind kept watchful." It was a technique that would prove invaluable in this flight and the many more demanding ones to come.

The *Chrysler 1* drifted on. Only the wind determined the balloon's course; the pilots could change their altitude in hope of finding a different wind, but that was all. As Verstraeten went to sleep, Bertrand took over the balloon. He had never piloted a balloon at night and was only 1,600 feet (488 m) above water he couldn't see, because of fog. But it was peaceful enough for him to put his head out of the capsule and look at the stars overhead. "The muffled atmosphere of that first night was magical."

Onwards over the ocean. On the third day of the race, the balloon came in range of coastal radio stations. Verstraeten called his mother, his voice trembling. "At that very instant, I missed my mother more than ever," Piccard wrote. Bertrand spoke to Michèle, told her he loved her and thanked her for letting him go. Thousands heard the message, but it felt like it was just the two of them. After the short messages, the cabin once again fell silent and *Chrysler I* drifted on.

Piccard calculated their position. *Chrysler I* had a narrow lead: it was in the middle of a storm that was pushing the balloon on. The German team felt it more, though, caught up in its wilder edges. Rain and ice forced their balloon ever further down, until they were level with the waves. Its propane burners could not keep it up in the air: they ditched in the ocean, 550 miles from the Canadian coast. The race continued without them.

Meanwhile, Bertrand was waxing philosophical, as would prove to be his wont when airborne with time on his hands. "There was no more contradiction between humanism and technology, between intuition and electronics, between man and nature, between the sky and ocean," he wrote. "It all existed side by side and we needed it all. Prejudice didn't hold any longer on the threshold of the unknown. I suddenly was being myself... I felt fully alive, with such deep consciousness and sensitivity that I wanted to crystallise them in me for the rest of my life." He put aside the official logbook and started writing in a personal notebook. "Extreme adventure, the real one, is not for showing off in public, nor is it an escape from reality or a wish, whether conscious or not, to get high on adrenaline... It is a life-sized mirror, and the opportunity to discover some new inner resources. Adventure is the breaking point when we realise that we can no longer be satisfied with reproducing automatically what we learned, that this won't do anymore."

Verstraeten wanted to sleep but couldn't, so Bertrand hypnotised him and stayed up himself. He thought of his father: he was following the same Gulf Stream that Jacques had explored twenty-three years before. He pictured Jacques telling him that it was possible to drift-dive all the way to England, then Spain. "In fact, I was taking over his expedition," Bertrand wrote. "I was too young at the time to understand what he must have gone through during those thirty days of scientific adventure, but I couldn't forget his beaming face when he watched the jets of water spouting from the fire boats celebrating the return of the mesoscaphe in New York Bay. He had gathered an impressive amount of oceanographic, biological and chemical data, but probably also a wealth of emotions, which I was now able to perceive." Bertrand had never talked with his grandfather about his voyages to the stratosphere, although he understood their impact. "But, as to the emotion my grandfather must have felt when being the first man to see the curvature of the earth, that incredible sensation of suddenly becoming part of space, of not completely belonging to our planet anymore, of not knowing which part of the world he was going to return to, that I didn't know. When listening to recordings, I was stunned by the absence of emotion in his speech. All his descriptions were rigorous, and always very technical, but there was no way you could guess, between the words, what he had felt." Bertrand had always thought of Auguste as the extra decimal point, the inventing machine. "That image stuck in my mind until the lift-off at Bangor, until that first night into which our balloon had melted, until I felt sure he couldn't possibly have been caught up only by his calculations. He must have experienced something else, some sensations which he never related. He may even have been afraid of mentioning them, but I suddenly discovered them, as he must have done. Almost motionless under the celestial vault, hanging from my lucky star, halfway between two worlds, the generation gap was getting narrower."

Before the race, a friend had sent Bertrand a letter, saying that he would maybe be able to chat with his grandfather "up there". "I definitely felt very close to him now and I understood what he must have felt. Here I was, watching the same stars as him, from the capsule of a balloon which was carrying me, as he had been, through a mass of simple, human emotions."

This was the first time Bertrand did not feel torn between medicine and the family tradition. "All of a sudden, it seemed that I could reconcile myself with everything: my relatives' career and my own, aeronautics and medicine, science and the wind. It was a bit as if I was paying a debt to my lineage in order to be my true self at last.

"I also felt utterly alive."

Bertrand Piccard at the controls

Bertrand woke Verstraeten up. They were coming up to 250 miles (400 km) off the coast of Portugal and were still in the lead, but their speed had decreased to 25 mph. In *Chrysler 4*, the Dutch were catching up from the North, travelling at 75 mph. At that rate, they were likely to reach northern Spain first, but the margin was small. The Americans had drifted far south and were out of the race. There was nothing any crew could do but trust the wind.

Night fell again and the fax in the gondola rattled: news that the Dutch were drifting in the Bay of Biscay. A storm had pulled them away from a finishing line in France and forced them to ditch off the coast of Cornwall. They sent a distress signal. Picked up by a Royal Navy helicopter, they were treated for shock and hypothermia. *Chrysler 1* would be victorious.

The balloon flew over Viana do Castelo in Portugal and the race was won. The pilots sent a telex: "We made it, we made it, we made it!" But the mood on board was more subdued. "We watched the streets of that little port go by slowly below our capsule, without feeling the emotional release we had expected. Five months of preparation, five weeks of waiting and five days of total concentration ended up in that instant. We had won the first transatlantic race, but history was now behind us."

Only two balloons had made it across safely, *Chrysler 1* and the British balloon. The Americans had continued their southwards tack towards Morocco and apparently had no intention of coming down, forgetting the race to attempt an endurance record instead. (Abruzzo was successful in this, staying in the air longer than anyone else had before, and would in 2004 win the Gordon Bennett cup. On September 29, 2010, however, he disappeared competing in the same race. His body and that of his co-pilot, Carol Rymer Davis, were found off the coast of Italy two months later. The race organisers estimated from radar that the pair hit the water at 50 miles per hour, somewhere in the Adriatic.)

When morning came, Wim found a field near a village and took the balloon down. They missed the landing, but made a second attempt. After 122 hours and 27 minutes in the sky, and 2,580 miles (4,152 km), neither pilot wanted to leave the gondola and come out of the dream. "I didn't want to think that the adventure was over, that I would have to resume the normal course of my life.

"But my life would never resume a normal course. I had

learned far too many things to be the same as before. When going back to my job as a psychiatrist, I felt my whole approach to life and medicine had changed. It was disconcerting, I found myself out of step with my own knowledge, my own conceptions and habits. Little by little, it dawned on me that the real adventure hadn't begun with the lift-off at Bangor but with the landing in Spain. No, the adventure wasn't over, quite the opposite: it had just begun."

When he returned to Geneva after the balloon flight, Piccard told his brother about his next adventure: to fly non-stop around the world in a balloon.

It wasn't an original idea: the first to attempt it had been Maxie Anderson, an American businessman and balloonist who had flown with Ben Abruzzo in *Double Eagle II*. In January 1981, Anderson took off in *Jules Verne*, from Luxor, Egypt, with another American, Don Ida, as co-pilot. The pair landed in Hansa, India, two days later. They didn't make another attempt: in 1983, taking part in the Gordon Bennett Cup as non-competitors, the two tried to land their balloon to avoid straying into East Germany. The bolts to release the gondola from the envelope failed at touchdown and the wind took the balloon back into the sky. The bolts then fired, balloon and capsule separated, and both pilots were killed in the fall.

Others had tried since then, but no one had come close to a circumnavigation. In the last days of the 20th century, there was one great adventure left for the Piccards.

Around

Wearing life jackets and helmets, Piccard and Verstraeten were bobbing in the sea. The huge silver fabric of their balloon floated around the gondola of *Breitling Orbiter*, tugged about by the currents. A coastguard plane flew low over the pilots. Six hours earlier, on January 12, 1977, the pilots had lifted off "like heroes" from Château-d'Oex, on a mission to fly around the world non-stop. Now they were "paddling in the Mediterranean", Bertrand later wrote in *A Trace in the Sky*, 20 miles off the French coast. A flange of a tube connected to the kerosene tanks had given way and more than a hundred litres of the gas had flooded the cabin, giving off toxic and flammable fumes. The weather conditions had promised the perfect flight path, but the pilots had taken the *Orbiter* down with an ignominious splash. Bertrand was living up to the Piccard name. Unfortunately he was exploring the sea, not the sky.

*

Piccard's transatlantic flight with Verstraeten four years earlier had taken him straight to the Mediterranean. When Piccard won the Chrysler Challenge five years earlier, he made sure a Breitling bag was on top of the gondola and thus in the hundreds of newspaper photos that were subsequently published. Thedy Schneider, who still runs the watchmaker and was delighted with the loyal publicity of Piccard, told Bertrand to call him if he had another project.

Bertrand did: "I'd like to fly around the world in a balloon," he told Schneider early in 1993. Schneider asked whether it was possible; Piccard said he didn't know. Schneider asked how much it would cost and when Piccard again said he didn't know, he agreed to fund it anyway: Schneider did not want merely to provide money and logos, but to be involved from the very beginning of such an audacious project.

Piccard went to the Swiss Institute of Meteorology (better known as Météo Suisse) and asked them how long it would take to fly around the world; they ran hundreds of computer simulations and estimated it would take about 20 days, if he launched in the winter at a latitude of 40 degrees north and a height of 32,800 feet (9,997 km) – near the bottom edge of Auguste's realm of the stratosphere. Piccard asked Cameron Balloons, who had supplied the experimental flyers for the Chrysler Challenge, to come up with a new type of craft: a pressurised gondola made from carbon fibre and Kevlar (a material commonly used to stop bullets), coupled to a huge balloon, large enough to keep the gondola and its occupants airborne for three weeks. Specialists would build the gondola itself, "but the general concept was mine," Piccard wrote in *Around the World in 20 Days*, "and I asked Cameron to use the system that had served my grandfather and father so well. The capsule would be a horizontal, pressure-tight cylinder, very similar to my father's last submarine. Inside would be a tank of liquid oxygen which would evaporate gradually, allowing the crew to breathe, along with lithium hydroxide filters to absorb the exhaled carbon dioxide." The *Breitling Orbiter* would be the most advanced balloon ever made, but Auguste Piccard would have been comfortable enough flying it. It was a Rozier balloon – the combination of hot air and hydrogen that Pilâtre de Rozier invented and was killed by in 1785. During the day, the helium in the envelope would expand under the heat of the sun. At night, Piccard would burn propane or kerosene to heat the air in the hot-air cone, which would in turn heat the helium, and keep aloft the balloon. Andy Elson, a "rather dishevelled-looking" Englishman who had flown the first balloon over Mt Everest, in 1991, and a friend of Wim Verstraeten, suggested using kerosene as the fuel rather than propane; the former is much lighter to transport, saving weight in the gondola. Another innovation seemed cosmetic but would also help performance: the balloons of the transatlantic race had been painted white, which meant they heated and cooled rapidly as day gave way to night; the new balloon would be covered in aluminium-coated plastic, to conserve the heat of the gas inside the bag, in the same way as silvered blankets keep marathon runners warm.

In June 1995, with the design approved, Schneider wired the money to Cameron Balloons from his office. Afterwards, Piccard set off on the hour's drive home, but had to stop at a restaurant on the way, "to recover from the intense motion I was experiencing. I felt I had just been given the green light to start building my life's dream, and that in future nothing would be the same."

The design and construction of the balloon, though, was probably less important than the work of the meteorologists who would plot its path through the winds. Piccard asked Swiss Météo for volunteers and they supplied Pierre Eckert, a specialist in planning the routes of sailing yachts. Piccard also approached Luc Trullemans, from the Royal Institute of Meteorology in Brussels – the same centre that had guided Auguste Piccard into the stratosphere. Trullemans, tall and outgoing, had already proved crucial during the Chrysler Challenge – Piccard says that he would have ditched in the ocean without Trullemans contradicting the official weather crew based in the Netherlands – "Those guys were absolutely useless. Trullemans really saved us. I owe him a lot." Eckert was small and shy, but the two got on from their first meeting. Having a pair of weathermen was unusual – the other balloon teams had only one forecaster. Each had his preferred source of weather data. Eckert relied on the European Centre for Medium Range Weather Forecasting; Trullemans on the American National Oceanographic and Atmospheric Administration. Both feeds stitched together myriad sources, from sounding-balloons, aircraft, ships, ground stations, and satellites – geostationary and polar-orbiting. Eckert and Trullemans crunched all these sources to come up with wind forecasts and specific flight trajectories. Trullemans used a model based on how nuclear fallout had spread, blown by the winds, after the Chernobyl disaster. As Piccard puts it: "The balloon was taken as the equivalent of a single particle [of radiation], blowing with the wind in different layers at different altitude, and the model proved incredibly effective." Trullemans and Eckert would prove to be "out and out winners", according to Piccard. The final touch was the balloon's name: *Breitling Orbiter*, the product of a pub session near the Cameron factory.

To circumnavigate the world was not just a challenge of design and engineering – it was also a race. It was more important to get things done than get them completely right. While the *Orbiter* was being built, in the winter of 1996–1997, the *Virgin Global Challenger*, piloted by Richard Branson and Per Lindstrand, was waiting on the weather in Morocco, ready to go. Steve Fossett, an American businessman who in his life would set 91 aviation records ratified by the FAI, was attempting to fly around the world alone in the *Solo Spirit* (a nod to Charles

Lindbergh's *Spirit of St. Louis*). Although the race was quite unofficial, it still had rules – set by the FAI. Each balloon had to begin and end its journey on the same longitudinal line; each balloon had to cover a minimum distance, roughly equal to two-thirds of the Earth's diameter, checking in with specified radar waypoints on its journey; and no balloon could land – each would carry an FAI-installed sealed altimeter that would be checked upon a balloon's landing to make sure it had not come down at any point. "I have to admit, the competition added a lot of pressure," Bertrand says today.

The race's start was false, though. In the winter of 1995–6, Branson's balloon didn't even take off; Fossett lifted off from St Louis in the USA and came down only 2,000 miles (3,220 km) later, in Canada. The next year, the *Breitling Orbiter* was ready and the race was still on; Branson was back in Morocco and Fossett in St Louis. Branson's balloon had a unique design: it was a vertical cylinder, which Piccard thought could prove dangerous ditching in the water, and had its sleeping quarters at the bottom of the balloon – the coldest place. The envelope lacked insulation, meaning the pilots would have to burn fuel constantly to keep the balloon in the air. "The balloon was really badly conceived," Piccard says. Branson, despite his obvious love for balloons, wasn't much of an expert. Brian Jones, who would later join the Orbiter team, says: "Richard is very courageous, and I have a lot of respect for him as a person. As a balloon pilot, not very much."

The gondola of the *Orbiter* had had its own problems during construction, though. The original version had failed its preliminary tests, with air leaking out of the cabin at various points. A new one was ordered, but finished only in September 1996, and final preparations in Switzerland were rushed. The race was between the constructors as much as the pilots: Lindstrand vs Cameron (who also made Steve Fossett's balloon). After Steve Fossett made one failed attempt, Lindstrand said it was clear that "the Cameron system doesn't do what it's supposed to do." No one was completely sure whether the circumnavigation was even possible; each million-dollar iteration of a team's balloon increased the odds, but the pilots were really flying blind and hoping that, this time maybe, their equipment would deliver.

On January 7, 1997, while the *Orbiter* team were still working to fit out their balloon, Branson took off. This "produced an atmosphere of desperation in the *Breitling* camp," Piccard wrote. It didn't last long: the next morning, he watched on TV as Branson was forced to ditch. The ground crew, flown in from the UK for a rushed departure preparation, had left the safety catches that fastened the six fuel tanks on the outside of the gondola: it would be impossible to jettison fuel tanks from inside the pressurised cabin. When the balloon took off, it rose very fast, losing a lot of helium. When night fell, there was not enough gas to keep the *Challenger* in the air, and it started to plummet. The crew desperately burned their fuel trying to stay in the air, and threw everything they could out of their gondola to unballast – food, water and equipment – before Alex Ritchie, the third co-pilot, crawled outside on top of the cabin, the balloon still in a death spiral, and loosened the tanks – all with impossible bravery. The tanks fell away and halted the balloon's descent, but with no food, water or fuel left, the circumnavigation attempt was over. "As I was sitting in the capsule while our balloon was plunging uncontrolled towards the earth," Branson told the *New York Times*, "the thought crossed my mind that maybe a round-the-world flight really is impossible." Safely delivered back to base, Branson returned to his normal optimism, betting that a balloon would complete the circumnavigation within 24 months.

The next Sunday, on January 12, 1997, the *Orbiter*'s turn came. Trullemans and Eckert spotted a good weather window and gave the go-ahead. The balloon was still not quite ready, but it would go. *Orbiter* rose up, emblazoned with the five Olympic rings; Piccard had talked the International Olympic Committee into supporting the project. The burner was lit with the Olympic flame, on exeat from the Olympic Museum in Lausanne. The conditions were perfect and "the wind at altitude was ideal as it would carry the balloon at a good speed straight towards the jet stream."

False hopes: half an hour later, with the balloon flying beautifully at 27,000 feet, a kerosene fuel tank overflowed, pushing the fuel across the floor of the gondola, contaminating the water reserve and filling the cabin with noxious vapours. Piccard and Verstraeten, ankle-deep in the toxic fuel, abandoned the flight and ditched into the Mediterranean. "The leak was the result of damage a hose clip sustained during the launch," Don Cameron said. "That clip cost 69 pence – less than one US Dollar – but it cost a million-dollar balloon a sporting chance at the big goal." Piccard was crushed, "the frustration immense... We felt we had destroyed our dream." The entire gondola, although recovered, was ruined.

Floating in the sea, Piccard looked at Verstraeten, who sat there, as if made mute: "he was mesmerised in his seat, just doing nothing," Piccard remembers. The two pilots' relationship had been tested in the previous months: Piccard thought Verstraeten wasn't training hard enough ahead of the flight. Verstraeten, who had invited Piccard, a completely novice balloonist, on board *Chrysler 1*, was disgruntled at what he perceived as the Piccard show.

To be fair, that's how Piccard saw it too: "I put together *Breitling*. [Verstraeten's behaviour] wasn't acceptable." Just like his father Jacques and his less successful great uncle Jean, Bertrand did not care for his authority to be questioned. Splashing around in the Med was breaking point. A few hours after the sea landing, Schneider had called Piccard to tell him they would try again, but it was clear that Verstraeten and Piccard could not fly and live together; something, or someone, would have to give. They flew back to Switzerland in a private jet, Piccard later wrote, "with feet bare, clothes still wet and carrying one square metre of the envelope which we had cut away for a souvenir."

Thedy Schneider quickly agreed to a new balloon, telling Piccard to "cheer up... Probably we'll need more than one attempt to go around it." Although the fuel system had failed, they recommissioned Elson to build the capsule. "We had specc'd what we genuinely thought was needed to fly around the world," Elson remembers. "When Wim and Bertrand had flown the Atlantic, they were flying in the equivalent of a Mini. They were hoping for a Mini Cooper to fly around the world and I had built them a Ferrari. It was one step too far in technology for where they were at." This time, Piccard was "determined to be more closely involved in its construction" – like Jacques, he would understand every nut and bolt of his vehicle – and he asked Verstraeten to try harder too.

Orbiter 2 would take a year to build; in between, Piccard returned to his psychiatric practice, to help "get some distance", he says. The other balloon teams were hardly going to wait, though. Fossett had made it as far as India, landing in a tree near Nonkhar; some of the villagers mistook him for Lord Hanuman, the Hindu monkey god, come down from on high. He had flown for six days and 9,940 miles (nearly 16,000 km), setting a ballooning record for distance and duration, and he had done so on his own – relying on an autopilot to let him snatch sleep – in an unpressurised capsule, enduring oxygen deprivation and extreme cold. It was an extraordinary feat. Fossett was building a new balloon and so was Branson. Two new crews had also entered the race. Barron Hilton, the hotelier, had put up a balloon called the *Global Hilton*. Dick Rutan would captain it. A highly decorated US Air Force pilot, Rutan had flown F-100s in Vietnam, until he was shot down, then had made the first non-stop flight around the world with his co-pilot Jeana Yeager, in December 1986, in the *Voyager*, a plane designed by his brother Burt (who would later design airplanes, then spaceships for Richard Branson). Yeager and Rutan travelled 24,985 miles and landed with only a few litres of fuel left. The *Global Hilton* planned to take off from Albuquerque, New Mexico. Another American, a 34-year-old architect and engineer called Kevin Uliassi, took Fossett's already extreme approach one step further: Uliassi would fly solo, in an unpressurised capsule, but one in which he could not even stand upright. He named his balloon the *J. Renee*, for his wife. To add to the sense of competition, in November 1997 US brewers Anheuser-Busch – the makers of beers including Budweiser and Beck's – put up $1 million in prize money to whoever made it round the world first. (Not enough even to cover the cost of a balloon, but enough to make it a sporting challenge.) They also set a deadline: December 31, 1999.

Orbiter 2 needed a redesign. The kerosene tanks which had nearly poisoned Piccard and Verstraeten would go on the outside of the capsule this time. This would, though, expose the fuel to temperatures as low as minus 56 degrees C. Halfway through construction, a personnel issue led to a more dramatic alteration. Piccard was worried that Verstraeten was too occupied with his own balloon business in Belgium, was not devoting enough time to the Orbiter project and "that he would never learn the gondola's systems thoroughly enough". So Alan Noble, the mission's flight director, and Piccard took the radical step of adding a third pilot to the balloon – "a partner who would be fully competent to fly the balloon while I was asleep and a technician able to carry out repairs if things went wrong." Andy Elson became part of the flight team, and the gondola was altered to accommodate an extra crew member.

That only served to increase the pressure though. Elson was responsible for building the capsule, as well as flying it, but never wrote down any of the technical details for others to examine. "The rest of us accepted his shortcomings because we were afraid that if we put too much pressure on him, he would walk out for good. Eventually we saw it was too late to call his bluff: we should have stood up to him earlier," Piccard wrote afterwards. "The technology was completely new, and they both needed to sit down and learn it," Elson says today. "But it never quite happened." For his part, Elson found Piccard "a bit stressy... He's frantic." (Piccard says that if he was busy, it was "correcting all the mistakes Elson was putting in... he also did not understand that the project wasn't just about building a capsule; I was trying to get money, media attention, overflight permissions, and the rest.")

Elson grew frustrated with Verstraeten's lack of commitment in particular, eventually telling Piccard that if the Belgian flew, he would not. "I love Wim, but it's a very technical environment, flying around the world in a balloon, and very different from what he was used to," Elson remembers. "Because I was still indebted to Wim, I could not possible stand him down," Piccard wrote. "I told Andy that if I succeeded without Wim, I might well see my face in the newspapers but I would never again be able to look at myself in the mirror." But Elson forced Piccard at least to remove Verstraeten from actively flying the balloon; he would be relegated to navigation and communications. Verstraeten was clearly just a passenger, in an undertaking that had no room for one: the extra food, water, oxygen and equipment for one person added 400 kg to the total flight load. "It was a transition situation," Piccard remembers. He was not very fond of Elson, either: "not someone I wanted to fly with," he says. Elson wound up many on the Breitling team. "Andy is a difficult guy to work with. And he upsets people for a pastime," remembers Brian Jones, who had joined *Orbiter 2* as a safety adviser but ended up becoming Elson's "user-friendly interface" (he had known him for years before). At one point, Elson threw his Breitling watch across the room in a meeting with the sponsors, then walked out. Don Cameron marched after him, shouting that he had no honour. "There were huge rows," Jones says. "We were already a month or two late," Elson recalls. "We'd been working hard and didn't need the media distractions."

While the *Orbiter* team bickered and made last-minute changes, Branson prepared, determined to be the first to take off in winter 1997. He asked the other balloons to delay while he sought permission to cross Chinese airspace (the Chinese were notoriously prickly about this; securing flyover rights was as difficult as finding the right weather). Branson didn't go to China, though, and the next the *Orbiter* crew knew, he was inflating his balloon in Morocco, on December 9. But with too much haste: he inflated the balloon during the day, since his weather slot was fast closing. In the desert, this was dangerous, because of the warm winds. The envelope took off, but without the cabin attached, and flew off. Branson phoned the Moroccan Air Force, asking the officers to shoot down the balloon with "neat" bullet holes in the upper part, enough not to make "such a mess that we couldn't patch it up", according to the *New York Times*. The envelope eventually landed in Algeria, but was ruined.

In the dying hours of 1997, both American balloons made their ascents. First was Fossett, from Busch Stadium in St Louis. Four hours later, Uliassi took off, but not nearly so well as his compatriot; shortly after his ascent from Loves Park, a city in Illinois, the bottom of his envelope ruptured, forcing the balloon down a few hours after lift-off. Fossett didn't last too much longer; he nearly reached the Black Sea, landing in a field in Krasnodar in Russia, on January 5, four days and 12 hours after take-off. According to the *New York Times*, the owner of the field complained: "I do all this work to plow this field and now this American tramples all over it." The heaters in Fossett's cabin had failed and the control for a gas burner had broken, leaving him half-frozen and unable to continue.

Next, it was Piccard's turn. In January, a crane lifted the gondola onto the launch-field at Château-d'Oex, but the cables gave way. The 270 journalists and thousands of spectators watched as the capsule fell awkwardly back onto its trailer. Piccard may have been following the tradition established by his grandfather of carelessly dropping pressurised gondolas just before launch; Auguste had done the same with the F.N.R.S. The burners, load-frame and some of the pipes were bent. Take-off would be delayed for repairs.

In the meantime, the *Global Hilton* balloon launched, on January 9. Piccard would certainly be the last in the sky now. But two hours after launch, Rutan and his co-pilot Dave Melton parachuted out of the gondola and into a cactus-filled field. They had heard a "boom", Rutan reported after. Melton had looked at his captain and said: "We're in trouble." The inner-balloon had ripped. Both pilots landed safely, if cactus-prickled; the balloon drifted for another eight hours, eventually coming down over Texas. It crashed into a power line and the balloon exploded.

That meant that Piccard had the skies to himself, for the 14th attempt to circle the Earth. The *Breitling Orbiter 2* took off, apparently without a hitch, on January 28 – Auguste Piccard's birthday. There was another, less welcome parallel with Bertrand's grandfather. At 6,000 feet up, "we heard a hissing, whistling sound from the rear hatch. It was leaking. A combination of haste, bitter cold and exhaustion had led to the hatch being fitted incorrectly – and this meant that until we could get it properly sealed, we would have to fly low, missing the fastest winds." Auguste had plugged a similar hole with Vaseline and tow; Bertrand, Elson and Verstraeten tried with a plastic bag and silicon sealant, but without success. That night, racked with anxiety, Elson and Piccard slept only a few hours; Verstraeten managed 11. The second day, the crew discovered that two of the six fuel tanks had emptied, dumping a tonne of kerosene and a third of the entire fuel supply – "Where the hell it went, I still don't know," says Elson. They never discovered why and by this stage Piccard was "really fed up with kerosene leaks", but decided not to say anything to Elson. *Orbiter 2* flew low and slow for four days, over the Mediterranean then into Iraqi airspace, hampered by the leak until Elson went outside the gondola. Suspended from a rope below the capsule, 5,000 feet (1,524 m) above ground, he removed the rear hatch and replaced it, fixing the problem.

The *Orbiter 2* was on its way, but, because of the delay, had missed its winds. The only strong ones available were blowing across the middle of China, and the Chinese had still not granted any balloon permission to fly over the country. As the *Orbiter 2* closed on the border, its crew knew that just ahead of them was a jet stream whose 160 mph winds could take them across the Pacific to California in only four days. *Orbiter 2* had flown over Iran, Syria and even Iraq, which was facing down a build-up of Western military forces over weapons inspections, without problem, but until now the Chinese would not budge, even after a year of negotiations.

Permission was eventually granted: a high-ranking Chinese official, who was in Switzerland at the time of the flight, had grown embarrassed with continually seeing "China refuses permission" on TV and newspapers, so started faxing Beijing. But it was Chinese New Year, and that permission only came through once *Orbiter 2* was over Burma and already out of fuel. Had the balloon not lost a third of its fuel, perhaps it could have completed its route by skirting China. But the mission was now "doomed", according to Piccard. They pushed on, at a very low altitude to avoid being swept into China: "we wanted to acquit ourselves as well as we could." At 1,000 feet up, the crew climbed out to sit on top of the gondola, idling along at 20 miles per hour, able to listen to the faint shouts coming from below and even to smell the spices from cooking rising up to them. "This was emphatically *not* what we were meant to be doing: we were supposed to be flying fast and high, inside a pressurised cabin, in pursuit of our dream – and here we were, flying slow and low in the warm air, going nowhere." Piccard found it liberating, though; Elson wanted to land: "he had had enough of Breitling and its balloons. He had already found another sponsor for future projects," Piccard wrote, in the belief that James Manclark, a Scottish property investor, had agreed to fund a balloon for Elson's own circumnavigation attempt before *Orbiter 2* even took off (perhaps unfairly – Elson insists he had no firm plans at this point – "I really thought the *Orbiter 2* was going to make it. I wanted to land because I wasn't even thinking about minor records on the way, anything other than the ultimate goal. I had always said that when I thought the technology was there, I was going to find my own sponsor, from the beginning – the reason that Wim came to me was because he knew I was trying to go around the world.").

But, as lackadaisical as the progress of the *Orbiter* had been, a record was in sight: that of the *Voyager* plane. Rutan's flight had lasted nine days and one hour. By the time *Orbiter 2* landed in Burma, on February 7, it had established a new duration record, for any form of aircraft, unrefuelled and non-stop, of nine days and 18 hours. "It's the icing on the cake, but, unfortunately, we haven't got the cake," Piccard told the ground crew. "When I saw our immense balloon neatly parked in that bean field, I felt both relieved and sad. I wanted to laugh and cry at the same time."

Orbiter 2 had flown 5,266 miles, nearly 8,500 km. Far, but not nearly far enough.

The Third Watch

The flying season was over. No one told Steve Fossett that, though. On August 7, 1998, he took off in the *Solo Spirit* from Mendoza in Argentina, where it was still winter and still, he hoped, the right conditions for flying. It was the first around-the-world attempt from the Southern hemisphere and an audacious one: Fossett's route would be mostly over water; ditching would be much more dangerous. Ahead of launch, he told the press: "My track this time will be far from the world's main shipping lanes and an ocean landing would be a serious matter."

On the other hand, flying over international waters neatly avoided the problem of getting flyover permission from those countries ill-disposed to grant it. Fossett used the same unpressurised gondola as in his previous three attempts, but attached to a new, much larger Cameron balloon, which allowed him to carry more burner fuel.

Soon after lift-off, two of the balloon's four burners caught fire, searing Fossett's face. He fought the blaze and repaired one of the burners, then continued east. He soon became the first balloonist to cross the South Atlantic Ocean and headed past the southern tip of Africa. After 10 days of flight he was halfway around the world and approaching the west coast of Australia; beyond that, the daunting tracts of the Pacific. But the balloon was picking up the right winds thanks to a meteorological team at Washington University in St Louis that was hitting every cue.

On August 15, though, with *Solo Spirit* 500 miles east of Australia and a new distance record of 15,200 miles

(24,462 km) set, meteorologist Bob Rice warned Fossett that he was approaching strong thunderstorms, and that there was no chance of avoiding them. Five hours later, shortly after he entered the lightning zone at around midnight, Australian time, the envelope ruptured and the *Solo Spirit* started going down, at a rate of 2,500 feet (762 m) per minute. Fossett cut away propane tanks to try and slow his fall. He rode the burner full-blast, desperately trying to reheat the balloon that had been cooled in the hail; a fire broke out inside the capsule. Just as the balloon was about to crash, Fossett abandoned the controls and lay on his bunk to minimise the force of the impact. It hit the ocean, went underneath and started filling with water. The burning balloon envelope collapsed on top. Fossett took the life raft in one hand and the emergency beacon in the other, but instead of switching this on, hit the test button. It transmitted only three beeps.

Back at mission control in St Louis, all the ground staff saw was the emergency locator beacon being triggered. Fossett was extremely lucky: he had been directly underneath a satellite when he pressed the test button on his beacon. Rescue ships were dispatched to the source of the signal. There was no information on Fossett himself: mission director Alan Blount said "a lot depends on how fast he came down."

Eight hours later, a patrol aircraft spotted Fossett, inside a life raft on the shark-infested Coral Sea. The plane dropped another raft with emergency supplies and Fossett climbed aboard. He was eventually picked up by a 60-foot ketch, uninjured. "I thought it would kill me," he told an Australian television journalist. "I was very surprised." Asked if that was the end of his adventuring, Fosett said: "Oh, no."

Fossett's next flight would not be on his own. He joined

Richard Branson's team, replacing Alex Ritchie, who earlier that year had died of injuries sustained in a sky-diving accident. A new sponsor, ICO Global Communications, was also signed up. A new team, RE/MAX, entered the race, bringing a fresh angle: its balloon would aim to be the first to complete the navigation, at the same time as setting a new balloon altitude record of 130,000 feet (39,624 m) and carrying out scientific studies. Its pilot Dave Liniger, who had founded RE/MAX, a property company, was a part-time Nascar driver and the owner of a Nascar track and an Arabian horse-breeding stable. He would take off from Australia. Cable & Wireless were also funding a balloon for launch in Spain. Kevin Uliassi and Jacques Soukup were each preparing a balloon.

Up against this stronger competition, the *Orbiter 3* mission was in disarray. Elson left and Piccard sacked Verstraeten from the team. Piccard felt sorry for Verstraeten, "but clearly a good friendship – even an important one – was not a sufficient basis on which to fly around the world," he later wrote. Losing Elson was easier: during *Orbiter 2*, the Englishman had "become a competitor inside the team", according to Piccard, planning his own circumnavigation. When he left, Elson took a key flight engineer with him, "to cock a snook", according to Jones. "We were pretty peeved." The Manclark-funded balloon came to nothing, but Elson joined the Cable & Wireless team as pilot. He was glad to be in control of his own team, seeing himself as different from Fossett and Branson, "a bunch of upstart millionaires trying to buy their way into our sport". He had been flying balloons since the 1980s. His first love had been sailing, but when he discovered his wife was easily seasick, he instead took up sailing in the sky and went ballooning with her. He disdained the publicity those new to his sport were attracting. Piccard had little time for Elson's balloon snobbery: "I was not the most experienced balloonist. But I was the most organised."

The *Orbiter* needed another co-pilot. The team initially considered asking a celebrity: Jochen Mass's name came up. Someone suggested broadcaster Terry Wogan. "That's when it got silly and we decided against choosing someone famous," Jones says. And taking a celebrity could have hampered the flight: Jones had learned that Branson's ground crew were unwilling to take risks that would put the billionaire in danger. Instead, Piccard chose Tony Brown, a Concorde flight engineer in his fifties, an excellent balloonist and the bearer of a formidable moustache. Jones had known Brown for years and thought from the start that "he and Bertrand would have problems getting on with each other," as he later wrote in *Around the World in 20 Days*. Jones himself would be the back-up pilot in case of injury.

This time, preparations went according to plan. More improvements to the balloon had been made. The gondola was more or less the same; two double-glazed, 30 centimetre portholes were added, one on each side of the pilot's desk. There was a new burner system, because Piccard had made a promise never to use Elson's kerosene system again – *Orbiter 3* would run on propane. The size of the envelope was increased and its shape modified for better insulation, using computer models from the École Polytechnique Fédérale de Lausanne. The researchers said that it would help to keep the balloon cool during the day, saving fuel. This led to another design change: on top of the central gas part of the envelope, the Mylar was reinforced with a layer of high-density foam a few millimetres thick. This would help prevent the helium from heating up, expanding and leaking out during the day, as well as cooling and contracting too much at night. According to Don Cameron, it was the "most important improvement" and one which none of the other balloons had. In daytime, solar heat would still warm the inner cell, so Cameron attached small electric fans around the top of the hot-air cone. Each had a solar panel; when the sun was out, the fans would whir and suck out the warm air. The gas cell was made from nylon, coated with a laminated barrier to prevent helium escaping. Twenty people were involved in making the envelope, whose construction was very complex. "It was strange to reflect that *Orbiter 3* was the most sophisticated balloon ever built, yet it could never be fully tested on the ground," Jones wrote. "The envelope was so huge that it had to be made in pieces and, although Cameron ran computer simulations, until the whole contraption took to the sky nobody knew exactly how it would perform."

Jones, with a military background, took pilot preparation more seriously than any mission before. They had a lot of practice in the decompression chamber, sitting there while the oxygen was reduced. The goal was to spot the symptoms of hypoxia – blue lips and fingernails. Its other main sign is a deterioration in mental faculties. However, owing to this deterioration, it is very difficult to spot oneself. During the training, a doctor asked Brown to remove his mask and count backwards in sevens from 100. Brown was so focused on the task that he ignored the doctor telling him to replace his oxygen supply. For his part, a hypoxic Jones would start "giggling, as if slightly drunk"; Piccard went "quiet and confused, tending to look around with a vacant expression on his face". They dived in a pool equipped with a water cannon and wave machine, and practised removing parachute harnesses and climbing into rafts. At Bristol Airport, they mocked up a box as the *Orbiter* gondola, then a fire crew filled it with smoke while the pilots rescued a dummy – "an unnerving experience". Jones invited the pilots of the other balloon missions to share in the safety training; they all did, apart from Branson and Lindstrand. Such training was much more intense than on the previous *Orbiter* missions. But Piccard nonetheless maintained his psychiatric practice, continuing to see patients (to this day, he takes sessions with a couple of longtime patients, albeit intermittently).

On November 16, the gondola and envelope were loaded on to two lorries, which transported them from Bristol to Château d'Oex. *Breitling Orbiter 3* was ready to go by the start of December. War – in Iraq – and weather delayed the start. As did the pilots' deteriorating relationships.

Brown was worried at the rag-tag nature of the operation. "For my part, I found that he brought with him some fairly rigid ideas," Piccard wrote. Brown was "straight down the line – he wanted everything specified according to British Airways standards," Jones says. But *Breitling Orbiter 3* was a prototype balloon, and its builders were in a rush: "he couldn't cope with something as experimental as the *Breitling Orbiter*," Piccard says. Testing, proper procedures and paperwork were not in place, which Brown disliked. "He was also quite a short chap," Jones remembers. One day, Brown came in to look at the balloon. When he sat in the pilot seat, his feet didn't touch the ground. He demanded the technicians change the seat, and so much of the design of the capsule. Brown was concerned about the new fuel system, asking to see diagrams and schematics that simply didn't exist. "We told him just to use your hands and listen." Brown was adamant, but Piccard told him that if the weather was good next weekend, they would fly. According to Jones, "that was the beginning of the problem."

These last few days put on the most pressure. Brown, like Verstraeten, objected to Piccard playing the role of chief too much – "he thought that I wasn't giving him enough room, I was arrogant, and not taking care of him," Piccard wrote. Brown himself came "with his big shoes on", as Piccard puts it.

"I always noticed with the experiences of my father, quite often there was someone in the team who tried to take the power and kick him out," Piccard remembers. "For the PX-8 it almost worked, this engineer made a big story, my father got ejected and eventually won, but it was a difficult period. For Grunman [the *Ben Franklin* mission], there was also a guy speaking behind his back. My father was aware and solved the situation completely. In that case, it was quite clear that Tony was trying to take more power and be the little king in the team, when actually, he had nothing, he had come in when everything was ready."

The atmosphere was oppressive. Jones's wife Joanna wrote in her diary: "The pilots seem very aggressive. It affects everybody. Living in Château-d'Oex is not much fun any more. No one is clear what the problem is. It just becomes very tense." On November 23, it spilled over. Piccard had deliberately increased the pressure of training to take Brown to the limit, thinking that it was better he broke down on ground than in the sky. ("From his psychiatric training, [Piccard] could be fairly devious in his approach," Jones says.) Over dinner, they argued again, and Brown told Piccard: "You're a nasty man. I won't fly with you." Piccard said: "OK, let's ask Brian then." Piccard said he would sleep on it, but he had already made his decision. In the morning, he told Brown that he would not fly. Jones would take his place. Piccard thought Brown seem "relieved. The fact is, I coped better with the pressure than him."

Piccard immediately felt "a feeling of tremendous liberation". He and Jones got on much better. This may be because Jones brought no ego to the mission. "The flight was the biggest deal of my life," he remembers.

Jones was born in Bristol on March 27, 1947. His father was a lawyer, his Scottish mother a school secretary. Jones was a shy child and bullied at school, which led to him playing truant. Ashamed of his behaviour, he set out to walk to Scotland, aged thirteen. He was found in a barn north of Bristol seven hours later. He enjoyed the Boy Scouts and the Air Training Corps at school, but flunked his exams, passing only one O-level, in English. He left school at 16 and took a job as a clerk at British Aerospace, in the suburbs of Bristol. "Soon, however, I realised that was a dead end, and I applied to join the Royal Air Force." Jones had no chance of becoming a pilot with just one O-level to his name (five was the minimum requirement) and so he became an administrative apprentice. At the same time, he entered himself into the RAF Education Section – "the force's equivalent of night school". One year later, with four more O-Levels, Jones applied for pilot training - but was refused once more. Instead, he became a loadmaster on the huge Hercules C-130 transport planes. He flew missions around the world, including rescuing the British embassy staff from Phnom Penh in the Vietnam War, wearing a flak jacket. Twice, he flew around the world, taking 15 days to complete each circumnavigation, stopping off along the way.

Jones then moved to Puma helicopters, serving three tours in Northern Ireland, flying sorties "into the border areas known as bandit countries – so dangerous that everything and everybody had to be moved by air". The helicopters picked up prisoners, delivered food and dropped off Special Forces. On these missions Jones always carried a machine gun and pistol. "We never knew when the weapons might be needed."

Aged 30, Jones quit the RAF to set up a wholesale catering firm with his sister Pauline. The business, Crocks, led to Jones meeting his future wife Jo and grew to include two retail shops. But nine years later, in 1986, Jones embarked on his first hot-air balloon flight, at a festival in Bristol: entranced, he sold his shops and bought a balloon.

In 1989, recession hit, and Crocks could no longer support two people, so Jones signed it over to his sister. At the same time, the Civil Aviation Authority granted commercial licences. Jones started flying balloons commercially, then became a balloon examiner. In 1994, he set up High Profile Balloons with Andy Elson and Dave Seager-Thomas (who would be a technician on the *Orbiter* capsule), operating balloons for companies such as the Royal Mail and Mitsubishi. Elson invited Jones to take charge of planning the *Orbiter 2*.

The first time Jones met Piccard, the Englishman was "slightly in awe of this slender, intense-looking man, with his receding hair, high intelligent forehead and penetrating eyes, because it was he who had initiated the whole *Orbiter* project." Unlike previous co-pilots, Jones deferred absolutely to Piccard. "I was very much the second man, and always felt like the second man, even though I was the expert balloon pilot. I never pushed myself forward." Maybe for this reason, Piccard and Jones got on well. "I felt drawn to Brian and saw that, besides having a calm temperament, he was extremely efficient," Piccard said. The two had very different characters. Jones was the down-to-earth, self-effacing British pilot; Bertrand was "more Latin" according to Jones. "I'm very practical. I'm not the slightest bit spiritual. Whereas Bertrand is the other extreme." The one dispute between the men happened when Piccard invited a French psychic to Château-d'Oex to bless the *Orbiter*. Jones rolled his eyes, but acquiesced. The medium went inside the gondola, waved crystals around, then went on her way. On entering the gondola, Jones found she had left piles of salt – a corrosive – in various corners. Jones went "berserk" and shouted at Piccard, who apologised. It was the only time "that I got really angry with him," Jones says.

The atmosphere inside the *Orbiter* team had improved,

but it was only on December 9, 1998 that Piccard held a press conference to announce the pilot change. The last-minute switch didn't play well in the papers. Verstraeten went on record saying that Piccard could not sustain a friendship, was jealous of others' aviation achievements and could not tolerate criticism. Elson had his say too: he told reporters that Piccard's only goal was to become as famous as his father and grandfather, but that he was not in their league; he had no chance of completing the circum-navigation because *Orbiter 3* was not carrying enough fuel. For Piccard, it was a time of "high anxiety and tension". He could not stop thinking about the attempt; even mowing the lawn in Lausanne he felt guilty that he was not checking some detail of the capsule.

Worse, the other teams were ahead. On December 18, 1998, Branson, Lindstrand and Fossett lifted off from Marrakesh and quickly crossed the Algerian border. Branson told reporters that practically every country on the route – including China, on strict conditions – had given overflight permission: "We hope to arrive in Britain by New Year's Day." (Fossett was less gung-ho: "Of course I'm scared. My fall into the Coral Sea in August reminded me how dangerous this is.") Branson did have permission from "practically" all countries – just not the tricky ones. The balloon was forced to fly a narrow passage between thunderstorms in Southern Turkey and the no-go area of Iraq; Russia and Iran had also refused permission, meaning the *Global Challenger* had to thread its way around their borders. As the balloon approached China, it was well out of the agreed position – the Chinese had offered only two narrow flight corridors in the north and south of the country – but Branson took the gamble to press on. As *Global Challenger* approached the Himalayas, the Chinese rescinded permission. The balloon could not land over the

Himalayas or alter course. "We're in a real jam," Fossett told reporters via satellite phone. "We're already over the Himalayas and there's no place to land. We have to keep going into China, and once over Chinese territory they could order us to land, or might even shoot us down." The ground crew frantically petitioned Beijing and Tony Blair even appealed to the Chinese government for permission. Permission was reluctantly and lately given, provided the balloon did not stray north of the 26th parallel. Branson simply cruised right across the middle of the country. China announced it would ban all future flights over its airspace – an unbelievable blow to the hopes of the four balloon crews waiting to go. "Now it looked as though Branson had finished our chances," wrote Jones.

But the *Global Challenger* had made it, and continued quickly on, the inconvenience of a total ban for everyone else costing them only a day's worth of fuel. On December 24, they left China and struck out over the Pacific, hitting nearly 90 miles per hour, then 200 miles per hour (322 km/h) soon after.

Two days later, they ditched in the ocean, ten miles off the Hawaiian island of Oahu. Of the more than 20 attempts made in the previous 20 years, this was the most nearly successful, even if no distance or endurance records were set. The *Breitling* team, though, had known that Branson's flight was over 36 hours before he came down. Eckert and Trullemans had run the weather models and were certain a jet stream would take the *Global Challenger* to Hawaii. Had Branson descended, he would have picked up a slower wind, but one going in the right direction. Jet streams are not continuous: they branch, like rivers do. They form when air is boxed in, between a cold front, a warm front and the last layer before the stratosphere, called the tropopause. When there isn't much space for the air to move, it goes fast; when there's more space, it dissipates, slows down and breaks into different currents, idling in different directions. The key to balloon navigation is to understand the whole river system of jet-streams, not just its fastest flow – hence the importance of meteorologists. As *Global Challenger* came down in the water, the envelope and gondola failed to detach, dragging the cabin along the surface at 20 miles per hour. The crew escaped and were unharmed, but the balloon was lost.

Branson was out, but Elson was just starting. On February 17, while *Orbiter* waited for good weather and Chinese permission, *Cable & Wireless* took off from Almería, Spain. Before lift-off, Elson said that he and his co-pilot Colin Prescot, the founder of an aeronautical filming company, stood "an 80 per cent better chance of achieving [the circumnavigation] than any other teams so far". As he had preferred for the first two *Orbiter* flights, he was using kerosene to save weight, and a huge, million-cubic-foot balloon. This meant Elson could fly longer than a propane balloon and so employ a "low and slow" strategy – there was little point in going quickly in a race no one had ever completed, and besides, Elson's was now the only balloon in the air. The low and slow strategy also included avoiding China, which was still refusing overflight permission. The balloon flew serenely, although a heater inside it broke, so Elson and Prescot donned arctic survival gear. The balloon stood up to strong thunderstorms over Thailand, then weaved their way over Indochina, avoiding Chinese air space. Fifteen days after take-off, they were over the South China Sea and had set a new balloon endurance record, beating the one Elson and Piccard had established in the *Orbiter 2*. They were now halfway round the world, with the second-most difficult part of the race, avoiding China, behind them; the most dangerous part was now directly in front of them: crossing the Pacific. Slow and low was working.

Orbiter would have to rely on a different strategy: pure speed. They had won permission to cross China, but only the south, below the 26th parallel. But the weather still prevented a take-off. "With another capable crew on its way and reports of good progress coming back, time seemed to slow to a snail's pace: every day that passed reduced our hopes of catching up, until finally our chance of winning the race appeared to have gone." February was waning: "normally the end of the month marked the end of the season for round-the-world ballooning attempts because thereafter wind patterns were not usually so favourable," Piccard wrote. He took his family skiing and the launch team went their separate ways from Château-d'Oex; Jones started driving home. Stefano Albinati called Piccard from Breitling to schedule the press conference announcing the cancellation of the attempt. They arranged a date of March 8. Piccard said: "I was in despair."

But a few days later, Trullemans called. He told Piccard there was a promising weather slot on March 1; he and Eckert had spotted a depression forming over the west Mediterranean. The *Orbiter* would have to be clever and travel anti-clockwise around it, starting out in the wrong direction over France, Spain and Africa, then swinging east. The launch process advanced through alerts. The first warning to stand by went out four days ahead of launch. Three days before, the alert would be confirmed, and the eight-strong launch team would leave Bristol for Switzerland. Launch minus two days, the remainder of the staff would convene. "And so, on February 25, our first warning went out."

Jones and his wife had made it as far as Mâcon when Piccard called with the good news, but they kept going, in case it was a false alert. They made it back to England at midnight and at 10 am the next day were boarding the plane for Geneva, and were upgraded to business class. Back at the launch site, Alan Noble was sceptical. "He was convinced that Bertrand and I were not really trying to go around the world," Jones wrote. "Rather, he thought, we were desperate to get the balloon into the air, just to make a flight of some kind." Jones had his own doubts: "I didn't think we'd do it." Nobody had come close to a circum-navigation yet: Fossett's had set the distance record, but his heroic attempt had ended before he tried the Pacific, the most dangerous part of the voyage. Branson had flown for longer than anyone else, but, in the end, without any hope of completing the circuit. Could it even be done?

By February 28, the gondola was on the launch field. The envelope was laid out. A decision had to be made. "I was completely *tiraillé* – torn apart inside," Piccard wrote. "My longing to go was dragging me forward, but my fear of failure was pulling me back." It was the last opportunity to fly in 1999. If they let the launch window go, they could keep the balloon and try again. Trullemans and Eckert esti-mated the flight would take 16 days. Noble liked that: "If you say 16 days, I say yes for the take-off. Any more, and you might not have enough fuel for safety." They took a vote and each member of the team raised his hand. It was a go. Piccard thought: "OK, now I'm playing my last card."

As the envelope was inflated, the pilots took some last-minute supplies – fresh food: bread, cheese, margarine and fruit. No alcohol on board, but they took two small tins of truffled pâté. Piccard and Jones had supper at the Hôtel de Ville, "our last meal on earth – well, for some time at least. To put it like that sounds as if we were going to the guil-lotine – and that was almost how it felt," Jones wrote. "It was a strange time altogether."

Piccard spoke with Michèle. They both knew the dangers of the mission; Fossett's near-death and the other failed circumnavigation attempts since had only reinforced this. "But we never spoke of the dangers, only the adventures," Michèle says. She knew that Bertrand would not do anything that did not allow him to come back. "When I met Bertrand, he was flying," she told me. "We were very young and I would go with him. We didn't realise then – it was serious between us, but you don't have the same attitude as when you are married and when you have children. Then you think of so many things, of consequences." The Piccard children were more fearless than the parents: a few days before launch, their eldest daughter Estelle came home from school and asked why her schoolmates and teachers were asking her if she was afraid. Was it dangerous? Michèle said it was, but that normally her father could manage everything. Still, she decided to take the family to the mountains for the first week of the flight, "because there were too many things like that." There was never any question of not flying. "I just realised it was part of his life and something I really liked – it brought him consciousness, awareness. I don't want to say I'm a fatalist. But I am someone who is very confident in life. I just think Bertrand certainly has something to do on this planet. And I just think his way cannot be stopped like that." Michèle herself enjoyed the excitement of the mission and being part of it. Her support let Piccard fly: "She helps a lot."

That evening in the hotel, Michèle thought: "I have no right to tell him to stop. I wouldn't like to do it. I love Bertrand like that, it's part of him. So to stop him would be to remove part of him."

At 6 am, with the go signal given, and after a few hours' sleep, both pilots were driven in their people mover to the airfield, dressed in their navy blue fireproof flightsuits. It was below freezing and mist obscured the mountains and stars above. As they turned onto the main road, the balloon, 170 feet high, came into view. "The sight stopped us dead," Jones said. "In a blaze of arc lights the slender, towering envelope was gleaming brilliant silver against the black sky... Escaping helium eddied round it in white clouds, like dry ice. At its base the chunky horizontal cylinder of the gondola, painted fluorescent red, was partially hidden by the double row of titanium fuel tanks ranged along each side. Men were swarming around it, some holding ropes, others manipulating hoses. The size of it was awe-inspiring. The volume of the envelope was 18,405 cubic metres, and the whole assembly, including the gondola and fuel, weighed 9.3 tonnes. This was the majestic giant in which we were going to commit ourselves to the sky." Piccard turned to Jones: "Can you believe it! That's ours!"

They walked to the balloon and the crowd surrounding it. "I think we look quite professional," Bertrand said to Jones.

Helium, pumped out of a tanker truck at minus 200 degrees celsius, was flooding the envelope, whistling as it poured through the vaporisers. Inside the gondola, Kieran Sturrock, the team's electronics specialist and technician, was going through the checks. He found one fault: a small leak from a nitrogen cylinder which operated the valve used to jettison helium from the top of the envelope. He tightened the connection, but didn't fully close the seal.

The two pilots said goodbye to their families, then climbed inside and began their own preflight checks. The balloon strained and tugged. In the high wind, the gondola was knocked about: "the screeching creaking sounds were appalling," Jones wrote. "The onlookers thought the gondola itself was cracking and coming apart... If the balloon had split or been flown over, several of them might have been injured as the fabric collapsed on them. Any one of our thirty-two propane tanks could have ruptured and then exploded. If it had, there would have been an instant, devastating fireball." One of the gas tanks was shaken free and caught in a cable: it jerked out and smashed against the side of the gondola. The balloon was in danger of being ruined as it took off: damage sustained on the ground might mean an almost immediate descent. It was time to go.

Noble waited for the gondola to bounce up once again and at 9.09 am local time cut the rope with his Swiss Army knife. Sky News called the take-off "not so much a launch – more of an escape". Bertrand's daughter Solange was four at the time. "I have only one memory," she says today. "It was the balloon taking off, and me waving goodbye."

The *Orbiter 3* went up, fast. The pilots closed the hatch and sealed the cabin. On *Orbiter 2*, Piccard had heard the whistling that would doom the flight within 20 seconds. This time, there was nothing: "only beautiful silence," Jones wrote. "We looked at each other and grinned. The hatch was airtight. The balloon was climbing. We were on our way."

Piccard remembered the *Orbiter 2* flight, how it had taken off on his grandfather's birthday. "I had felt then that it was a sign of fate, that I was going to succeed. The intuition proved false."

Now, on his 41st birthday, Bertrand thought: "Maybe this is something I have to do myself, and not count on family fortune."

The Last Great Adventure

When balloons ascend too quickly, they explode. As the air became thinner and the sun warmed it, the helium in the gas cell at the top of the *Orbiter* was expanding. Piccard and Jones needed to vent the gas, but they were quickly running out of the nitrogen which powered the release valve. The same had happened to the *Global Hilton* balloon, which took off in January 1998, forcing its pilots to parachute out. It had also forced the *J-Renée* down in December 1997. More than 200 years before that, de Rozier had come up with the hybrid design Piccard was now using. His ascent had been too quick and the hydrogen had expanded. Because of a faulty valve, it could not immediately escape and the pressure built up. When de Rozier finally opened the valve, the sudden discharge of static created a spark which ignited the gas; the explosion killed him.

Now, though, Piccard economised with the nitrogen and gradually stabilised the balloon. They radioed Geneva: "Everything on board OK." The reply was quick: "Good morning, *Breitling Orbiter 3*. I read you loud and clear. Report flight level two two zero. Good luck."

The balloon approached the Matterhorn, where Piccard had performed his hang-gliding acrobatics a couple of decades before. The skies were clearing and the balloon flew south. Jones went to his bunk for a nap as Piccard manned the controls. "In complete silence I watched the mountains file past the portholes. I knew I was taking the biggest gamble of my life, but for the first time in months, maybe even years,

I was feeling fabulously well and confident. All our team had done their very best, and now, alone in the cockpit, I had no option but to trust the wind and the unknown."

The *Orbiter 3* was guzzling its propane; Piccard wrote in the logbook that they were having to burn fuel 60 per cent of the time. At that rate, the propane would run out in less than a week. The fuel gauges for the outside tanks were crude: a strain gauge measured the weight of each tank. But this varied according to outside temperature and pressure, so it was difficult to calculate exactly how much fuel was being used. "Everything had started so well," Piccard wrote, "and now this first night was turning into catastrophe."

The fax was broken too. On the ground, Kieran Sturrock, still in Château d'Oex, was furious at the Geneva mission control's delay and sent his own message: "What the fuck are you playing at in the Control Room? You are supposed to be responsible for the lives of two men in an experimental balloon, not running a social club." The pressure was getting to everyone. The problem was only an overload at the routing station, and was soon fixed.

Under a full moon, the balloon flew over the Balearic islands. The pilots relaxed more and made themselves at home in the gondola. This resembled a giant stubbed cigar: it was 4.8 m (16 ft) long, and had a two-metre diameter. At the front was the cockpit, with two racing-car seats facing a transparent desk, which afforded a view through the forward porthole below. Each pilot had his own porthole directly in front too, with the instrument panel spanning the width above. The most watched instrument was the GPS, which displayed the position of the balloon. There were VHF and HF radios, for short- and long-range communication, a satellite telephone and two fax machines, operated by laptop computers. Three altimeters were the pilots' most important navigation tool, and a variometer gave the rate of climb. A sealed barograph took the balloon's altitude every few seconds; this had been installed and sealed by an FAI observer.

The kitchen area was directly behind the right-hand seat – only two square feet, with a sink, two small kettles and a water heater mounted above. It took half an hour to heat, then the pilots would put in their bagged, pre-cooked meals to cook. Behind that were the bunks. One was reserved for sleeping, with a rubber mattress and safety harness. This was a safety measure installed after Steve Fossett's dive into the Pacific. The other bunk was covered in survival equipment – life rafts, immersion suits and parachutes – all laid out ready for use at a moment. The corridor rang along the centre of the gondola, back to a small lavatory next to the stainless steel cylinders of liquid oxygen and nitrogen. The life-support system drew oxygen from the tanks, passing it around the gondola, and lithium hydroxide filters, known as scrubbers, absorbed the carbon monoxide produced by the pilots – the same system, in principle, as Auguste Piccard had used 70 years before. (Jones took much delight in pointing out to Piccard that scrubber was English slang for prostitute.) Another breathing system provided 100 per cent oxygen, delivered through masks connected to the flying helmets, in case cabin pressure failed. And each parachute had an oxygen supply too. The nitrogen was on hand to repressurise the cabin if necessary. Warning lights would flash if the pressure in the gondola grew either dangerously low or high. The *Orbiter 3* trailed a line of 20 solar panels below the cabin to power the electrics. It was more than cosy, but big enough for the two men. As Jones put it: "In such cramped quarters there was almost no possibility of getting physical exercise – but the view from the toilet was spectacular."

Breitling Orbiter 3 had filed a flight plan, as all aircraft must. "Ours was extremely unusual in that we did not know exactly where we would be going." Instead, they gave a rough outline: "Château-d'Oex, Switzerland - crossing the Alps - Nice - the Balearic Islands - Morocco - Mauritania - Mali - Niger - Chad - Sudan - Saudi Arabia - Oman - India - Burma - South of China - Pacific Ocean - California - Crossing USA - Crossing Atlantic Ocean - Canaries - intended landing in North Africa east of 10 degree lat." In the box for "estimated duration of flight", they had entered: "20 days".

Life on board was comfortable. The balloon itself flew very quietly. Apart from the hum of a couple of fans, it was peaceful inside; turbulence was not a problem, as *Orbiter 3* didn't cut through swathes of air at different pressures, but flew with the wind. Inside, it didn't seem to move. Jones slept naked, Piccard wore pyjamas and slept with a special pillow which he had taken from the Town & Country Hotel in Bristol. "In our domestic habits, we were very gentlemanly: whenever I got up, I would clear the bed and leave it ready for Bertrand, and he did the same for me. On one occasion he even left a chocolate on my pillow." The pilots slept at different times – Jones from 2 am until the middle of the day, Piccard the first part of the night. When Jones woke Piccard, he would do so with a cup of tea. They spent the afternoons together and watched the sunset. They ate whenever they felt like it, but were more sparing with lavatory breaks: they would only use the lavatory for "a major call of nature", as it sacrificed some of the cabin air pressure (Jones nearly blocked it on his first attempt), and employed red plastic bottles the rest of the time. Jones started taking a clinical interest in these, telling Piccard when his urine was too dark. "He was delighted I was looking out for him so well." They each took a book – Bertrand an account of his grandfather with the title *Auguste Piccard: Professeur de Rêve* – which neither had time to open, along with a talisman text – a copy of *Une Vie*, which its author Guy de Maupassant had given to Jules Verne. Jean-Jules Verne, the author's great-grandson, had lent it for the flight. It was a high accolade: Verne had dismissed Branson, telling *Le Figaro*: "What they are doing is closer to a millionaire's whim than a genuine scientific inquiry." Verne thought that only the *Breitling* team shared the true love of adventure that characterised his great grandfather; he saw "that we were neither money-grubbers nor record-hunters." They played music: Piccard liked a French new age group called Era, "who play a mythical kind of music – half religious, half mysterious." One can imagine Jones's sighs. Piccard, having more truck with modern music than his father did in the *Ben Franklin*, also listened to Elton John and the Eagles.

A pleasant enough way to pass one's time, but there was also a race on. On day two of the flight, *Orbiter 3* was still dawdling above Spain, where Elson had taken off 12 days before. On the ground, Trullemans and Eckert were studying Elson's route intensely. Their predictions were accurate, even as Elson was thousands of miles ahead, in India. "It did not help to know that Andy's balloon was so far ahead – but it seemed to us that he was advancing even more slowly than we were," Jones wrote. There was little they could do, though, but follow the met instructions from the ground.

The two were in constant contact with the ground and their families. Piccard, always more emotional than Jones, sometimes found these exchanges hard to bear. One fax from Michèle "went like an arrow to the heart". At home, she was plotting the *Orbiter*'s course on a large map with pins, exactly as Piccard's mother had done with Jacques as he made his way in the Gulf Stream. Jacques himself was broadcasting updates of the *Orbiter*'s progress every day on Swiss radio. He messaged the *Orbiter* itself in typically paternal fashion: "Boys, remember to exercise," he wrote in one dispatch. "Jacques was probably living again his own adventures, through Bertrand," Thierry Piccard says. "And I think that Bertrand was extremely happy at that moment to be able to give Jacques this opportunity. At no moment was my father ever jealous to see Bertrand succeeding, not at all. They were both extremely close in both directions."

Over the Sahara, the pilots stretched their legs. Piccard and Jones had to jettison four tanks of propane: Piccard had added these to the exterior of the gondola, after calculating that the original Cameron design did not allow for sufficient fuel. There was no automatic release system for these additional tanks, so they would have to cut them free themselves. They took the balloon down to 10,000 feet, then opened the hatch and went out, without any harness. Outside, they discovered that ice had covered the burner and was hampering ignition. Piccard attacked the icicles, feeling "like a boy again, smashing the icicles around the eaves of the family chalet". Then, his parents had said it was a shame to break such beautiful objects, but now Piccard flew at them. Jones hung over the edge, Piccard holding his ankle, and cut the white nylon to free the tanks, which tumbled into the empty desert below. They thought about cutting away the remaining pipework to save weight, but thought the gear looked too expensive, so kept them on board. It would prove a useful decision.

The *Orbiter* was receiving constant updates on the *Cable & Wireless* balloon's progress; "Latest news on Andy: flight time 15 days 22hrs 44 minutes so far. Alt. 18,000 feet, 19.06N 112.12, east of Hainan, over South China Sea." But finally Piccard and Jones could start heading east. They made their way towards Libya and Egypt, and over

Sudan, where they received a message.

> Hello brian and bertie
> Congratulations on joining us in the air, We heard your inflation was a bit iffy? What do you expect if I'm not there?
> Now we hear you are having trouble with the ice. What's the problem not enough gin
> So you've decided to follow us and be second well done, lets all have a party at the end? I think cameron's should pay they have made most money from these adventures.
> Sorry you missed your jet stream to Iraq. What will you do now? We anticipate our flight lasting 26 to 28 days depending on how long we have to wait for the pacific and Atlantic weather systems. Currently waiting at Taiwan for 48 hours for the pacific route to open for us.
> Very best wishes from both of us for a safe and enjoyable flight.
> Colin and Andy
> Sorry lost your number then been too knackered swimming the formosa straight towing a balloon is bloody hard nothing like training at Swindon pool loads of hugs andy.

Elson's tone was confident, but Jones saw an opportunity. "That message made my spine tingle. Andy was stuck over Taiwan, forced to loiter for a couple of days for fear that the wind would sweep him south and dump him near Hawaii, as it had dumped Branson. In a couple of days we should reach China, and we might not be all that far behind. We were catching up fast..."

Orbiter 3 left Sudan, approaching either Saudi Arabia

or Yemen. The latter could be a problem. The ground crew at Geneva were improvising flight clearances as they came: although they had permissions, they still had to announce themselves as they approached each country's airspace, often only just in time. Not doing so could be dangerous: in 1995, the organisers of the Gordon Bennett race had over-flight permission for Belarus. But civil aviation had failed to informed the military, which put a helicopter in the air, forcing one balloon to land and shooting down another, killing both its pilots.

Yemen had never been part of the original flight plan, and so *Orbiter* did not have clearance. And they were heading straight for a prohibited military zone, over which, according to the aeronautical charts, intruders would be fired upon without warning. Piccard was blasé about the danger: he was "fairly cynical about the locals' ability to take out high-flying aircraft, reckoning that their heaviest armament would be a few shotguns normally used for riot control," according to Jones. The ground crew made calls and made contact, but never got the OK. The *Orbiter* diverted north, still passing over the no-fly zone. While the *Orbiter* was changing tack, losing time over Yemen, the *Cable & Wireless* balloon was south of Osaka and preparing to cross the Pacific. The pilots never made contact with Yemeni ground control, but the transponder flashed orange, a sign that "we were being interrogated as we went over." At 2.30 am, with the danger past, Jones woke Piccard and went to bed himself. The *Orbiter* was four days behind *Cable & Wireless*.

On March 7, at 4.30 am GMT time, Jo Jones, Brian's wife, sent a fax to Piccard, who was at the controls:

I've just had a telephone call from Alan, who has

been contacted by the Cable & Wireless Control Room to say that their balloon is landing 70 miles off the coast of Japan. The reason given is that the balloon is "iced up". They plan to land in the sea, and search-and-rescue are with them now. We are checking the website and watching CNN on television, but as yet we have no further information. Will keep you posted.

Elson's balloon had flown into snowstorms. It climbed through the thunderclouds until it was spat out of the top, taking damage. Flying through another storm would now be impossible. They had also damaged their satellite phone. Elson finally fixed it, then spent the night transferring images and flight data back to England – draining the batteries in the expectation that they would climb into the sun and recharge them the next day. Unlike Piccard and Jones, Elson and Prescot had not taken back-up batteries (there was a reason the balloon was nicknamed Able & Careless). Over the sea of Japan, Elson had a choice: go up to recharge, but be taken on a perilous heading, towards Hawaii and its thunderstorms, or fly three days staying under the clouds, over the Pacific. "The balloon just died and he was forced to ditch," Piccard wrote. Elson maintains that he could have flown without power, but he needed electricity to communicate and get weather information. Three days flying blind, underneath the clouds through complex weather systems across the Pacific made for an easy choice. There was another factor: "Bertrand didn't have enough fuel to get around, so we said we might as well ditch and do it the next year. And... the buggers!" Elson took the balloon safely down. Had he known how competitive the *Orbiter 3* was, his decision would have been different. "Yeah, we would have gone for it," he later told me. "Under the clouds."

Piccard "could hardly believe it" and thought: "If we do get round, we're not going to be second." But if Elson had been forced to ditch, maybe so too would the *Orbiter*. Piccard faxed control: "This is unbelievable news. I take no pleasure out of it, as it must be very frustrating for them. But of course it gives us more chance to be the first around. It also brings fear that the same problem could happen to us."

The race was over, but the task ahead of *Orbiter 3* remained immense. Another flight-endurance record had, yet again, been broken, but Elson hadn't even attempted the Pacific. *Orbiter* kept on, over India then Burma, where *Orbiter 2* had come down. Jones radioed air traffic control for clearance. "They had trouble grasping the idea of a round-the-world flight, and we had a splendid exchange:

Air traffic control: Hotel Bravo – Bravo Romeo
Alpha, what is your departure point and destination?

Myself: Departure point, Château d'Oex,
Switzerland. Destination, somewhere in Northern
Africa.

Air traffic control, after several seconds' silence: If
you're going from Switzerland to northern Africa,
what in *hell* are you doing in Burma?"

The balloon did 90 mph (145 km/h) across Burma, straight on to China. "The Chinese had seen us coming and their first reaction was entirely characteristic. They called Control and said: 'Your balloon's heading for the prohibited zone. It must land.'" Eckert and Trullemans reassured the Chinese air traffic control that this would not be the case. Jones and Piccard flew on, keeping to half a degree – thirty miles – of the agreed limit. *Orbiter 3* sailed the 1,500 miles across China, always within its corridor. In the end, thanks to skilful piloting, "China was a bit of a non-event," Jones said. Up next was the Pacific – a stretch of water wider than the route the *Orbiter 3* had already traced. It was "a point of no-return", Jones wrote.

Before take-off, Jones and Piccard had discussed the dangers of the flight: "We agreed that there were only two areas of the world that would probably kill us, where the chance of survival was negligible," Jones remembers. The first was the Tibetan plateau, too high to survive without acclimatisation: altitude sickness there could lead to fluid in the lungs and swelling of the brain; both often proved fatal. The second was the Pacific. The balloons that had so far ditched in that ocean had done so relatively close to shore. There were precedents from sailing, though, that showed the dangers of the the remote waters. Two years before, Tony Bullimore, a British sailor, had capsized during the Vendée Globe, a single-handed around-the-world race, 1,000 miles south-west of Australia. He was assumed drowned, until his upturned yacht was spotted by an Australian navy ship five days later and he was rescued, barely alive. Another competitor, Gerry Roufs, disappeared in the South Pacific, west of Chile; pieces of his boat were found on the shore of Chile five months later; his body was never recovered.

Midway over the Pacific, the *Orbiter 3* would be 4,000 miles (6,400 km) from anywhere. The chances of being rescued would be as good as zero. And although the gondola floated well, it would probably turn over thanks to its weighting. Escape would be difficult: "our only chance would be to pile all loose equipment at the front and hope that the gondola would tilt nose-down at a steep enough angle to bring the rear hatch clear of the water," Jones calculated. "Even then, we might easily drown trying to escape: with a hatch open, the gondola could fill with water and sink, taking us to the bottom with it. If we had to parachute from a height – forget it."

Piccard was frightened: "really scared", although he didn't say anything to Jones. Problems with the burner also developed; the electrically operated valve jammed open, sending long flames into the hot-air cone which threatened to burn a hole in the envelope. Piccard and Jones switched them off and switched to the three burners on the other side of the balloon. There was now no backup. "The possibility of total burner failure was infinitely more alarming than when we had been over land," Piccard wrote. He resorted to self-hypnosis to get to sleep.

The valves remained a worry, but the *Orbiter* started out over the blue. On March 13, the 13th day of the flight, the balloon passed over the Marianas Trench. For Piccard, it was a "big moment". Bertrand had been too young to see the *Trieste* make its remarkable dive. But he "had read newspaper articles describing how keen the competition to reach the deepest part of the ocean was, and I was very proud that my father had won the race. Now, overflying the Marianas Trench, I was taking part in another international contest of the same kind, against very rich and well equipped competitors. Could I add one more victory to my family's tally? At some moments I was confident it would be my fate to succeed, but at others I began to think it impossible that my generation could continue the success story. As in the preparation of the project and the flight, I was oscillating between hope and anxiety. To have lived in that state for five years had been a most exhausting experience – but at least I was now close to the moment of truth."

The plan had been to keep to the north, then fly across the USA. But the meteorologists announced a drastic revision: Trullemans and Eckert wanted to send the *Orbiter* south, to pick up a jet stream which would start to build off Hawaii in a few days' time: "the jet stream they were talking about existed only on their computer models, three days in the future." They had rerun their calculations. If the balloon headed north, the balloon would fly faster over a shorter course. But the bad weather behind the balloon would catch it and perhaps bring the *Orbiter* down in thunderstorms. Heading south meant keeping low and slow, and adding 2,000-odd miles to the journey. This was what Branson had done: started on a northern route, then diverted south, and it hadn't ended well for the billionaire. Piccard and Jones distrusted their weather men's judgment. Piccard told Jones he was "a little afraid". "Thank God! I've been wanting to tell you – I'm shit-scared too!" They decided to follow Trulleman and Eckert's advice.

On March 10, *Orbiter 3* lost contact with the control centre at Geneva. The balloon was directly under their Pacific satellite; the envelope was blocking the antennae in the gondola below. Other, small problems were increasing the pressure: the pilots were struggling to stay above the clouds, which were unusually high. Flying high meant flying cold. At night, the cabin was only a degree above freezing. The pair were constantly de-icing equipment and the burners were still broken: "I was scared that all the burners would soon be out of action and that our flight would come to an abrupt end," Jones wrote. Tanks 11 and 12 of propane ran out after only a day of use, because of their constant burning to stay high. Huge cumulonimbus clouds towered around the balloon, "any of which might contain wind-shear and hail violent enough to destroy our envelope by ripping it to shreds. It was vast clouds of exactly this kind – bigger than any that form over land – that had nearly killed Steve Fossett the previous summer." At sunset, Piccard and Jones looked out of the portholes at the dark storm clouds ahead. At night, they would dim the cabin lights, scrape the windows of ice and look for the stars. If they couldn't see them, they were in cloud and in trouble. "I thought that we were probably going to die in the next 24 hours," Jones said. "I really did think that."

Two days later, contact was re-established. Noble instructed the pilots to do an EVA to shed excess weight. For the first time in ten days, they felt fresh air and spent six hours outside. They threw overboard anything no longer needed – food, scrubbers and rubbish, a total of 128 kilograms. They fixed a leaking tank using the hoses they had decided not to jettison during the first EVA. The balloon was heading south-east at its highest altitude so far – 30,500 feet (9,296 m). Piccard and Jones received a message from Steve Fossett: "Dear Bertrand and Brian, Your flight is truly impressive. Your patience with the launch and slow trajectory are paying off. I hope you will enjoy a safe flight to Mexico." They had no plans to stop in Mexico, but the balloon was progressing leisurely, at 40 mph – with a lot of sea to cover. Other messages came through; Neil Armstrong wished them luck and so did Richard Branson, who wrote: "It really does look like you could do it this time... Have a safe and very uneventful journey across the Atlantic." Piccard thought of Peter Bird, who had twice tried to row the Pacific by himself. He had succeeded on the third attempt, taking four months. When he tried again, in the opposite direction, he disappeared. Piccard had received an award set up in Bird's honour, and was "really impressed by the knowledge that at some point we would cross Peter's track". Piccard also received a message addressed to him, from a Devon-based astrologer: she told him that the relevant planets for March 1 (when *Orbiter* had launched) aligned with his own birth charts and, what's more, the chart of the first-ever manned balloon flight, in 1783. As the *Orbiter* passed the 20,000-kilometre mark (12,427 miles), Piccard was delighted. He handed over to Brian, went to sleep and dreamt that he was flying in a commercial airplane which crashed in the ocean.

At 2 am GMT on March 15, Orbiter was flying at 80 miles per hour and increasing its speed. "We were finally entering the jet stream, and all around us were gorgeous colours." Pinked cirrus clouds had replaced the cumulo-nimbus towers. Now, the worry was fuel: "Every push of propane is something we're losing forever," Piccard wrote in his journal. They had 12 tanks left to cover the remaining thousands of miles. By the end of the day, they were heading for Mexico – exactly the track Trullemans and Eckert had predicted. Trullemans advised Piccard to move one degree south, into the centre of the jet stream to pick up more speed. "None of us could know it at the time, but that was the only mistake Luc or Pierre ever made, and it was the beginning of our worst problem."

That night, *Orbiter 3* broke the distance record of 14,236 miles that Fossett had set before crashing into the Coral Sea and Piccard had a strange dream, where he and Brian had gone around the world, but could not tell anyone of their accomplishment. There were 8,000 miles to go. But the *Orbiter* was inching too far south; Trullemans and Eckert told them to adjust four degrees north. On March 17, *Orbiter* overflew the coast of Mexico. The Pacific was done with, but it had cost a lot of fuel – maybe too much. They had been flying high, causing the balloon to vent helium, in the process reducing its lift and requiring more propane to be burnt. Noble told them to come down to 33,000 feet (10,058 m):

> It is VITAL that you do not push the ceiling. You need to squeeze every last gasp of propane from each tank,

and monitor fuel use constantly. Our programme still says you can complete the circumnavigation with a little to spare, but we need good wind speeds and no further increase in fuel consumption.

The *Orbiter*'s speed dropped dramatically and its course veered horribly away from the best heading: the balloon was making its way not to Africa, but Venezuela, "and final disaster threatened," Piccard wrote. He phoned and asked for advice. "For some reason I couldn't explain, I was completely out of breath, panting even when I made no physical effort." Jones was the same. Piccard gave an interview to Swiss radio. "When they heard me gasping and hardly able to talk, everyone on the ground became extremely anxious and started to call doctors and specialists for advice. It was all too easy for them to visualise horrific scenarios: the two pilots falling unconscious and silent as the balloon drifted away southwards, out of control, to vanish forever in the wastes of the ocean." The pilots weren't hypoxic, nor were they suffering from carbon dioxide poisoning. All the cabin monitors showed normal. "We were suffocating," Piccard told me. They donned oxygen masks and continued. Doctors on the ground thought the problem could be pulmonary oedema – a build-up of fluid in the lungs – or exposure to styrene, the glue used in the shell of the gondola. The oxygen made them feel better in any case, but the balloon was still on the wrong tack. Eckert told Piccard, at the controls, to take the balloon as high as possible. "Go to the extreme limit. I think you'll find the wind a little more to the left, and you'll escape Venezuela. As high as you can – that's the last chance of saving the flight."

As he took the balloon up, Piccard knew he was trying the last possible action. He saw his dream dying in the South

Atlantic. He took note as *Orbiter* penetrated different layers, always watching the wind, while he called Michèle. Speaking to her made him feel better, but Piccard told her: "The wind is going to the right. We're not going to make it."

With only 660 feet before the balloon reached its maximum altitude, the GPS showed a degree to the north. Piccard couldn't believe it: "If it continues like this, we're safe!" It was two degrees, then three, and eventually 15 degrees and "we're back on track! That's absolutely amazing!"

Orbiter 3 was on course and the jet stream ahead stretched out over the entire Atlantic. Piccard and Jones felt their luck had turned; the cold, asphyxiating misery of the Pacific and Mexico was behind them now. They received another message, from Jacques Piccard:

> My dear Bertrand and Brian,
> You have victory in your grasp. You are tired, stressed out, impatient to reach the end. Who wouldn't be in these conditions? The whole world is backing you with every possible kind of support.
> While remaining prudent, in the midst of your success, have the courage to help all those who are helping you here with all their strength, with all their heart, and with all their might. If you take into account the years you have devoted to this project, you only have to accomplish a thousandth of what you have achieved already.
> Less than three days to go before you arrive at your meridian – with a wind that's going to keep accelerating all the way.
> Courage. Everyone loves you and embraces you.
> Papa, Wednesday evening, 17 March.

PS. Maybe a little physical exercise would do you good? (I'm judging from afar.) What about a descent to 2,500 metres and a good airing for a few hours with the hatch open, before the Atlantic crossing? (Again, I'm speaking from a distance!) Forgive me for offering advice. It's just to tell you how much everyone is thinking of you.

As a scientist and explorer, Jacques had never been afraid for himself. His letters back home had been long on factual description and short on feeling. But as a father, he was scared for and protective of his children. "When my father was doing his adventures or explorations, his accounts were very scientific," Bertrand says. "And when I began doing my explorations, then he was not a scientist, he was a father and he was writing very, very tender words and messages."

Now, there was one more decision to make. The balloon had only four fuel tanks left, from the original 32: a quarter of the world to fly around, on an eighth of the fuel. *Orbiter 3* could land safely over Puerto Rico, or risk the Atlantic. Go or no-go. Noble asked Piccard and Jones for their decision, saying: "I think you can go for it." Jones said: "Bertrand! Tell him we're going anyway." Piccard replied to Noble by quoting Dick Rutan, the pilot of *Voyager*: 'The only way to fail is to quit' – and we're not going to quit. Even if we have to ditch in mid-Atlantic, we go for it."

The risk was a calculated one. Ditching in the rolling waves of the Atlantic would be risky, but nothing like as dangerous as coming down in the Pacific: they were sure they would at least make it three-quarters of the way across, within range of rescue helicopters. As Jones cheerily put it: "If we ditched, the chances of dying were quite small."

The flight was fast and smooth. "We went out over the Atlantic like a rocket," Piccard wrote. "I'm really starting to think we're going to do it, but I'm not allowing myself to believe it. And I think that even if we do succeed, I still won't be able to believe we've done it." They raced on to Africa in the dark. They were on tank pair number five, which was showing 55 kg. Five had long been Piccard's favourite number; five in his family, before his mother's death, and he says that fives had always appeared at important moments in his life. Now, he noted in his journal: "Such coincidences cannot happen by chance. Once again I really have the impression we're being guided."

At 5.56 am on March 19, *Orbiter 3* reached the coast of Africa. There was no way of telling, apart from the GPS: no lights below. At 6.15, the sun came up and Piccard looked out on the desert he had last seen 20 days ago. The finishing line was 9 degrees 27 minutes West; they would cross it at 10.30, according to Control's estimation. As Piccard and Jones approached the end, their telephone went dead, the antenna frozen. They crossed the line without realising, noticing only afterwards on their GPS that they had completed the first circumnavigation of the Earth by balloon. Jones and Piccard stood up, hugged and shouted ecstatically. They had done it.

In mission control, champagne was popped, cheers went up and tears came down the ground crew's faces. One person who did not indulge in the shared, joyful release was Jacques Piccard, who sat quiet in the control room unable to relax. He kept his emotions in check and telephoned his son, his voice measured and low. "Bertrand, it's fabulous, what you've done. But you still have to land, and I want to remind you of something very important. Probably, you've thought of this, but in case you haven't, when you land, *you must bend your knees*."

"As a teenager, it had sometimes annoyed me to be treated as a little boy, but now I knew how important it was for my father to give any advice that would help keep me safe," Bertrand wrote. "It was also a way for him to cope with his emotions. I myself find it so much easier, so much more natural, to let feeling show, to let it out. But that is not my father's style. He had broadcast live on Swiss radio every day and made frequent visits to the control centre, but although he had been terribly afraid for us all through the flight, all he did was to reassure others, saying there was nothing to worry about. For three weeks he slept badly and probably suffered more stress than Brian or me." When they were later reunited, Jacques told Bertrand that he would himself not have gone on so many of his expeditions, had he known how hard it was for those left behind.

But for now, the balloon was still flying on in blissful anticlimax. Piccard and Jones retrieved their truffle pâté, which they had saved the whole flight. To open it, Piccard used the Swiss Army knife that every Piccard always kept in a pocket, whether to the stratosphere or the bottom of the ocean. They started a descent towards Egypt, which took the whole day, and set another record: in the history of aviation, no one had flown longer or further without refuelling.

On March 21, the balloon came down as it crossed the border from Libya to Egypt. Jones started the descent, venting helium. Piccard stowed all the free equipment. They came down fast, and they both bent their knees. They smashed onto the ground and bounced straight up again. Ten minutes later, they tried once more, this time with barely an impact. The cabin skidded along the earth and came to a stop. "For a moment we looked at each other, speechless with the realisation that we were safe. The flight was over, and we were surrounded by utter silence."

Piccard scrambled out of the rear hatch to film the envelope as it deflated and collapsed. He was overcome, finally exhausted. He left a camera outside and re-entered the cabin, then emerged again with Jones for the benefit of posterity. "We stood there, alone in the silent desert." Piccard's dream had come true: they had made the circumnavigation, but there was no one around to tell. Piccard phoned his wife in Cairo: "Can you imagine, *Chérie* – we made it!"

"These were the words I had dreamt of saying for five years, and I am sure the power of the moment will stay in my mind and my heart for all my life." In the tanks, there was only enough fuel for another two hours' flight. Piccard sat and turned his face to the warm desert breeze. The wind had carried him around the world and now he felt it fill his whole body.

*

In Cairo, Jones and Piccard were reunited with the world. Piccard's three children ran into his arms. He kissed Michèle. Once back in Geneva, his father hugged him. "My father came to greet us, just like my mother and I used to do when he came back from an expedition," Piccard later said. "Only in the meantime, I had become a father and he was a grandfather. When I shook my bunch of flowers under the ovation of thousands of people crammed on the runway at the airport, I had a thought for my father and grandfather. They had broken all vertical records, upwards and downwards. As if to form a cross, I had added the horizontal record of the longest flight in history. The circle had gone round but it was still the same circle. I wondered what my father, in his eighties, felt about the circle having turned so much. I sincerely hoped that he perceived the centre as I did."

Jacques did. At a later ceremony, at the National Geographic Society in Washington.

Jacques made a short speech. "I have always been proud to be the son of my father," he said. "Now I am proud to be the father of my son."

A Greater Adventure

Before dawn, in the cold air of a clear spring sky in March 2012, Bertrand Piccard steps onto the runway of an airfield in Payerne, a 40-minute drive from Lausanne. Wearing a dark blue flight suit, and carrying his helmet, he climbs a short stepladder into the cockpit of an extraordinary prototype airplane, one that he has been building with his partner André Borschberg for nearly a decade. The wings of the *Solar Impulse HB-SIA* arch more than 63 metres – the same as an Airbus A340 – but the plane weighs only 1,600 kilograms – less than half a Range Rover. Exactly 11,628 photovoltaic cells cover the wings and power four ten-horse-power propeller engines, which now start spinning with an electric whirr. The ground crew remove the wheeled struts that support the frail-looking wings as the *Solar Impulse* begins taxiing forwards, slowly and quietly, drowned out by the engines of the support cars following. As the plane hits 22 miles per hour (30 km/h), it noses up and takes off, sailing into the sky. With air beneath them, the spindling wings now look sturdy; the fuselage that on the ground seemed flimsy becomes elegant, and the *Solar Impulse* looks alive, like a crane vaunting in its flight. It seems not to fly, though, so much as float.

Piccard spends the day arcing the solar-powered plane around the Matterhorn, and lands shortly before sunset. But the *Solar Impulse* is a plane that would fly for ever.

*

"If *Solar Impulse* succeeds, it will be about the same level as my father and grandfather," Piccard says. "The balloon flight around the world is not at the level of going to the Mariana trench, or being the first in the stratosphere. *Breitling Orbiter* was a personal dream – it didn't change the world. *Solar Impulse* is clearly a big thing."

As remarkable as the *Orbiter 3* flight was, it was also anachronistic. The first non-stop aerial circumnavigation of the Earth was completed in 1949, ; the first non-refuelled circumnavigation was in 1986 by Dick Rutran. To make the undertaking epic, Piccard had to impose constraints, flying in a technologically advanced form of a technologically redundant vehicle: a great adventure by virtue of the clauses attached to it. "*Orbiter 3* was the end of 200 years of ballooning," Piccard says. "But *Solar Impulse* is the beginning of a new cycle in the history of aviation."

The *Orbiter* was necessary for the *Impulse,* though. When he landed in Egypt and checked the near-empty propane tanks, Piccard swore that if he flew around the world again, he would do so without fossil fuels. Piccard's mission with the *Solar Impulse* is modern and grand: he wants to circumnavigate the world in a fixed-wing aircraft using only solar power. And, in the true tradition of the Piccards, this time Bertrand is imagining a new type of vehicle – inventing the very means for a new type of adventure. When Auguste Piccard returned from the stratosphere for the first time, he said: "The question facing us today is not so much whether man will be able to go even further and people other planets, but how to organise ourselves so as to make life on earth more and more worthy of living." *Solar Impulse* would not be a 20th century exploit of conquest. For the grandson too, a greater feat of exploration would consist of "preserving, if not improving, the quality of life on our planet. I think the pioneering spirit is not anymore to conquer the planet, because it's been done.

There have been 12 people on the moon. Is it useful to be the thirteenth or fourteenth one? I don't care. I think now the pioneering spirit should be more about the quality of life, better governance of this planet. *Solar Impulse* is a symbol of this mindset. We can do better now."

In 2001, Piccard and Jones travelled to the USA to visit solar pioneers across the country. They saw Helios, the latest in a line of prototype unmanned solar planes flown by Nasa. Piccard studied how much extra energy it would use to put a pilot in a plane. A year later, the Helios prototype broke up in mid-air and fell into the Pacific: according to the crash report, the fragile aircraft hit turbulence and the subsequent spin ripped off the plane's long wing. But Piccard and Jones met Fred Militky and Paul MacCready, who had pioneered solar flight in the 1970s. They offered enough advice and encouragement that Piccard went to the Swiss Federal Institute of Technology in Lausanne (EPFL). Its director, Stefan Catsicas, commissioned a feasibility study, supervised by André Borschberg, an engineer and former Swiss Air Force pilot. Jones and Piccard would be pilots. When he told his brother Thierry of his plan, Thierry thought to himself: "Here we go again."

Piccard had toyed with the idea of a Zeppelin-like airship, thinking it might be easier to build, or a hybrid of airplane and airship, but the feasibility study showed that it was equally difficult to build all three, and an airplane would be quicker through the air. They came up with a model which met the minimum requirements of the mission: that each square metre of solar cells could transport 8 kilograms. On November 28, 2003, armed with just the study and a model airplane, Piccard held a press conference to announce *Solar Impulse*, alongside Borschberg and Jones. "Why did we announce it so early? Because we wanted to make sure we would never give up. If you burn the bridges behind, you can never withdraw, only move ahead," Piccard says. He didn't even have a pilot's licence.

What he needed now was the money. Piccard enlisted some extra help in raising it. His wife Michèle signed up to *Solar Impulse* to run the corporate identity and branding. "Michèle is not behind me, like my grandmother and mother were behind their husbands' work," Piccard says. "She is next to me. What you see from me is a large part from her." Together they enlisted their first financial partner, Semper, a Geneva-based asset-management firm, in summer 2004. In October that year, the Piccards signed Solvay, a chemicals and plastics company. Its founder, Ernest Solvay, had invited Auguste Piccard to the Solvay Institute in the early 20th century and had been the main benefactor of the Fonds National, which had funded balloon and bathyscaphe. "It was symbolic for me," Piccard says. "And the Solvay people said it was logical to support the following part of the story." The money was crucial: Piccard decided to scrabble funds each year, rather than raise all the money in one go – "if we had waited for all the money, we would never have started." Other sponsors, including Omega and Deutsche Bank, joined later, and Borschberg set up a company and production facility in Dübendorf, a suburb of Zurich. "It's extremely close to running a startup," Borschberg says, who himself has founded three technology businesses.

Borschberg was doing more and more, and Jones less and less, until eventually he left the project. Piccard says that he was not dedicated enough and was unwilling to relocate to Switzerland, but that the separation was amicable: "Originally, he was supposed to be involved, but the only way to be involved is to be here and work on it. He was living in England and didn't speak French. He thought we could subcontract the construction of the airplane to André, but it wasn't in André's character to do so. He wanted to just show up and fly the plane. He did absolutely nothing." Jones feels harshly treated, though. "André came in as project manager and then it all started going downhill. It didn't make any sense," he says. "He was a bit inflexible I have to say: if I'd moved to Switzerland I would have been penniless. Bertrand was doing talks for $20,000 a time. It's a wee bit glib." Did Piccard manipulate Jones out, the same way he did Elson on *Orbiter*? "I don't know," Jones says. "I don't know. In the back of my mind, I believe there were people around the project saying: 'What do you need a Brian for, what does he know about aeroplanes, and anyway, he's a Brit, and this is a Swiss project.' I am sad about it actually." Piccard says: "I was as sad as him."

Before they could build the prototype, Piccard and Borschberg started making virtual flights – unlike *Orbiter*, whose tests began with launch. "With the *Breitling Orbiter*, it was trial and error," Piccard says. "We made one balloon... tried, failed, another, tried, failed, and so on. At the end we succeeded. With *Solar Impulse*, the project is much more difficult, but we go much more progressively – step by step, we test everything. We make test flights, longer flights and so on. With *Breitling Orbiter*, it was just inflate the balloon and go. So the way we proceed is much more scientific, there is much more technology, and the goal is probably more difficult to achieve."

The virtual flights proved the plane should be able to fly at night and in May 2008, both pilots, equipped with oxygen masks, helmets, parachutes and supplies, "flew" the plane for 25 hours, in a simulator equipped with five huge projector screens, inside a hangar in Dübendorf. The flights proved that the weak link in the project would be human. For the round-the-world attempt, each pilot will alternate with the other, in five-day stints. At the same time, plans for two planes were drawn up: the first, *HB-SIA*, would be a rudimentary, barebones technology demonstrator and training vehicle; the second, *HB-SIB*, would be a refined and more durable version for the round-the-world attempt.

By September 2008, *Solar Impulse* had 50 employees, including Formula One racing technicians and a former NASA astronaut who had flown Space Shuttle missions. Construction on the cockpit, fuselage and wing began. The design for the first prototype had been finalised: a central wing, composed of carbon-fibre beams made by a specialist shipyard, would run 63 metres. Carbon-fibre ribs spaced at 50-centimetre intervals would support it. The underside would be covered with a resistant film; on top, 200 square metres of photovoltaic cells; 22 per cent of the light energy captured by these would be converted to propulsion for the four motors, delivering over 24 hours an average of 6 kW or 8 horsepower – about the same as Orville and Wilbur Wright had available to them for the first-ever powered flight in 1903, which covered 37 metres. Four underwing pods would each contain a 3.5-metre-wide carbon-fibre propeller, turning at a maximum of 400 revolutions per minute; together, they would give the plane a cruising speed of 44 miles per hour (71 km/h). The cabin would not be pressurised. The stark honeycomb spars and ribs of the fuselage and wings, as they were put together, began to take the *Solar Impulse*'s arching shape; Piccard's five-year-old dream of solar-powered flight was becoming real, and so was his status as an inventing, pioneering Piccard, worthy of the line.

Nearly two months after construction began, Jacques Piccard was taken to the hospital in Lausanne with heart difficulties; on November 1, he died. Before that, his family took their chance to say goodbye to a head of the family who was, at that late stage of his life, "a little bit alone", according to Phillip Rathle, Bertrand's brother-in-law.

Bertrand thanked his father for the curiosity he had taught him, and for letting him be different, for letting him argue with him. "It was important for each of us to say, that despite the fact there were different points of view, differing ways of doing things, there was a lot of love between us," Bertrand says. "When we had big arguments, it was not because we did not love each other. In a way, my father was always very respectful and devoted to his own father. In that sense, I don't think my father would have allowed himself to have an argument with his own father. I know for him it was not easy, because he could not understand that his son was not as dependent and devoted to him as he was to his own father." Jacques spent the last four days of his life unconscious, with his sons, daughter and grandchildren taking turns to sit by his side. Bertrand was with him when he died, holding his hand. "I was saying, everything has been done, everything has been achieved, you can go. We're with you to help you and the family is now ready for you to pass away."

For all Bertrand's achievements with *Breitling Orbiter*, Jacques had been the head of the family. "With *Solar Impulse*, I am now the leader of the project and the family. Which is not the same as before – I have to make my own way."

Bertrand's brother Thierry says that the mantle had already been passed to Bertrand: "In a sense, Bertrand was already leading the show in terms of Piccard activities. My father had been sick and getting tired for many years. It was a difficult moment. When somebody passes away, all the hope that we can live again what we have lived with them disappears. A good bit of our lives disappears." For Thierry, the *Solar Impulse* is a way for Bertrand to honour his father, as the *Auguste Piccard* mesoscaphe was for Jacques: "Bertrand is probably supported by the memory of our father and grandfather in continuing what they started. Even when your father is dead, you want to make him proud: this does not change at all." It is simpler than that for Bertrand: "He would love the *Solar Impulse*. I feel his absence, very much."

*

Just over a year after Jacques Piccard died, on December 3, 2009, the huge door of the Dübendorf hangar groaned open and the *HB-SIA* was slowly wheeled out onto the tarmac. Two dozen people watched as Markus Scherdel, the German test pilot, fired up the four propellers and started down the runway. As the plane reached 21 mph, it nosed up and took flight for the first time. 370 metres and 28 seconds later, it touched back down again – as Piccard described it, "a flea hop, but in reality it is the entry into a totally new and uncharted domain of flight".

The short-hop was the first of an important series of breakthroughs for *Solar Impulse*. On April 7, 2010, the plane made its first flight, circling above Payerne for an hour and a half at 3,900 ft. In July, Borschberg took to the cockpit and piloted the *HB-SIA* on its first-ever night flight. He flew for 26 hours from 6.51 am to 9.02 am the next day, without using a drop of fuel. He saw the dawn: "Just sitting there and watching the battery charge level rise and rise thanks to the sun... And then that suspense, not knowing whether we were going to manage to stay up in the air the whole night. And finally the joy of seeing the sun rise and feeling the energy beginning to circulate in the solar panels again," Borschberg said as he left the cockpit.

The *Solar Impulse* doesn't fly like any other plane, and certainly not the military jets Borschberg is used to: more like steering a sailboat than an aircraft. "The airplane reacts extremely slowly," Borschberg told me. "If you turn the flight controls to the right, it will start turning in maybe one or two seconds, and then you will have to stop the turn at least five or ten seconds before. This kind of flight relationship between the pilots and plane has to be developed." (Piccard still didn't have permission from Swiss Civil Aviation to fly the *Solar Impulse* and was busy logging hours in other planes.)

The flight was the longest in the history of solar aviation and the first at night, and earned three FAI-certified world records. On May 12, 2011, *Solar Impulse* made its first international flight, from Switzerland to Belgium. A month later, it flew to Paris for the Air Show there.

In December 2011, Borschberg spent three days straight in the flight simulator, which was by then a full-scale mockup of the cockpit of the second plane, under construction. The tests measured the ergonomics and lavatory facilities in the cockpit, how much the pilot could exercise, vigilance and tiredness of the pilot. Borschberg wore electronics that monitored his brain waves and heart functions. He slept for 20 minutes at a time in a seat that reclined for these naps. The test was an important one. According to Borschberg, it "demonstrated that our concept of flying single-handed for several days in a row is viable."

On May 24 the next year, Piccard put some of those lessons into practice, with the first intercontinental flight of the *Solar Impulse* and a "dress-rehearsal" for the final, 2014 round-the-world attempt. He and Borschberg alternated pilot duties over the eight legs of the 3,728-mile flight that took exactly two months, because of unexpected headwinds and turbulence on various flights.

The *HB-SIA* was only intended to fly over Switzerland: its fragility increased fears for its pilot's safety; less dress-rehearsal than a script read-through. The final plane for the world record attempt, the *HB-SIB*, will be built entirely for its mission, to fly around the world. "The second airplane is a step up as big as the first one," Borschberg says. It must fly many days and many nights in wildly differing conditions, in the sun and rain, and across oceans: according to Piccard, "it is an airplane made for travels." Its cockpit is also unpressurised and the plane cruises at 27,000 ft (9,000 metres). It features a seat that reclines, so that the pilots can catch sleep in bursts, and has proper lavatory facilities, unlike the prototype. It has watertight wings, so that it can fly in rain and clouds (the *HB-SIA* would short-circuit in similar conditions and lose power). It took eight stages to fly to Morocco and back in the *HB-SIA*: the round-the-world flight will be done in only five, each stint lasting four to six days. (The only limiting factor for the *Solar Impulse* is human endurance: a two-seater version is planned once solar technologies are efficient enough to allow the extra weight.) The second plane relies on cutting-edge, experimental tech: Solvay has created electrolytes that increase the energy density of the batteries. The carbon-fibre sheets to build the new plane weigh only 25 grams per square metre (writing paper weighs around 80 grams per square metre). Bayer Material Science is contributing nanotubes to glue the carbon fibres together, making the wings stronger and lighter at the same time. Omega has developed a new, extremely precise bank indicator for the *Impulse*'s sensitive turning, accurate to within one degree, rather than the five used in most commercial planes. Most importantly, the avionics are more sophisticated, and tougher; its systems are built to continue if one part of them fails. If one engine gives up, the battery power can be rerouted to the others.

The *HB-SIB* is pushing the science of solar-powered vehicles forward and is a technological marvel, but the round-the-world flight is nonetheless very dangerous. The physical demands of flying for five days straight are themselves extreme. The risk of hypoxia is more real, without a co-pilot to observe the symptoms. "You don't notice it," Piccard says. "You start to faint progressively and you just stop thinking." In one simulation in a decompression chamber at ground level, Piccard took his oxygen mask away and shut the supply off. On the instruction to put his mask back on, Piccard did so and said he was perfectly able to fly. He hadn't turned the oxygen supply back on, though. In 30 seconds, he would have been dead. "You're completely stupid and you don't notice it." Storms and turbulence are a threat: "You cannot fight it, you have to correct," Piccard says. "When it's too turbulent, it's scary – it's not like in a passenger plane, when it passes quickly. For *Solar Impulse*, we cannot have turbulence." Over water, the *Solar Impulse* pilot would have to parachute out, as landing on water is not a possibility: "if you ditch in the ocean, you will be electrocuted," Piccard says. And as with *Orbiter*, the vast blue of the Pacific is the most forbidding challenge: any problem that brought the *HB-SIB* down over that ocean would likely mean death for the pilot. "We are very aware of the risks."

In mid-2012, the main spar of the second plane broke under torsion testing, delaying the round-the-world attempt until 2015. Piccard and Borschberg used the year delay to fly the *HB-SIA* across the United States in the summer of 2013. He began in San Francisco and, like his father, was delighted with American attitudes: "In Silicon Valley, you don't need to teach people how to innovate." Tim Koogle, the first CEO of Yahoo!, and Elon Musk, who co-founded PayPal, electric car maker Tesla and private space transport company Space X, visited. So did Larry Page, the cofounder of Google. He sported his Google Glass, the wearable computer with a heads-up display contained in a pair of glasses (which, depending on your view, is either the "Segway for your face" or possibly the next great revolution in personal computing) and recommended Piccard take them flying. "All these mythical names," Piccard told me over Skype. "They're living here!" Michèle came with Bertrand for most of the trip. She flew back to Lausanne for a month, while her daughters sat school and university exams; then the whole family flew out. It reminded Piccard of his own childhood with his father, mother, brother and sister in Florida. "Some great memories." Over the course of its staggered journey over the US, *Solar Impulse* set the record for the greatest distance of a manned solar-powered flight. When the plane landed in Washington DC, Ernest Moniz, the US Secretary of Energy welcomed its pilots, saying: "I believe in 10 years we're going to see the fruits of all these technologies changing the world." Meanwhile, the second plane was readied; flight tests begin in 2014.

An extra year in a decade-old project – and 15-year dream – was acceptable. "We didn't lose one year; we won one year." Piccard's mission is not one of conquest, but of education, and the North American tour helped just that. "The goal is to change the mindset of people through *Solar Impulse*. If an airplane can fly around the world with no fuel, nobody can say that we cannot reach incredible goals with clean technology. You have a lot of resistance to change, a lot of people saying: 'I don't believe in that' – because of dogma. They are afraid of change and they are not pioneers." Piccard's publishers called his and Jones's account of the *Orbiter 3* mission *The Greatest Adventure*, against Piccard's wishes: *Solar Impulse* is the greater adventure, he says.

"Adventure is about the unknown. The goal is not to make something impressive that will make the breaking news of CNN and everyone says that's impressive, that's dangerous

"But if you do something that really faces the unknown,

faces the doubts, the uncertainties, and you have to develop new skills to make it happen – that's interesting."

The *Solar Impulse* flies in 2015 – an adventure begun nearly a century ago by Auguste, passed on to Jacques and taken up by Bertrand. If the flight succeeds, the Piccard name will once more stretch beyond sky and sea.

The first, prototype Solar Impulse *in flight*

Epilogue

All the children of Bertrand and Thierry Piccard are daughters: it is likely then that the Piccard name, on Auguste's side, will not exist in a living descendant (although Bertrand points out with a shrug that mooted changes to Swiss law might allow them to pick this name for themselves). Nor does Bertrand expect his daughters to continue his adventures – Estelle is studying law, Oriane economics and Solange medicine – or at least not in a facsimile way: "I would like them to be pioneers in what they do," he says. "If they are bakers, at least they should make a special type of bread, and not just do what everyone else has done without asking questions." For their part, Estelle, Oriane and Solange "all refuse to say what they want to become precisely, to avoid any pressures from the outside."

Letting go of the Piccard name, which serves as an intensifier of the explorer meme, would relieve some of that pressure. Auguste did not force Jacques down into the Marianas Trench; Jacques did not bully Bertrand into a balloon. But perhaps tradition and a famous family name did: Bertrand flew, in his words, "to realise the potential I had. It was not a question of competition – there was never any rivalry between my grandfather, father and me. It was more a question of continuing the tradition of exploration, each one had the potential in his education, in his name, in his family tradition and it was nice to continue in the best way possible." That circumnavigating the world non-stop in an experimental aircraft is a "nice" way to maintain a family tradition shows the great weight Bertrand must feel.

Thierry Piccard's life offers an alternative Piccard existence: the explorer genes without the explorer meme. With his elder brother living up to tradition, he was free to pursue a less adventurous existence. Today, he is a corporate finance director at Tetra Leval, the makers of Tetra Pak, and also married with three daughters. He is not envious of Bertrand: "No. I'm only happy in fact. I even feel a bit comfortable, because it's nice to have someone carrying on an adventure that can be linked to the Piccard family, without having to be that guy myself. If I had to do it… I wouldn't. I'm more comfortable on the ground."

Most of us are more comfortable on the ground. The Piccards can carry on the adventure for us. But the example of three generations – their attitude, their endeavour and their inventiveness – can teach the rest of us to be pioneers, to challenge ourselves, and perhaps to make a special type of bread, if we want. We all have explorer genes; we don't have to go the highest, the deepest, or the furthest, to make use of them.

Appendix

Poem by Robert Underwood Johnson on the occasion of Auguste Piccard's birthday, 1933

Many have mounted with the lark
And drowned his morning hymn
With din that might affright dark
And startle cherubim

Many since Chavez won – and fell –
Have topped the Alpine crest,
Or viewed, as Dante looked on hell,
Untrodden Everest

Imagination's magic mood
Has caught within its ken
A miracle of fortitude
That makes of women men

Danger nor death has given pause
To these adventurers
How far, how swift the daring was:
How its remembrance stirs

Them have I honored as I may
With wreaths that bards must bring
To heroes. Let me rather say
They live that bards may sing

Come now, ye comrades of the air
And you from 'neath the sea.
Bring here of praise your generous share
In friendly rivalry

For here is one whose beckoning star
Showed a new firmament
Who, following no one by Piccard
Made his own precedent

Let me come near this noble fame –
Discoverer of a zone,
The first that might not place his name
On what was once Unknown.

And let me grasp the unflinching hand
That held his course on high
Not knowing what were Fate's demands
Above the safer sky.

And let me hear that reverent voice,
Hushed in a dream of awe,
As silent sages do rejoice
Finding a newer law

And let me fathom those brave eyes
That saw what sees the sun.
And gazed upon God's mysteries
As only God has done.

Acknowledgements

Many thanks to Beatrice Perry and David Isaacs, whose casual remarks turned out to be the genesis of this book. I am indebted to Rebecca Nicolson and Aurea Carpenter at Short Books, and to my editor Emma Craigie for her close reading and lucid suggestions. Apologies to the London Library for abusing their generous lending limits. Thank you to Bruno Giussani for introducing me to Bertrand and revealing that he didn't have a pilot's licence, despite having flown around the world. Thank you to Tamara Pelège, Karen Hansson and Lorraine Dupart at Solar Impulse for fielding so many requests. Thanks to Carinne Bertola, curator of the Musée du Leman, for letting me browse the Piccard archives there. I owe a great deal to Jean-François Rubin: for his time and friendly conversation, for his two wonderful books in French on the Piccards, and for letting me sit at the controls of an actual Piccard submersible, the *F.-A. Forel*.

It was a privilege speaking to those who have achieved the most remarkable aerial and subaquatic feats: thank you to André Borschberg, Brian Jones, Wim Verstraeten, Andy Elson, Don Kazimir and especially Don Walsh.

Thank you to my colleagues at *WIRED*, in particular Greg Williams, Madhumita Venkataramanan and Olly Figg, and to my editor David Rowan, for giving me my start in writing. They caught many faults in style, clarity and accuracy. Nonetheless I slipped much past them; the mistakes that remain are all mine. Thank you Kimberly, Charlie, Tim, Rhodri and Jason for all the good times. Thank you to Mum, Dad, George and Alice for their love and support. Thank you to my other reader, Claire, the without-which-nothing, both in writing this book and more generally.

Finally, thanks to the Piccard family, especially Philippe Rathle and Thierry, Michèle and Bertrand Piccard, for welcoming me into your home and sharing so many stories. It has been an inspiration. Bertrand, the best of luck as you follow your trace in the sky.

Bertrand, Jacques and Auguste Piccard

Bibliography

Addor, Jacques-Henri and Piccard, Bertrand *Solar Impulse HB-SIA*, 2011

Ballard, Robert D. *The Eternal Darkness: A Personal History of Deep-Sea Exploration*, 2000

Becker, Jean *Hot Air Balloons: History, Evolution and Great Adventures*, 2010

Biddle, Wayne *Dark Side of the Moon: Wernher Von Braun, the Third Reich and the Space Race*, 2009

Branson, Richard *Reach for the Skies: Ballooning, Birdmen and Blasting into Space*, 2011

Broad, William J. *The Universe Below: Discovering the Secrets of the Deep Sea*, 1998

Cousteau, Jacques-Yves *The Silent World*, 1973

Crouch, Tom *Wings: A History of Aviation from Kites to the Space Age*, 2004

Dwiggins, Don *Riders of the Winds: The Story of Ballooning*, 1973

Field, Adelaide *Auguste Piccard: Captain of Space, Admiral of the Abyss*, 1969

Flammarion, M.C. *Travels in the Air*, 1871

Gillespie, Charles *The Montgolfier Brothers*, 1983

Gould, Carol Grant *The Remarkable Life of William Beebe: Explorer and Naturalist*, 2006

Hart, Clive *The Prehistory of Flight*, 1985

Holmes, Richard *Falling Upwards: How We Took to the Air*, 2013

Honour, Alan *Ten Miles High, Two Miles Deep: The Adventures of the Piccards*, 1957

Huot, George and Willm, Pierre *200 Fathoms Down*, 1955

Kittinger, Joe *Come Up and Get Me: An Autobiography of Colonel Joseph Kittinger*, 2010

Kunzig, Robert *Mapping the Deep: the Extraordinary Story of Ocean Science*, 2000

de Latil, Pierre and Jean Rivoire *Le professeur Auguste Piccard*, 1962

Marine Technology Society Journal 43 Into the Trench: Celebrating the Golden Anniversary of Man's Deepest Dive, 2009

Marx, Robert F. *The History of Underwater Exploration*, 1990

Matsen, Bradford *Descent: The Heroic Discovery of the Abyss*, 2006

Paccalet, Yves *Auguste Piccard: Professeur de Rêve (une Vie)*, 1997

Piccard, A. *Au fond des mers en bathyscaphe*, 1954

Piccard, A. *In Balloon and Bathyscaphe*, 1956

Piccard, Bertrand *A Trace in the Sky*, 2009

Piccard, Bertrand and Brian Jones *The Greatest Adventure: the Balloonists' own epic tale of their round-world-voyage*, 1999

Piccard, J. *Seven Miles Down: The Story of the Bathyscaphe*, 1962

Piccard, J. *The Sun beneath the Sea*, 1973

Polmar, Norman *The Death of the USS Thresher: The Story behind History's Deadliest Submarine Disaster*, 2004

Rolt, L.T.C. *The Balloonists*, 2006

Rubin, Jean-François *La Famille Piccard entre Ciel et Mer*, 2007

Rubin, Jean-François and Arnaud Schwartz *A la Conquête du ciel et des abysses: Auguste Jacques Bertrand Piccard*, 2009

Ryan, Craig *The Pre-Astronauts: Manned Ballooning on the Threshold of Space*, 2003

Smith, Patrick. *The Romance of Ballooning: The Story of the Early Aeronauts*, 1972

Sóbester, Andras *Stratospheric Flight: Aeronautics at the Limit*, 2011

Van Pelt, Lori *Amelia Earhart: The Sky's No Limit*, 2006

Vulpe, Nicola *The Extraordinary Event of Pia H.* , 2009

Ward, Bob *Dr. Space: The Life of Wernher Von Braun*, 2009

Yeager, Jeana, Rutan, Dick and Phil Patton, *Voyager,* 2001

Index

Abersold, Erwin 191

Abruzzo, Ben 208, 215

Abruzzo, Richard 208–209, 214

Ackerman, Robert 82–83

Albanati, Stefano 243

Alexander the Great 90

Anders, Bill 199

Anderson, Maxie 215

Andrée, Salomon 4

Andrews, Roy Chapman 73

Apollo II 192

Armstrong, Neil 261

Auguste Piccard, the
baptism 184–185
construction of 181–184, 198
dives 185–186
fitness to dive 185
sale of 186

Bailly-Cowell, Marc 187

Balbo, Italo 63

Banks, Joseph 28

Barton, Otis 94–97

Bathyscaphe 89
Japanese 149
Trieste see Trieste

Bayly, Rob 208

Becquerel, Henri 22

Beebe, Charles William 73, 93–97, 99, 133

Ben Franklin, the
construction and launch 189

ejection from Gulf Stream 192

end of mission 193

interior 190

life on board 191–192

pilot's station 190

Bernasconi, Captain 62

Bird, Peter 261

Bishop, Charles 152

Bjerknes, Vilhelm 11

Blount, Alan 232

Bohr, Niels 13

Bombard, Alain 192

Borschberg, André 272–274, 277–280

Bourne, William 90

Boyle, Robert 27, 90–91

Bradley, Troy 208

Branson, Richard 176, 184, 207, 226, 232–233, 240–241, 261
Virgin Global Challenger 219–221, 224, 240–242

Breitling Orbiter
abandonment of flight 222
balloon, coating 218
capsule 217
design and construction 218
gondola 217, 220
meteorologists, importance of work 218–219
Rozier balloon, as 217
sponsorship 222
take off 222

Breitling Orbiter 2

China, permission to cross 229
construction 223
duration record 230
leak 228
redesign 224
take off 227–228
Breitling Orbiter 3 196, 216
  Africa, reaching 266
  anachronistic flight of 271
  Brown's concerns 236–237
  bunks 250
  burners, problems with 259
  China, over 257–258
  China, permission to cross 243
  circumnavigation of the Earth
  216–230
  co-pilot, choice of 234
  cockpit 249
  control entre, losing tough with 260
  descent 267
  disarray, mission in 233
  distance record, breaking 262
  envelope 234–235
  flight 248–268
  flight plan 251
  gondola 234
  instruments 249
  jet stream, picking up 260, 262
  kitchen area 250
  life on board 251–252
  launch, preparations for 244
  Pacific, over 258–259
  pilot change, announcement of 240
  pilot preparations 235
  preparations 234
  propane, running on 234
  psychic blessing 239
  size 246
  success of mission 266
  survival equipment 250
  take off 247
  wrong track, on 263
  Yemen, over 255
Breitling watches 208
Brown, Tony 234–237
Bullimore, Tony 258
Buono, Guiseppe 156, 159, 165–168
Burke, Admiral Arleigh 146–147,
160–161
Busby, Frank 191
Bushnell, David 92
Byrd, Admiral Richard 73

Cable & Wireless 242, 253–256
Cameron Balloons 207, 217, 220
Cameron, Don 208, 222, 226, 234
Cameron, James 176–178
Catsicas, Stefan 272
Cavendish, Henry 25
Cayley, Sir George 10
Century of Progress
  construction 77
  Dow Chemicals, removal of logo
  by 80
  first take off and wreck 79
  inflation 78
  Jean and Jeanette taking control
  of 79
  Jean Piccard relinquishing right to
  fly 78
  Piccards' flight 81–82
  record height 79
  second take off 79
  sponsorship 80–81
Century of Progress International
Exposition 77
Challenger Deep 150–151, 155–156,

160–161, 163
bottom, Trieste reaching 171
Cameron's decent to 176–178
dive 164–176
life in 172–173
observations on 174
return from 174–176
target zone 164
Charles, Jacques 27–28
Chun, Carl 88
Cosmic rays 61–62, 64, 71, 74, 89, 120, 174
Cosyns, Max 114–115, 117, 125
Kipfer's place, taking 60
plastic balloon, creating 83
second flight by 65
stratospheric balloon, work on 66
war, in 66
Cousteau, Jacques-Yves 117–118
Coxwell, Henry Tracey 30
Curie, Marie 13

Da Vinci, Leonardo 25
de Bort, Léon Teisserenc 11, 23
de Henriquez, Diego 127
de Lattre de Tassigny, General Jean 112
de Rozier, Jean-François Pilâtre 26, 28–29, 217, 248
Deep sea deposits, minerals in 177
Deepsea Challenger 177
Dempster, Arthur Jeffrey 13
Denis, Ernest 20–21
Denis, Marianne see also Piccard, Marianne
background 20
marriage 21
DeVorkin, David 79
Dietz, Robert 110, 144–145, 148, 150,

156, 170
DOER Marine 176
Dorian, Sylvestre 70–71, 73
Drazen, Jeffrey 173
Drebbel, Cornelius 90–92

Earhart, Amelia 72
Eckert, Pierre 218–219, 222, 241, 244, 252, 257, 259, 262
Einstein, Albert 12–14, 58–59
Eisenhower, President 179
Electrometers 22–23
Elson, Andy 218, 223, 225–226, 228–229, 233, 239, 242, 252, 254, 256–257
Enderis, Guido 6

F.-A. Forel 194–195
F.N.R.S. balloon
ballast 34–36
Bavarian bureaucracy, problem of 38
construction of 36
destruction of 66
Dräger apparatus 33–34
envelope, construction of 37
failure to take off 40
gas-bag 36
inflating 36–37
pressurised cabin 31–33
rival project 41
spherical chamber 32–33
sponsorship 29
third flight 65
F.N.R.S. balloon (first flight)
account of 43–51
ballast, jettison of 48
certificate of airworthiness, refusal of 38

INDEX

CH 113, flight designated 43
criticisms 42–43
descent 48
first inflation of 40
glacier, landing on 49
heat in cabin 47
helmets, Swiss rules requiring 38–39
high mountains, in 49
mercury, leak of 46
public doubt as to contribution of
flight 57-58
scientific contribution of flight 55
view from 45
F.N.R.S. balloon (second flight)
account of 61–63
captain's log 61
descent 62
inflation 60
landing 62
launch site 60
new gondola 59
postponement 60
preparation for 59
scientific results 64
take off 61
view from 62
F.N.R.S. 2
ballast 103–105
Boa-Vista, journey to 118
cabin 99–101
command, division of 114
construction 115
criticism of experiment 124-125
diving site 116–117
first manned dive 118–121
first voyage 107
French Navy, receipt by 126
funds for 97

gasbag 101–103
idea for 97
launch practice 117–118
material for 99
petrol reservoirs 115–116
petrol, running out to sea 122
petrol use of 101–103
Piccard stripped of authority as to
126
propellers 105
reconstruction, funds for 125–126
requirements for 98
return to post-war 114–115
Scaldis, on 116
strength of 98
testing 98
trail rope 105
travel to the deep 101
unmanned, tests on 121–123
windows 99–100
F.N.R.S. 3 129, 131, 143, 157
first dive 133
Fedoseenko, Pavel 67
Folger, Timothy 188
Ford, Henry 80–81
Fossett, Steve 176, 227, 240–241, 261
Solo Spirit 219–220, 223–224,
231–232
Franklin, Benjamin 27, 188

Gas ballooning 10
Geiger, Herman 198
Gibbon, Edward 139
Gilruth, Robert 75–76, 86
Glaisher, James 30
Global Hilton 224, 227, 248
Gordon Bennett Cup 15–16, 80, 215
Gordon Bennett, James Jr 15
Gray, Captain Hawthorne C. 30–31

Grunman's Ocean Systems 187, 191
Guillisen, Jean 100, 105
Guillisen, Professor 100
Gulf Stream
  drifting in 188
  effect of 188
  mesoscaphe for exploration of
  187–189 see also Ben Franklin, the
  nature of 187
  study of 187

Haigh, Ken 191–192
Hansen, Asmus 41
Harris, Denvol 156
Helios prototype 272
Hergé 16–17
Hersell, Hugo 42
Hess, Victor 22–23
Heyerdahl, Thor 188
Hill, Charles 156
Hill, Edward 80
Hilton, Barron 224
Holmes, Richard 24–25
Hoogeslag, Gerhard 208
Hoover, George 85
Hot-air balloons
  Aérostat Réveillon 24
  altitude records 30
  American 67–68
  ascents in 14–16
  Bartsch von Segsfeld 67
  Cable & Wireless 242, 253–256
  Cameron-Rozier 77 208
  Century of Progress 67, 77–82
  Chrysler 1 208–215
  circumnavigation race, rules for 220
  density and pressure of gas in 16
  development of 25–29
  Explorer 67–68

F.N.R.S. see F.N.R.S. balloon
first manned flight 28
first recorded flight 25
funeral rituals 25
German 67
Global Hilton 224, 227, 248
Helvetia 14
history of 24
J. Renee 224, 248
Montgolfiers, displays by 26
Osoaviakhim-1 66–67
Pleiades 83–84
Polish 68
pressurised cabin 31–33
Project Helios 85
Solo Spirit 219–220, 231–232
Soviet 66
speed of light, experiment as to 14
sport 15
Star of Poland 68
trail rope 105
trans-Atlantic race 207–215
USSR-1 66–67, 79
USSR-1 bis 67
Versailles, launch from 24
Virgin Global Challenger 219–221,
  224, 240–242
Houot, Captain Nicolas-Maurice 133
Hypoxia 235, 280

Ida, Don 215
International Solvay Institute for
Physics 13
J. Renee 224, 248
Jair, Kenneth 156
Johnson, Robert Underwood 73, 285
Jones, Brian 220, 226, 234–235,
  237–240, 243–268, 272, 274
Jones, Joanna 237, 255

Kaech, Donald 180
Kaiser, Edmond 113
Kazimir, Don 110, 191–192
Kepner, Major 67–68
  Explorer II 68
Kipfer, Dr Paul 3–5, 38, 43
  F.N.R.S. flight see F.N.R.S. balloon
  Innsbruck, journey from Obergurgl
  56
  second flight, forbidden to go on 60
  wicker helmet 38–39
Koogle, Tim 280
Kraft, Erich 208

L'Hoir, George 33
Lindbergh, Charles 56, 72, 87, 199
Lindstrand, Per 219, 221, 240
Liniger, Dave 233
Louwman, Evert 208
Lovell, Jim 199
Lunardi, Vincenzo 28

MacCready, Paul 272
Mackenzie, M. Kenneth 180
Maillard, Marie-Claude
  background 142
  marriage 142 see also Piccard,
  Marie-Claude
Maillard, Olivier 17
Manclark, James 229
Marianas Trench 169, 176, 259
Masaryk, Thomas 21
Mass, Jochen 208, 234
Masuch, Dr Hermann 67
May, Chester 189, 191
Melton, Dave 227
Messner, Colonel 56
Meteorology 11
Michel, John 158, 166

Michels, Professor 100
Michelson, Albert 14
Militky, Fred 272
Millikan, Robert 22–23, 82
Moniz, Ernest 281
Monod, Professor Théodore 119–120,
124
Montgolfier, Etienne 26
Montgolfier, Joseph 25–26, 28
Morley, Edward 14

Nasa Manned Space Center 75
Navy Electronics Laboratory, San
Diego 152–155
Nero Deep 159
Niagara Falls hydroelectric power
  station 9
Noble, Alan 225, 244, 247, 262, 265

Obergurgl 51–52, 56
Oceanography, science of 149
Office of Naval Research, US 149–152

Page, Larry 280
Pflaum, John 156, 175
Phelps, Captain John 146
Pic-Pic cars 9
Piccard Aviation 204
Piccard family, history of 8
Piccard, Auguste
  absent-minded professor, as 18–19
  aeronautics, interest in 14
  air travel, predictions of 74–75
  America, in 69–
  bad publicity, generating 69–70
  bathyscaphe see F.N.R.S. 2
  Belgium, honoured by 63
  birth 8
  celebrity, attaining 56

Chexbres, move to 105
childhood 9–10
children, raising 22
clothing 18
cosmic rays, study of 22, 29
death 182
description of 17
diving balloon, plan for 87–89
doctor of science, as 12
doctoral thesis 12
ecologist, as 19–20
Einstein, description of 13
F.N.R.S. see F.N.R.S. balloon
first F.N.R.S. flight, account of
52–55, 58
Free University of Brussels, at 13
French Academy of sciences, lecture
to 12
glacier, coming down from 50–51
height 17
Helvetia, going up in, 14
hot-air balloon 29
ascents in 14–16
experiments with 10
identical twin, as 9
Innsbruck, journey from Obergurgl
56
Institute of Technology, professor
at 13
interviews after flight 53
Italians, collaboration with 128
Jacques, tribute to 113
last dive 139
lectures 19
marriage 21
matriculation 12
mechanical engineering degree 12
North American ascension,

planning 76–77
Order of Leopold, award of 57
outdoors, love of 19
personal interests 19
physical demeanour 18
prefabricated houses, proposal for
106
Professor Calculus, as 16–17
promise to Marianne not to fly
again 65
public scrutiny 57
reckless, believed to be 42
Remi's description of 16–17
Scaldis see Scaldis
scientific curiosity 17
scientific papers 12
Second World War, in 105–106
secondary education 11
smoking, view of 71, 73
sport, ballooning for 15
stratosphere, flying balloon in 3–7
Swiss Army's Lighter-then-Air
Service, joining 16
Trieste see Trieste
Washington, lectures in 74
wicker helmet 38–39
Piccard, Bertrand 113, 128, 182, 184,
186, 194–195
appearance 197
balloon race, flying in 207–215
Ben Franklin, work on 199
birth of 152, 197
circumnavigation of the Earth
216–230 see also Breitling Orbiter
attempts at 196
early life 197–199
flying, sensation of 201
hang-gliding 200–201, 204–205

INDEX

head of family, becoming 276
Jacques, rebelling against 202–203
marriage 204
psychiatrist, as 204, 206, 236
purpose of life, pondering 202
Solar Impulse HB-SIA, flying see
Solar Impulse HB-SIA
trauma, interest in 206
Piccard, Denise 18, 20
birth of 21
ordination 21
Piccard, Don
hot-air ballooning as sport,
pioneering 87
Piccard, Estelle 245, 283
Piccard, Geneviève
birth of 21
Piccard, Hélène
birth of 21
Piccard, Jacques
America, in, 149
appearance 110
Auguste, idolising 108, 113
Auguste's death, effect of 183
awards 179, 181
bathysphere, comment on 96
birth of 21
Breitling Orbiter 3, message to
264–266
Captain Nemo, as 111
Challenger Deep dive 161, 164–176
death 275–276
description of 110
education 109–110
Free Territory of Trieste, paper on
127
French Resistance, joining 112–113
funding for Trieste, seeking 143

international ecology institute,
launch of 194
marriage 142
marriage, end of 183
mesoscaphe, building 181–184 see
also Auguste Piccard, the
Navy Electronics Laboratory,
working at 152–155
Office of Naval Research, contract
with 149–150
sea, at 109
Second World War, in 112
tribute by Auguste 113
Piccard, Jean Felix
Auguste's return from stratosphere,
reaction to 57
aviation, contribution to 86
Baltimore, in 69
birth 8
cellophane balloon, designing 83
Century of Progress 77–78
flight 79–82
supervision of construction 67
childhood 9–10
children 76
cluster balloon, designing 83–85
death 86
doctor of science, as 12
General Mills and US Navy, fired
by 85
General Mills, consultant to 84–85
hot-air balloons, experiments with
10
identical twin, as 9
marriage 75
matriculation 12
plastic balloon, creating 83
Pleiades, flight in 83–84

secondary education 11

stratospheric flight, financing 80

Swiss Army's Lighter-then-Air Service, joining 16

teaching post, seeking 82–83

US citizen, becoming 76

US, moving to 12

Piccard, Jeanette

Century of Progress flight 79–82

death 87

female altitude record 81

General Mills and US Navy, fired by 85

General Mills, consultant to 84

learning to fly 79–80

licensed balloon pilot, becoming 80

Nasa, consultant to 86

ordination 86–87

teaching post, seeking 82

Piccard, Jules 8

outdoors, in 10

scientific background 9

Piccard, Marianne

Auguste Piccard , naming 185

danger, put in 21

marriage 21

promise from Auguste not to fly again 65

Piccard, Marianne (Auguste's daughter)

birth of 21

Piccard, Marie 8

Piccard, Marie-Claude 175, 202

death 183, 194, 205

marriage, end of 183

Piccard, Marie-Laure 183

Piccard, Michèle 205, 210, 245, 252, 264, 268, 273, 281

Piccard, Noelle 181, 183

Piccard, Oriane 283

Piccard, Paul (brother of Auguste) 8

Piccard, Paul (uncle of Auguste) 8–9

Piccard, Rodolphe 8

Piccard, Solange 283

Piccard, Thierry 183, 186, 193, 199–200, 202–203, 253, 272, 276

occupation 284

Piccard-Pictet 9

Planck, Max 13

Plexiglas 100

Pollini, Professor A. 149

Prescot, Colin 242

Priestley, Joseph 25

Project Nekton 146–148, 155–158

Putnam, George 73

Rathle, Michèle

marriage 204 see also Piccard, Michèle

Rathle, Phillip 275

Rechnitzer, Dr Andreas 156–158, 160–162, 164, 166–167, 173, 179

Regener, Erich 42, 64

plastic balloon, creating 83

Remi, Georges Prosper (Hergé) 16

Reveillon, Jean-Baptiste 26

Rice, Bob 232

Ridlion, Jeannette

background and marriage 75–76 see also Piccard, Jeanette

Ritchie, Alan 221, 232–232

Robert, Nicolas-Louis 28

Rolt, LTC 25

Roufs, Gerry 258

Rozier balloon

Breitling Orbiter as 218

fuel 218

INDEX

Rubin, Jean-François 17–18, 183, 186
Rutan, Burt 224
Rutan, Dick 224, 227, 230, 271
Ryan, Craig 82

San Diego Trough 154
Santos-Dumont, Alberto 138
Scaldis
  crew 116
  Dakar, voyage to 116–117
  preparation of 116
Scheiber, Angelus 52
Scherdel, Marcus 277
Schmidt, Eric 176
Schneider, Thedy 216–218, 223
Schrenck, Martin 67
Schrödinger, Erwin 13
Seager-Thomas, Dave 239
Settle, Thomas "Tex" 77–79, 81
Sheehan, John 97
Shelley, Percy Bysshe 28
Shumaker, Lieutenant Larry 161, 179
Simultaneous inventions 26
Solar Impulse HB-SIA
  construction 275
  employees 275
  first flight 277–278
  first intercontinental flight 278
  flying 278
  funding 273
  greatest adventure, as 281
  mission 271
  photovoltaic cells 270
  records set by 281
  test flights 274
  virtual flights 274
  weight 270
Solar Impulse HB-SIB
  construction 279

round-the-world flight, dangers of
  279–280
  turbulence, effect of 280
Solo Spirit 219–220, 231–232
Solvay, Ernest 13, 273
Soukup, Jacques 233
Stewart, Patrick 197
Stratosphere 11
  air pressure 31
  balloon attempts 29–32
Stratospheric air travel, safety of 65
Sturrock, Kieran 246, 249
Submarines
  balloon, tethered by 96–97
  bathyscaphe 97
  bathysphere 94–97
  Beebe, designed by 94–97
  Deep Flight Challenger 176
  deep-sea pressure 92
  First World War, in 92
  history of 90–92
  military service, in 92
  PX-44 194–195
  spherical 94
  Turtle 92
Submersibles, history of 90–92
Swiss Aero-Club 14
Swiss Army's Lighter-then-Air Service
  16

Terechkova, Valentina 81
Tesla, Nikola 9
Thermocompressions, salt-making
  device based on 8–9
Tintin 16–17, 20
Todd, Anthony 188
Trieste
  Free Territory, paper on 127
  bottom of Challenger Deep,

reaching 171

cabin 129

Capri, dive in 135–137

Challenger Deep dive 160–161, 163–176

Challenger Deep, return from 174–176

christening 133

construction 129–131

Dietz visiting 144–145

first voyage 133

flags on 162–163

Ischia, dive in 141

Nero Deep, descent into 159

observational dives 142

Office of Naval Research, backing by 149–150

Pacific, deep dives in 156–159

plan for 127–128

Ponza, dives in 137–140

Project Nekton 146–148, 155–158

retirement 180

sale of 151–152

Southern California, dives off 153–155

Thresher, search for 180–181

towable, being 129

upgrade 180

work on 129

Trieste II 180–181

Triton Submarines 176

Troposphere 11

Trullemans, Luc 218–219, 222, 241, 243–244, 252, 257, 259, 262

Uliassi, Kevin 224, 227, 233

United Kingdom Meteorological Office 11

Uranium 235 13

USS Thresher 180–181

Valdiva 88

Van Orman, Ward T. 77

Vasenko, Andrey 67

Verne, Jean-Jules 252

Verne, Jules 88, 93

Verstraeten, Wim 207–216, 222–226, 228, 233

Virgil, Ernest 156

Virgin Galactic 176

Virgin Global Challenger 219–221, 224, 240–242

Virgin Oceanic 176

von Baeyer, Adolf 12

von Braun, Wernher 19, 116, 189, 199–200, 203

Walpole, Horace 28

Walsh, Don 152–153, 156, 160–162, 167–179, 181

Weis, Pierre 12

Wilkins, Bishop John 91

Willm, Pierre-Henri 133

Winzen, Otto 84

Wolf, Theodor 22

Yeager, Jeana 224

Zhuge Liang 24